John F. Porter

WAITING FOR CHRIST

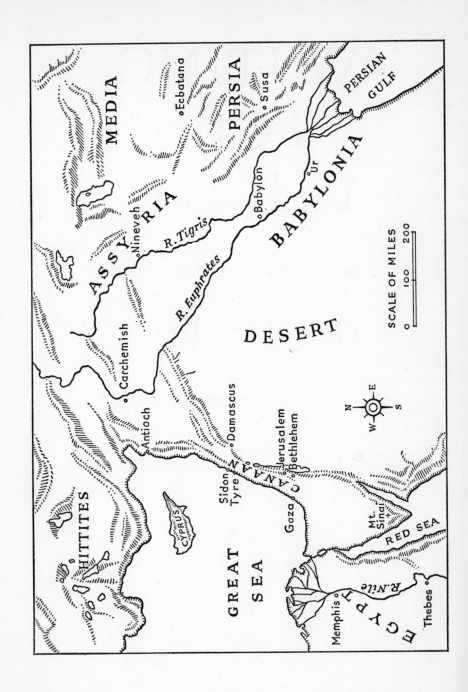

WAITING
FOR
CHRIST

based on the translation of the
Old Testament Messianic Prophecies by
RONALD KNOX

arranged in a continuous narrative
with explanations by
RONALD COX, C.M, S.T.L., S.S.L.

SHEED AND WARD — NEW YORK

IMPRIMI POTEST: J. P. WILKINSON, C.M.

VISITOR AUSTRALIAN PROVINCE

1 April, 1959

IMPRIMATUR: ✠ JAMES M. LISTON, D.D.

BISHOP OF AUCKLAND

21 APRIL, 1959

Contents

	PAGE
MAP OF BIBLICAL LANDS	FRONTISPIECE
INTRODUCTION	1
1. THE WITNESS OF MOSES	5
2. THE KINGSHIP OF DAVID	27
3. THE DIVIDED KINGDOM	55
4. THE BABYLONIAN CAPTIVITY	115
5. THE RESTORATION	187
6. TYPES OF CHRIST	262
7. OUR LADY IN THE OLD TESTAMENT	275
INDEX OF MESSIANIC TEXTS	279

Introduction

THE title of this book is taken from Martha's confident act of faith in Jesus just before he raised her brother Lazarus from the dead: 'I have always believed that you are the Messiah; you are the Son of God; the whole world has been *waiting* for you to come.' For almost two thousand years the Jewish people had been watching eagerly for the coming of the Saviour promised by the Lord God himself to their father Abraham. That is why these Messianic prophecies, scattered all through the Old Testament, are essential reading if the portrait of Christ in the four Gospels is to be appreciated.

As in the other Knox-Cox volumes, the Scripture passages flow continuously on the left-hand pages, with a matching commentary, paragraph by paragraph, on the opposite pages. I have made a few slight changes in the Knox text here and there when the Latin Vulgate, from which he translated, differs from the original text. For example, 'She shall crush thy head' (Gen. 3, 15) is now 'He shall crush your head' (p. 10). The second person singular has been replaced by the more common modern usage of the plural. I have quotation marks for direct speech; I have paragraphed the text more frequently than Mgr. Knox did; for easier reading I have omitted chapter and verse numbering; the layout is that of a modern book.

The Jewish rabbis list some 458 Messianic texts; a recent Catholic author, Heinisch (*Christ in Prophecy*), restricts the number of literally Messianic texts to 50. I have followed a middle course with 120 literal and 30 typical references. Not all of them can be established with equal certainty; where there is proof of fulfilment in the New Testament, I have indicated it in the commentary.

This book is divided up into six chapters; the first five treat of the literally Messianic passages, the sixth deals with the

types of Christ (with an appendix on our Lady in the Old
Testament). Each chapter opens with a list of contents and
an historical introduction, outlining the main developments
of Jewish life and thought during that period. Then follow
the Messianic excerpts in chronological order. In an index at
the back of the book all Scripture passages are listed in biblical order: first the historical books, next the didactic books,
and finally the prophets. Of the 54 books of the Old Testament 35 are represented in *Waiting for Christ*; the bulk of
those omitted belong to the historical books. The outstanding
contributors to the Messianic picture are Isaias and the
Psalms; between them they have almost half (66 texts) of the
total content. The most famous individual passage is the fifty-
third chapter of Isaias (p. 170).

These prophecies were the subject of much of our Lord's
instruction to his apostles: 'This is what I told you, while I
still walked in your company; how all that was written of me
in the law of Moses, and in the prophets, and in the psalms,
must be fulfilled' (Lk. 24, 44). There are about 100 references
in the New Testament to our Lord fulfilling what was written of him in the Old Testament. The early Christian apol-
ogists, like SS. Peter and Paul, often appealed to the Old
Testament to prove that Jesus was the Messiah, and the Lord
God himself.

To understand the prophecies it must be remembered that
they are a New Testament picture in an Old Testament
frame. The background of the times in which they were
written colours the different presentations of the Messiah; the
Gospel fulfilment gives new light for a correct interpretation.
That is what is meant by the saying: 'What is latent in the
Old is patent in the New.'

The two outstanding characteristics of the Messiah are:
He will be a conqueror, and his kingdom will embrace all
peoples. Both the Messiah and the Lord God are spoken of

as coming to save their people; these two divergent lines converge in Christ, who was both Messiah and God. The divinity of Jesus Christ is the key to understanding much of the Old Testament prophecies.

R. J. Cox

Feast of Christ the King   Holy Cross College

1958   Mosgiel, N. Z.

CONTENTS: Chapter 1

GEN. 2, 4—3, 24	He shall crush the Serpent's Head	6
GEN. 22, 1-18	Son of Abraham	12
GEN. 49, 1-12	Lion of the Tribe of Juda	16
EX. 12, 1-13	The Lamb of God	18
NUM. 24, 12-19	A Star out of Jacob	20
DEUT. 18, 9-20	The Prophet of the Lord	22

1. The Witness of Moses

WHEN our Lord began his public ministry by the Jordan River, the apostle Philip announced the good news to his friend Nathanael: 'We have discovered who it was Moses wrote of in his law; it is Jesus the son of Joseph, from Nazareth.' The importance of Moses as a witness to Christ is also seen later at the Transfiguration, when he appeared alongside our Lord. And Jesus himself appealed to the witness of Moses against the unbelieving Jewish leaders: 'If you believed Moses, you would believe me; it was of me that he wrote.' On Easter Sunday afternoon, on the way to Emmaus, our Lord began his discourse on the Old Testament, beginning with Moses: 'Then, going back to Moses and the whole line of the prophets, he began to interpret the words used of himself.'

Moses was the great leader who brought his people out of their four hundred years' bondage in Egypt in the thirteenth century B. C. This Exodus was the greatest and most spectacular event in the lives of the Jewish people; it was accompanied by such mighty signs that showed how the Lord protected his chosen race. Moses first led them to mount Sinai, where God made a covenant by which they bound themselves to serve the Lord God alone (monotheism). At this time they were given the ten commandments, with many other laws and obligations; these were called the Mosaic law. This was their way of life, teaching and guiding them in their every action.

All this, as well as the story of the patriarchs from the time of Abraham, plus an introduction on the beginnings of the human race, is set down in the first five books of the Bible. Moses wrote down the story under inspiration; in the course of time this original deposit was added to by other inspired writers to suit the changed conditions in which the Jewish people had to live. The same is true of the Book of Daniel, which was rewritten in Machabean times. Other inspired writings, notably the psalms, were also retouched by later authors; some authorities think that Psalm 21 was retouched three times.

GENESIS 2, 4—3, 24

When heaven and earth God made, no woodland shrub had yet grown, no plant had yet sprung up; the Lord God had not yet sent rain upon the ground, that still had no human toil to cultivate it; there was only spring-water which came up from the earth, and watered its whole surface. And now, from the clay of the ground, the Lord God formed man, breathed into his nostrils the breath of life, and made of man a living person.

God had planted a garden out in the East, in Eden, in which he now placed the man he had formed. Here, at the bidding of the Lord God, the soil produced all such trees as charm the eye and satisfy the taste; and here, in the middle of the garden, grew the tree of life, and the tree which brings knowledge of good and evil. The garden was watered by a river; it came out from Eden, and went on to divide into four branches. One is called Phison; it is the river which surrounds all the country of Hevilath, a gold-producing country; no gold is better; bdellium is found there too, and the onyx-stone. The second river is called Gehon, and is the river which surrounds the whole country of Ethiopia. The third river, which flows past the Assyrians, is called Tigris, and the fourth is the river Euphrates.

So the Lord God took the man and put him in the garden of Eden, to cultivate and tend it. And this was the command which the Lord God gave the man, 'You may eat your fill of all the trees in the garden except the tree which brings knowledge of good and evil; if ever you eat of this, your doom is death.'

HE SHALL CRUSH THE SERPENT'S HEAD

MAN IN THE GARDEN OF EDEN. It was Moses who set down in writing this account of the creation and fall of Adam and Eve. He wrote it under divine inspiration, a guarantee that everything in it is what God wanted written. This does not mean that every detail is to be taken as a literal, factual description of events as they really happened; the human author of Scripture may use imagery and symbol just as any non-inspired writer does; and he writes as a man of his own time, not of ours, with modes of writing normal then.

According to scientists there was a gap of hundreds of thousands of years between Adam and Moses. In his narrative of what happened when Adam was created, Moses depended on facts revealed by God plus his own observation of the world in which he lived.

The "clay of the ground" and "the breath of life" express the truth about man, that he is composed of two elements, a body and a soul. It is not meant to be an actual description of the creative act of God; it is a picturesque presentation in oriental imagery. Whether Adam's body was formed from inanimate matter or from some existing animal, Moses did not know and does not state because God does not reveal scientific truths.

The Garden of Eden is a symbol of the state of sanctifying grace. The picture is an oasis (garden) in a desert (Eden). That it is not meant to be taken literally is clear from the four rivers that water it: the Phison (Ganges?), Gehon (Nile), Tigris and Euphrates were the four great streams known to the Hebrews. They could not be located in any one area; they are only meant to symbolize the good life with God, the blessings of divine friendship.

But the Lord God said, 'It is not well that man should be without companionship; I will give him a mate of his own kind.' And now, from the clay of the ground, all the beasts that roam the earth and all that flies through the air were ready fashioned, and the Lord God brought them to Adam, to see what he would call them; the name Adam gave to each living creature is its name still. Thus Adam gave names to all the cattle, and all that flies in the air, and all the wild beasts; and still Adam had no mate of his own kind. So the Lord God made Adam fall into a deep sleep, and, while he slept, took away one of his ribs, and filled its place with flesh. This rib, which he had taken out of Adam, the Lord God formed into a woman; and when he brought her to Adam, Adam said, 'Here, at last, is bone that comes from mine, flesh that comes from mine; it shall be called Woman, this thing that was taken out of Man.' That is why a man is destined to leave father and mother, and cling to his wife instead, so that the two become one flesh. Both were naked, Adam and his wife, and thought it no shame.

Of all the beasts which the Lord God had made, there was none that could match the serpent in cunning. It was he who said to the woman, 'What is this command God has given you, not to eat the fruit of any tree in the garden?'

To which the woman answered, 'We can eat the fruit of any tree in the garden except the tree in the middle of it; it is this God has forbidden us to eat or even to touch, on pain of death.'

And the serpent said to her, 'What is this talk of death? God knows well that as soon as you eat this fruit your eyes will be opened, and you yourselves will be like gods, knowing good and evil.'

THE FORMATION OF EVE. The march past of animals is not meant to be an actual description; it signifies the lordship of man over the animal kingdom. To a Hebrew the naming of anything meant ownership. That woman is of the same nature and dignity as man is clearly taught in this paragraph; this was important in ancient times, when women were commonly held to be inferior.

The symbolism of Eve's formation from Adam expresses their identity of nature; the imagery is taken from a mason or a builder constructing a house of the same materials as the foundation. The story teaches monogamy (one man, one wife) as God's basic plan for family life (Mt. 19, 5-6). It also emphasizes that in the family man is the divinely constituted head to whom all members are subject; a central authority is required in every society.

Adam and Eve possessed the gift of integrity: a special gift by which their physical powers and emotions were under the control of their reason and will. It was only after they sinned, and their passions were out of control, that they felt the need of clothing.

TEMPTATION AND FALL. The serpent symbolizes the devil: 'The great dragon, serpent of the primal age, he whom we call the devil, or Satan, the whole world's seducer' (Apoc. 12, 9). The cleverness of a snake in alertness to danger and ability to escape from it was proverbial in the East; that is why our Lord himself told his followers, 'You must be wary as serpents.' Also serpents were the objects of Chanaanite worship in ancient times; Moses could warn the Hebrews of the danger of this practice by showing them that the devil chose serpent form.

It is commonly assumed that the fruit Adam and Eve ate was an apple. This opinion is based on a false interpretation

And with that the woman, who saw that the fruit was good to eat, saw, too, how it was pleasant to look at and gave desirable knowledge, took some fruit from the tree and ate it; and she gave some to her husband, and he ate with her. Then the eyes of both were opened, and they became aware of their nakedness; so they sewed fig-leaves together, and made themselves girdles.

And now they heard the voice of the Lord God, as he walked in the garden in the cool of the evening; whereupon Adam and his wife hid themselves in the garden, among the trees. And the Lord God called to Adam: 'Where are you?' he asked.

'I heard your voice,' Adam said, 'in the garden, and I was afraid, because of my nakedness, so I hid myself.'

And the answer came, 'Why, who told you of your nakedness? Or had you eaten of the tree, whose fruit I forbade you to eat?'

'The woman,' said Adam, 'whom you gave me to be my companion, she it was who offered me fruit from the tree, and so I came to eat it.'

Then the Lord God said to the woman, 'What made you do this?'

'The serpent,' she said, 'beguiled me, and so I came to eat.'

And the Lord God said to the serpent, 'For this work of yours, you, alone among all the cattle and all the wild beasts, shall bear a curse; you shall crawl on your belly and eat dust all your life long. **And I will establish a feud between you and the woman, between your offspring and hers; he is to crush your head, while you lie in ambush at his heels.'**

To the woman he said, 'Many are the pangs, many are the throes I will give you to endure; with pangs you shall give

of the Song of Songs: 'It was under the apple tree where sore distress overtook your own mother, where she that bore you had her hour of shame' (8, 5). But the tree of knowledge in Genesis is only a symbol; it means that God forbade Adam and Eve to commit sin. If they did offend him, they would learn by experience (knowledge) how good it is to serve God and how evil to disobey him. That is what God meant by the prohibition, and that is the knowledge Adam and Eve got from their fall. But the phrase as used by Satan means the divine right to decide for themselves what is right and wrong.

This desire to rise above their created state and be 'like gods' was a sin of pride: 'Of all sin pride is the root' (Ecclus. 10, 15). It was also a sin of disobedience to God's express command: 'A multitude, through one man's disobedience, became guilty' (Rom. 5, 19).

As a result of their sin, Adam and Eve lost the close friendship of God and were cast out of the garden; this means that they lost the supernatural life of sanctifying grace. They also lost their bodily immortality; God had expressly told them that the penalty of sin was death; this is symbolized by their inability to approach the tree of life in the garden. The loss of the gift of integrity is indicated by the fig-leaves.

PUNISHMENT AND THE PROMISE OF A REDEEMER. In the midst of this picture of disaster just one verse stands apart by itself because of its promise of redemption. It is called the Protoevangelium, the first good news that Christ would win the victory over Satan: 'By his death he would depose the prince of death, that is, the devil.'

In this verse, Genesis 3, 15 (printed in bold in the text opposite), there is a threefold contrast between individuals:

birth to children, yet you shall be devoted to your husband; he shall be your lord.'

And to Adam he said, 'You have listened to your wife's counsel, and have eaten the fruit I forbade you to eat; and now, through your act, the ground is under a curse. All the days of your life you shall win food from it with toil; thorns and thistles it shall yield you, this ground from which you win your food. Still you shall earn your bread with the sweat of our brow, until you go back into the ground from which you were taken; dust you are, and unto dust shall you return.'

The name which Adam gave his wife was Eve, because she was the mother of all living men.

And now the Lord provided garments for Adam and his wife, made out of skins, to clothe them. He said, too, 'Here is Adam become like one of ourselves, with knowledge of good and evil; now he has only to lift his hand and gather fruit to eat from the tree of life as well, and he will live endlessly.' So the Lord God drove him out from the garden of Eden, to cultivate the ground from which he came; banished Adam, and posted his Cherubim before the garden of Eden, with a sword of fire that turned this way and that, so that he could reach the tree of life no longer.

GENESIS 22, 1-18

God would put Abraham to the test. So he called to him, 'Abraham, Abraham'; and when he said, 'I am here at your command,' God told him, 'Take your only son, your beloved son Isaac, with you to the land of Moria, and there offer him to me in burnt-sacrifice on a mountain which I will show you.'

Rising, therefore, at dawn, Abraham saddled his ass, bid-

'You' (Satan) v. 'the woman' (Mary); 'your offspring' (sin) v. 'hers' (Christ); 'he' (Christ) v. 'your head' (Satan). It is the final contrast that is the climax; it quite clearly refers to the victory of our Lord over the empire of Satan by his death on the cross. It will be a decisive victory because the head is a vital organ; it will not be without hurt to the victor (heels are not vital organs); Christ will have to suffer in order to redeem mankind.

Mary alone is the woman—not Eve, as some authors hold. (1) If Eve was the woman, why is there no mention of Adam? He was as guilty as she. Christ's mother alone is mentioned because he was to have no human father: he was to be born of a virgin, which Eve was not. Isaias 7, 14 refers to Mary and Jesus in the same way: 'Maid shall be with child, and shall bear a son, that shall be called Emmanuel.' (2) It would be strange that 'a feud' should be described only as between Satan and Eve. The general feud between Satan and the human race would normally be expressed as between Satan and Adam. This therefore is a special feud. It is the same enmity that exists between Christ and Satan, and so must refer to complete sinlessness; this fits Mary alone, who was conceived Immaculate.

SON OF ABRAHAM

ABRAHAM COMMANDED TO SACRIFICE ISAAC. Abraham was the founder of the chosen people: 'We have Abraham for our father' (Mt. 3, 9). About 1800 B.C. God told him to leave his native land, Babylon, and migrate to a foreign country; and so he came to settle down by the Mediterranean Sea, in a land later known as Palestine.

He was seventy-five years old at the time of his migration.

ding two of the men-servants and his son Isaac follow him; he cut the wood needed for the burnt-sacrifice, and then set out for the place of which God had spoken to him. It was two days later when he saw it, still far off; and now he said to his servants, 'Wait here with the ass, while I and my son make our way yonder; we will come back to you, when we have offered worship there.'

Then he took the wood for the sacrifice, and gave it to his son Isaac to carry; he himself carried the brazier and the knife. As they walked along together Isaac said to him, 'Father.'

'What is it, my son?' he asked.

'Why,' said he, 'we have the fire here and the wood; where is the lamb we need for a victim?'

'My son,' said Abraham, 'God will see to it that there is a lamb to be sacrificed.'

So they went on together till they reached the place God had shown him. And here he built an altar, and set the wood in order on it; then he bound his son Isaac and laid him down there on the altar, above the pile of wood. And he reached out, and took up the knife to slay his son.

But now, from heaven, an angel of the Lord called to him, 'Abraham, Abraham.' And when he answered, 'Here am I, at your command,' the angel said, 'Do the lad no hurt, let him alone. I know that you fear God; for my sake you were ready to give up your only son.'

And Abraham, looking about him, saw behind him a ram caught by the horns in a thicket; this he took, and offered it as a burnt-sacrifice, instead of his son. So Abraham called that spot, 'The Lord's Foresight'; and the saying goes to this day, 'On the mountain of the Lord it shall be seen to.'

He arrived first at Sichem (where his grandson Jacob would later dig a famous well, John 4), then moved to Hebron, and finally to Beersheba in the extreme south. And there he was when the incident here recorded took place. By this time Abraham was more than a hundred years old. God had promised him that he would make a great people of his descendants, and still at this great age Abraham had only the one son, Isaac (his other son, Ishmael, was born of a wife of inferior status, and so had no right of succession to his father), through whom this promise could be fulfilled.

St. Paul praises Abraham for his faith in God under the most trying tests (Rom. 4, Gal. 2, Heb. 11). As he made his way for fifty miles from Beersheba to Moria (the mountain is identified later as Jerusalem, 2 Paralipomena 3, 1) his trust in God never wavered; his only purpose was to carry out the divine will.

We are reminded of another more famous Son of Abraham, who would walk Jerusalem with the wood of a cross on his shoulders. That is why the Church sees in Isaac a type of Christ (p. 264): 'He did not even spare his own Son, but gave him up for us all' (Rom. 8, 32).

ABRAHAM REWARDED FOR HIS OBEDIENCE. Of all the millions of men in the world, God chose out Abraham to be the ancestor of the promised Redeemer who would crush the serpent's head; it was through his line that our Lord would eventually be born at Bethlehem.

Late in his public life, Jesus would make mention of this happy day in Abraham's life: 'As for your father Abraham, his heart was proud to see the day of my coming; he saw, and rejoiced to see it' (Jn. 8, 56).

We have the word of St. Paul (Gal. 3, 16) to prove that

Once more the angel of the Lord called to Abraham out of heaven; and he said, 'This message the Lord has for you: I have taken an oath by my own name to reward you for this act of yours, when you were ready to give up your only son for my sake. More and more will I bless you, more and more will I give increase to your posterity, till they are countless as the stars in heaven, or the sand by the sea shore; your children shall storm the gates of their enemies; **all the races of the world shall find a blessing through your posterity,** for this readiness of yours to do my bidding.'

GENESIS 49, 1-12

Then Jacob summoned all his sons to him: 'Gather about me,' he said, 'to hear what awaits you in the days still to come; gather about me, sons of Jacob, and listen; it is Israel, your father, who speaks.

'You, Ruben, are my first-born, my pride, my manhood's first-fruits; yours was the privilege, yours the right to rule, but all went to waste like water.

'Simeon and Levi are brothers indeed, warriors both, and ready tools of violence. Never may this soul of mine take part in their conspiracy, this heart be of their company; raging, they slew their enemy, recklessly they hamstrung oxen. A curse on this unrelenting rage of theirs, this bitter spite! I will distribute them here and there in Jacob, I will scatter them throughout Israel.

'But you, Juda, shall win the praise of your brethren; with your hand on the necks of your enemies, you shall be reverenced by your own father's sons. Juda is like a lion's whelp;

the word 'posterity' (zera in Hebrew), in this promise to Abraham, refers to the person of Christ, and not merely to the sons of Abraham in general: 'The promises you know of were made to Abraham and his offspring; (it does not, by the way, say, "To your descendants," as if it meant a number of people; it says, "To your offspring," in the singular, meaning Christ).'

Jesus is called 'Son of Abraham' at the beginning of the genealogy in St. Matthew's Gospel. Descent from Abraham was an essential condition for any true Jew; Matthew had first of all to establish this truth of Jesus before he could present him as the Messiah.

LION OF THE TRIBE OF JUDA

JACOB'S DYING PROPHECY ABOUT HIS SONS. Jacob was a grandson of Abraham. During a long famine in the Middle East, he and his sons settled in Egypt, where his son Joseph had become Prime Minister. It was there, just before his death, that he summoned his twelve sons and spoke these prophetic words to them.

The eldest son, the first-born, usually succeeded his father and was the main recipient of paternal blessings. But Jacob passes over his first three sons because of their evil doings. It was the fourth son, Juda, to whom the right of primogeniture was to come. He promises Juda a position of pre-eminence among the twelve tribes until the coming of the Messiah, whose office it will then be to rule all nations, not the twelve tribes only. From this prophecy it is quite clear that the Messiah will come from the tribe of Juda (Mt. 1, 3; Apoc. 5, 5).

The blessings and graces of Messianic times are pictured under the image of an abundance of wine (it is not meant to

on the hills, my son, you roam after your prey; like a lion
couched in his lair, a lioness that none dares provoke. Juda
shall not want a branch from his stem, a prince drawn from
his stock, **until the day when he comes who is to be sent to
us; he shall have the obedience of the nations.** To what tree
will he tie his mount; the ass he rides on? The vine for him,
the vineyard for him; when he washes his garments, it shall
be in wine, all his vesture shall be dyed with the blood of
grapes. Darker than wine his eyes shall be, his teeth whiter
than milk.'

EXODUS 12, 1-13

It was while they were still in the land of Egypt that the
Lord said to Moses and Aaron, 'For you the month Nisan is
to lead in all the months, to be the first month of the year.
Make this proclamation to the whole assembly of Israel:
On the tenth day of this month, each family, each household, is to choose out a yearling for its own use. **It must be a
male yearling lamb, with no blemish on it.** These victims
must be kept ready till the fourteenth day of the month, and
on the evening of that day, at set of sun, the whole people
of Israel must **immolate.** They must take some of the blood,
and sprinkle it on the doorway, jambs and lintel alike, of the
house in which the lamb is being eaten. Their meat that
night must be roasted over the fire, their bread unleavened;
wild herbs must be all their seasoning. All of it must be eaten
under the same roof; you must not take any of the victim's
flesh elsewhere, **or break it up into joints.** No part must be
eaten raw, or boiled, it must be roasted over the fire; head,
feet, and entrails, all must be consumed, so that nothing re-

be a literal description; it is only vivid oriental metaphor).
Vines shall be everywhere; on every terraced hillside there will
be a vineyard; wine will be so plentiful that it may be used
to wash clothes in. 'A time is coming, the Lord says, when
never a mountainside but shall run with sweet wine' (Amos
9, 13).

The description of the person of the Messiah, in the final
sentence, is also a figure of speech; it refers to his interior
grace of soul, not his external appearance: 'Yours is more than
mortal beauty' (Ps. 44, 3).

THE LAMB OF GOD

THE PASCHAL LAMB.   Towards the end of their four hundred
years' stay in Egypt, the people of Israel lost favour with the
ruling dynasty. At this time the Lord raised up Moses to lead
them into the promised land. The slaughter of the first-born
was the last of a series of ten plagues; these were marvels
worked by Moses at the command of God to force the unwill-
ing Pharoah to let the Israelites depart from Egypt and offer
sacrifice at Sinai.

When Jesus returned to the Jordan River after his forty
days' fast in the desert, he was greeted by John the Baptist
with these words: 'Look, this is the Lamb of God who takes
away the sin of the world.' This expresses two aspects of our
Lord's person already foretold in the figure of the paschal
lamb of the Exodus. First, our Lord's sinlessness ('a lamb
without blemish on it'): 'No lamb was ever so pure, so spotless a victim' (I Pet. 1, 19). Second, our Lord was to be immolated as a victim in place of guilty mankind: 'Has not
Christ been sacrificed for us, our paschal victim?' (I Cor. 5,

mains till next day; whatever is left over, you must put in the fire and burn it.

'And this is to be the manner of your eating it; your loins must be girt, your feet ready shod, and every man's staff in his hand; all must be done in haste. It is the night of the **Pasch**, the Lord's passing by; the night on which I will pass through the land of Egypt, and smite every first-born thing in the land of Egypt, man and beast alike; so I will give sentence on all the powers of Egypt, I, the Lord. **The blood on the houses that shelter you will be your badge; at sight of the blood, I will pass you by,** and there shall be no scourge of calamity for you when I smite the land of Egypt.

'And this command is to be kept as an observance by you and your sons for ever.'

NUMBERS 24, 12-19

Their next encampment was in the plains of Moab, on the further side of Jordan opposite Jericho. It was in Moab that Balac himself bore rule at this time. So he sent envoys to Balaam son of Beor, the soothsayer who dwelt on the Ammonite border, desiring his presence. 'Here is a people on the march from Egypt,' he said, 'whose hosts darken the face of earth, and they are encamped at my doors; come and lay your curse on them, or they are too strong for me. I would fain overthrow them, drive them out of my country; and I know well that a blessing falls where you bless, a curse where you curse.'

And Balaam answered, 'Did I not warn the messengers you sent to me, "Though Balac should fill his house with

7). It was by his blood that the sentence of death would be removed: 'You have ransomed us with your blood and given us to God.'

The paschal lamb was to be roasted entire; the Israelites were ordered specifically not to 'break it up into joints.' God saw to it that this minute detail was fulfilled to the letter on Calvary, when the soldiers broke the legs of the two thieves, but not our Lord's (p. 266): 'Not a single bone of his shall be broken' (Jn. 19, 36).

The paschal feast was perpetuated among the Jewish people as their most important feast; it was held annually on the same day that it was first celebrated in Egypt. In the fulness of time this was to be the very day of our Lord's death on the cross, and the day on which he celebrated the last paschal feast and instituted the Mass as the permanent sacrifice for his Church.

A STAR OUT OF JACOB

THE PROPHECY OF BALAAM.   At the end of their forty years in the desert, the Israelites were ready to enter the promised land. They were now camped on the east bank of the Jordan, opposite Jericho. At a loss how to defeat the victorious Israelite army, king Balac of Moab decided to send for a neighbouring witch doctor to curse them.

This man, Balaam, is unique in Old Testament prophecy: he is the only non-Jew through whom the Lord revealed some aspect of the Messiah to come. His character is well summed up by St. Peter: 'They have gone far astray, leaving the true path, and following the path of Balaam, the man who was content to take pay in the cause of wrong, and was rebuked for his perversity, when the dumb beast spoke with a human

silver and gold and offer to give it me, I have no power to go beyond the Lord's bidding by uttering any word of my own, for good or ill; I can only deliver the Lord's message?" I will go back, then, to my own folk; but not till I have instructed you about what this folk shall do to your folk in the days that are coming.'

And once more Balaam prophesied: 'Thus speaks Balaam, the son of Beor, thus speaks the man whose eyes were opened; who heard speech of God, most high, the Almighty, knew his mind, had vision of him, and in a trance, learned to see aright! My vision is not of this time, is not of the things that meet my eyes. **I see a star that rises out of Jacob, a stem that springs from Israel's root;** one who shall lay low the chiefs of Moab, shall bring devastation on all the sons of pride. Edom shall fall into his hands; the men of Seir will yield their lands to the enemy. Brave deeds in Israel; such a ruler for Jacob as shall leave no remnant in the captured city.'

DEUTERONOMY 18, 9-20

It was thus Moses spoke to the people of Israel while they were still on the other side of Jordan, in the desert plain. It was the first day of the eleventh month of the fortieth year, when Moses handed on to the Israelites the commands which the Lord had entrusted to him. Moses, then, began to expound the law, with these words: 'When you reach the land which the Lord your God means to give you, take good care not to imitate the abominable ways of the men who dwell there. None must be found among you to consecrate son or daughter by making them pass through the fire, to consult soothsayers, or keep watch for dream-revelations and omens; there must be no wizard, or enchanter, none who consults

voice, to bring a prophet to his senses.' (The story of the talking donkey is one of the most charming in literature.) Eventually Balaam made contact with the Israelites and made known to them the contents of his four prophecies; he was slain by them when he later led them into idolatry.

Balaam spoke his prophecies from the mountain range to the east of the encamped Israelites, looking down upon them from a height of three thousand feet. The metaphor of a star indicates that the Messiah will be a king of great glory and splendour: 'I, Jesus, the bright star that brings in the day' (Apoc. 22, 16). It was a bright star shining in the heavens that announced to the three wise men that the Messiah had been born (Mt. 2, 2).

The two nations, Moab and Edom, represent all the enemies of Christ and his Church. They are selected here because they were at that moment opposing the chosen people in their advance to, and conquest of, Palestine.

THE PROPHET OF THE LORD

MOSES' PROMISE TO THE CHOSEN PEOPLE. God's original plan was that the Israelites should enter the promised land direct from Sinai. It was only because of their want of faith in him that he condemned them to die in the desert. Eventually a new generation grew up; and it is to these new Israelites that Moses addressed these words, while they were camped across the Jordan River, opposite Jericho. The whole book of Deuteronomy (The second giving of the law) is taken up with Moses' words of explanation of the laws which God had given the chosen people at mount Sinai, forty years before.

Moses had been their mediator with God at Sinai; the

familiar spirits and divinations, and would receive warnings
from the dead. All such things are hateful to the Lord; it is
to punish them for such evil doings that he means to destroy
these nations at your onslaught. Yours to stand before the
Lord your God perfect and unreproved; let them listen to
soothsayer and diviner, these other nations you will dispossess; not such is the schooling you have received from the
Lord your God.

'No, the Lord your God will raise up for you a prophet like
myself, of your own race, a brother of your own; it is to him
you must listen. Was it not your own plea, that day when all
were publicly assembled at mount Horeb, that you might
hear the voice of the Lord your God no longer, have sight of
that raging fire no longer, lest it should be your death? And
the Lord told me, "All that they have said is well said. I will
raise up for them a prophet like yourself, one of their own
race, entrusting my own message to his lips, so that he may
instruct them at my bidding. Whoever refuses obedience to
these commands which he gives in my name, shall feel my
vengeance. If anyone is so presumptuous as to prophesy in
my name when I have given him no message to deliver, or
prophesy in the name of alien gods, his life must pay for it." '

Lord spoke to him, and he handed on the message to the people. He now assures them that God will never cease to communicate his will to Israel all through the rest of their history. For this purpose he will establish a permanent line of prophets: 'No day dawned but I was at work betimes, sending my servants to prophesy to them.' There was always the danger that the Israelites would dabble in the occult sciences of their pagan neighbours in an attempt to communicate with the Deity. Moses' promise makes this both unnecessary and sinful: God will communicate directly through his prophets.

When our Lord fed the five thousand with five loaves and two fish by the lake of Galilee, the crowd said: 'Beyond doubt this is the prophet who is to come into the world' (Jn. 6, 14). The apostle Philip told his friend Nathanael: 'We have discovered who it was Moses wrote of in his law; it is Jesus, the son of Joseph, from Nazareth' (Jn. 1, 45). Later, Peter will also state that Jesus was the prophet foretold by Moses (Acts 3, 22); and Stephen also draws the same conclusion (Acts 7, 37). These witnesses show that Moses' prophecy refers to the person of our Lord, over and above the promise of a prophetic order: 'In old days, God spoke to our fathers . . . through the prophets; now at last in these times he has spoken to us with a Son to speak for him' (Heb. 1, 1-2).

CONTENTS: Chapter 2

2 Kg. 7, 1-16	Son of David	28
Ps. 2	Christ the King	30
Ps. 109	Eternally a Priest	32
Pss. 19; 20	An Eternal King	32
Ps. 8	Jesus, the Second Adam	34
Ps. 15	Resurrection of our Lord	36
Ps. 21	Jesus' Prayer on the Cross	38
Ps. 30	Father, into Your Hands	42
Ps. 39	The Obedience of Christ	44
Pss. 40; 54	The Traitor, Judas	46
Ps. 68	The Enemies of Christ	48
Ps. 108	An Innocent Soul Misjudged	52

2. The Kingship of David

ST. MATTHEW begins his Gospel: 'A record of the ancestry from which Jesus Christ, the son of David, was born.' This title was frequently on the lips of those asking favours of Jesus; it was more common than Messiah. When our Lord asked the Pharisees, in the temple, just a few days before his death: 'What is your opinion concerning Christ? Whose son is he to be?' They told him, 'David's.' And on Palm Sunday, the crowds acclaimed Jesus as he rode into Jerusalem in triumph: 'Hosanna for the son of David.' From the time of David until the coming of Christ this title remained the most popular designation of the Messiah. He is never called son of Solomon, or Ezechias, or Josias, or any other king. David remained the greatest name in the history of the chosen people. All their desires and hopes were centred in the glorious reign of David's most illustrious son, the Messiah king.

David reigned about 1000 B.C. for a long period of forty years. He was a warrior who had been renowned for his personal courage since he slew the Philistine giant Goliath. He united the twelve tribes of Israel into a powerful nation under his sole rule. He captured the strong fortress of Jerusalem and made it the capital of his kingdom. In his reign Israel enjoyed the period of its greatest prosperity; a like reign would not again be experienced under any other king until his son the Messiah should come to rule Israel and all nations for evermore.

David had troubles too during his long reign. He was a fugitive from king Saul for years in the desert of Juda, and later his eldest son Absalom rose up against him in revolt. Both these phases, his glorious reign and his suffering at the hands of enemies, are reflected in the Messianic psalms, which make up this chapter. Under divine inspiration David expressed his feelings in words which he accompanied on the harp; these are the psalms, the finest example of the prayer life of the Hebrews in the Bible. The best proof of this is the fact that our Lord died with David's psalms on his lips.

2 KINGS 7, 1-16

King David had now a palace of his own to dwell in, and the Lord kept him safe, on every side, from all his enemies. Whereupon he said to the prophet Nathan, 'Here am I dwelling in a house all of cedar, while God's ark has nothing better than curtains of hide about it!'

And Nathan answered, 'Go your own way, fulfil your own purpose; the Lord is with you.'

But that same night the divine word came to Nathan, 'Go and give my servant David a message from the Lord: Do you think to build a house for me to dwell in? House was never mine, since I rescued the sons of Israel from Egypt; still in a tabernacle, a wanderer's home, I came and went. This way and that the whole race of Israel journeyed, and I with them; now to this tribe, now to that, I gave the leadership of the rest, and never did I reproach any of them for not building me a house of cedar.

'This message, then, you will give to my servant David from the Lord of hosts: Out in the pasture lands, where you were tending the sheep, I summoned you away to bear rule over my people Israel; go where you would, I was ever at your side, exterminating your enemies to make room for you, granting you such renown as only comes to the greatest on earth. Henceforth my people are to have a settled home, taking root in it and remaining in undisturbed possession of it, no longer harassed by godless neighbours, as they have been ever since I first gave Israel judges to rule them. No longer shall your enemies trouble you; and this too the Lord promises, that he will grant your line continuance.

'So, when your days are ended, and you are laid to rest beside your father, I will grant you for successor a son of your

SON OF DAVID

THE PERMANENCE OF DAVID'S HOUSE. On the death of
Moses, Joshua led the Israelites across the Jordan and began
the conquest of the promised land. Within thirty years the
twelve tribes were in substantial possession of the whole of
Palestine. For several hundred years they lived apart as sep-
arate tribes, without any close unity of action; this was the
time of the Judges. Their desire for closer co-operation and
organization, especially in time of war, led them to ask the
Lord for a king to rule over them. The first king was Saul;
he disobeyed the Lord, and David was chosen in his place.

David was most successful in uniting the scattered tribes
and in defeating all Israel's enemies. He chose Jerusalem as
his capital, and there lived in state in his palace. Although he
had brought the Tabernacle and the Ark of the Covenant
into Jerusalem, he was unhappy at the contrast between his
own lodgings and the lowly shelter for the Lord his God. So
he determined to right matters and build a fitting temple to
house the Ark.

In God's plan, the temple was to be the work of Solomon,
David's son. But he was pleased with David's thoughtful-
ness: in return the Lord would build David a house, not a
dwelling of wood and stone but a line of sons that would last
forever. At times the prophecy concerns Solomon only, sometimes the whole posterity of David, and especially Jesus
Christ who was to fulfil God's promise completely.

At the Incarnation, the angel Gabriel announced to Mary:
'He shall be great, and men will know him for the Son of the
most High; the Lord God will give him the throne of his
father David, and he shall reign over the house of Jacob
eternally; his kingdom shall never have an end.' That his son-

own body, established firmly on his throne. He it is that shall build a house to do my name honour. **I will prolong for ever his royal dynasty; he shall find in me a father, and I in him a son.** If he plays me false, be sure I will punish him; ever for man the rod, ever for Adam's sons the plagues of mortality; but I will not cancel my merciful promise to him, as I cancelled my promise to Saul, the king that was banished from my favour. **Through the ages, far as your thought can reach, dynasty and royalty both shall endure; your throne shall remain for ever unshaken.'**

PSALM 2

What means this turmoil among the nations? Why do the peoples cherish vain dreams? See how the kings of the earth stand in array, how its rulers make common cause, against the Lord, and against **the King he has anointed,** crying, 'Let us break away from their bondage, rid ourselves of the toils!'

He who dwells in heaven is laughing at their threats, the Lord makes light of them; and at last, in his displeasure, he will speak out, his anger quelling them: **'Here, on mount Sion, my sanctuary, I enthrone a king of my own choice.'**

Mine to proclaim the Lord's edict; how he told me, **'You are my son; I have begotten you this day.** Ask your will of me, and you shall have the nations for your patrimony; the very ends of the world for your domain. You shall herd them like sheep with a crook of iron, break them in pieces like earthenware.'

Princes, take warning; learn your lesson, you that rule the world. Tremble, and serve the Lord, rejoicing in his presence, but with awe in your hearts. Kiss the rod, do not brave his

ship is different from that of all other men is St. Paul's argument in the Epistle to the Hebrews (1, 5). Our Lord is the divine Son of his heavenly Father: 'My Father and I are one' (Jn. 10, 30).

Son of David became the official title for the Messiah to come; it expressed all the hopes and desires of the chosen people down through the thousand years before our Lord actually did come to the land of Palestine. The title appears again and again, especially during the Babylonian exile in the prophecy of Ezechiel (37, 24) and Psalm 88. In the Gospels it is commonplace on the lips of those acknowledging Jesus as the Messiah.

CHRIST THE KING

REVOLT AGAINST THE MESSIAH. David was primarily a warrior king who fought against the surrounding pagan nations. In this psalm he presents a picture of the opposition of hostile forces to the Messiah king. The kings of the earth will not succeed in their attacks on the Messiah, because the Lord has decreed otherwise; at the request of his Son, the Lord will come to his aid.

That David is thinking of the Messiah, not himself, is proved from the universality of the king's rule over all nations (always a Messianic characteristic) and from the citation of this psalm in Acts 4, 25-26, with the following explanation: 'Herod and Pontius Pilate, with the Gentiles and the people of Israel to aid them, made common cause against your holy servant Jesus, so accomplishing all that your power and wisdom decreed.'

The phrase 'the king he has anointed' is a translation of a single Hebrew word, Messiah. In course of time it became a technical designation of the Redeemer to come. It is better

anger, and go astray from the sure path. When the fire of his vengeance blazes out suddenly, happy are they who find refuge in him.

PSALM 109

To the Master I serve the Lord's promise was given, 'Sit here at my right hand while I make your enemies a footstool under your feet.'

The Lord will make your empire spring up like a branch out of Sion: 'You are to bear rule in the midst of your enemies. From birth, princely state shall be yours, holy and glorious; you are my son, born like dew before the day-star rises.'

The Lord has sworn an oath there is no retracting, 'You are a priest for ever in the line of Melchisedech.'

At your right hand, the Lord will beat down kings in the day of his vengeance; he will pass sentence on the nations, heap high the bodies, scatter far and wide the heads of the slain. Let him but drink of the brook by the wayside, he will lift up his head in victory.

PSALMS 19; 20

The Lord listen to you in your time of need, the power of Jacob's God be your protection! May he send you aid from his holy place, watch over you, there on mount Sion; may he remember all your offerings, and find savour in your burnt sacrifice. May he grant you what your heart desires, crown your hopes with fulfilment. So may we rejoice at your deliverance, rallied in the name of the Lord our God; abundantly may he grant your prayer.

known to us by its Greek equivalent, Christ. Psalm 2 is the
first mention of this title. The Messiah's divinity is also indicated in the title 'Son' (Heb. 1, 5) and the eternal generation
('this day') of the Second Person of the Trinity.

ETERNALLY A PRIEST

KING AND PRIEST. This psalm gives something new in the
Messianic revelation: the priesthood of Christ. He will not
be a Jewish priest of the line of Levi but a Melchisedechian
priest; that is, he will have his priesthood directly from God,
not from human descent, and he will not hand it on to another; he will be a priest forever in his own Person (Heb. 7).
Melchisedech was a contemporary of Abraham (Gen. 14,
8-20); he offered a sacrifice of bread and wine, foreshadowing
the sacrifice of the Mass, instituted by our Lord at the Last
Supper (p. 264).

Jesus himself argued from this psalm that the Messiah
would be more than human: 'David calls Christ his Master;
how can he be also his son?' (Mt. 22, 42-46). The phrase
'born before the day-star' also indicates his generation from
all eternity, before creation began.

AN ETERNAL KING

VICTORY IN BATTLE. The first two paragraphs (Ps. 19) are
a prayer for victory; the third and fourth paragraphs (Ps. 20)
are thanksgiving for victory after the battle. Both these
psalms were written to be sung by the people in the temple
in time of war. In the first and fourth paragraph the king is
addressed in the second person; in the second and third the
psalm is addressed to God, and the king is spoken of in the
third person.

Shall I doubt that the Lord protects the king he has anointed, will listen to him from his sanctuary in heaven? Is not his right hand strong to save? Let others talk of horses and chariots; our refuge is the name of the Lord our God. Stumbled and fallen they, while we stand firm on our feet. O Lord, save the king, and hear us in the hour when we call upon you.

Well may the king rejoice, Lord, in your protection, well may he triumph in your saving power! Never a wish in his heart have you disappointed, never a prayer on his lips denied. With happy auguries you meet him on his way, set a crown of pure gold on his head. Prays he for life? **Long continuance of his reign you grant him; to last unfailing till the end of time.** Great is the renown your protection has won for him; glory and high honour you have made his. An everlasting monument of your goodness, comforted by the smile of your favour, he stands firm, trusting in the Lord; the favour of the most High is with him.

Ay, but your enemies—they shall feel your power; that right hand will not leave their malice unpunished. At your frown, they will wither away like grass in the oven; whirled away by the Lord's anger, burnt up in its flames. You will rid the land of their breed, their race will vanish from the world of men. See how all their false designs against you, all their plots come to nothing! You will rout them; bent is your bow to meet their onslaught.

Stand high above us, Lord, in your protecting strength; our song, our psalm, shall be of your greatness.

PSALM 8

O Lord, our Master, how the majesty of your name fills all the earth! Your greatness is high above heaven itself. You

Both psalms are attributed to David. Was he writing only
of himself as the leader of his people in battle, or was he
thinking too of the Messiah? Although not quoted in the
New Testament, both psalms are used of our Lord in the
liturgy, and the Fathers of the Church frequently apply them
to Christ. Since David was a type of Christ (p. 268), it is a
simple step from his temporal victory over the enemies of
the chosen people to Christ's final victory over the forces of
evil: 'His reign must continue until he [God] has put all his
enemies under his feet' (I Cor. 15, 25).

The Holy Spirit, the primary author of Holy Scripture,
often intended more than the human writer understood. It
seems that a phrase like 'to last unfailing till the end of
time' cannot be restricted to David alone (although flattering
titles were used of kings in ancient times) but refers to the
eternal kingship of Christ. One whose every prayer is always
answered, who is crowned with glory and honour, and who
enjoys the divine presence permanently, can be no other but
God's only Son. Also the complete conquest of enemies is
one of the characteristics of the Messianic king (Ps. 2); their
defeat is essential to the universal reign of the Messiah.

If David was thinking of himself alone, it seems rather
strange that he never uses the first person singular (a characteristic of his other psalms). He either addresses the king
in the second person or speaks about him in the third person. This would be normal procedure only if the king was
someone distinct from David.

JESUS, THE SECOND ADAM

MAN CROWNED WITH GLORY AND HONOUR. Compared with
the wonders of God's created universe, especially the starry

have made the lips of children, of infants at the breast, vocal with praise, to confound your enemies; to silence malicious and revengeful tongues. I look up at those heavens of yours, the work of your hands, at the moon and the stars, which you have set in their places; what is man that you should remember him? What is Adam's breed, that it should claim your care?

You have placed him only a little below the angels, crowning him with glory and honour, and bidding him rule over the works of your hands. You have put them all under his dominion, the sheep and the cattle, and the wild beasts besides; the birds in the sky, and the fish in the sea, that travel by sea's paths. O Lord, our Master, how the majesty of your name fills all the earth!

PSALM 15

Keep me safe, Lord; I put my trust in you. The Lord, whom I own as my God, confess that in him is all my good! There are faithful souls in this land of his; wondrous delight he gives me in their companionship. What do they do but lay up fresh store of sorrows, that betake themselves to alien gods? Not with these will I pour out the blood of sacrifice; I will not take forbidden names on my lips. No, it is the Lord I claim for my prize, the Lord who fills my cup; you, and no other, will assure my inheritance to me. Portion is none were more to my liking; welcome the lot's choice.

Blessed be the Lord, who schools me; late into the night my inmost thoughts chasten me. Always I can keep the Lord within sight; always he is at my right hand, to make me stand firm. Glad and merry am I, heart and soul of me; my body, too, shall rest in confidence that you will not leave my soul in

heavens at night, man seems an utterly insignificant creature. Yet God deigned to give Adam dominion over the works of his hands: 'Take command of the fishes in the sea, and all that flies through the air, and all the living things that move on the earth.'

St. Paul sees a deeper meaning in this psalm: 'We can see one who was made a little lower than the angels, I mean Jesus, crowned, now, with glory and honour because of the death he underwent' (Heb. 2, 9). This dominion of the Second Adam is over the souls of men, not over fish, birds, and animals. Jesus won the right to rule by his Passion and Death; although he now reigns at the right hand of God, his dominion will not be complete until the Second Coming at the end of time (I Cor. 15, 24-28).

RESURRECTION OF OUR LORD

CONFIDENCE IN GOD'S PROTECTION. In this psalm, king David addresses his prayer to God. He expresses his detestation of the idolatry around him; he will have no part in it; he places all his confidence in God, the supreme Good and the foundation of all his hopes. He is happy in the knowledge that God will not abandon him; after death both body and soul will share in the delights that come from the intimacy of God's presence.

Peter, in his first sermon on Pentecost Sunday, quotes the latter part of this psalm to prove the resurrection of Jesus: 'It is in Jesus' person that David speaks. My brethren, I can say this to you about the patriarch David without fear of contradiction, that he did die, and was buried, and his tomb is among us to this day. But he was a prophet: it was of Christ he said, foreseeing his resurrection, that he was not left in

the place of death, or allow your faithful servant to see corruption. You will show me the way of life, make me full of gladness in your presence; at your right hand are delights that will endure for ever.

PSALM 21

My God, my God, why have you forsaken me? Loudly I call, but my prayer cannot reach you. You do not answer, my God, when I cry out to you day and night, you do not heed. You are there none the less, dwelling in the holy place; Israel's ancient boast. It was in you that our fathers trusted, and you rewarded their trust by delivering them; they cried to you, and rescue came; no need to be ashamed of such trust as theirs. **But I, poor worm, have no manhood left; I am a byword to all, the laughing-stock of the rabble. All those who catch sight of me fall to mocking; mouthing out insults, while they toss their heads in scorn, 'He committed himself to the Lord, why does not the Lord come to his rescue, and set his favourite free?'**

What hand but yours drew me out from my mother's womb? Who else was my refuge when I hung at the breast? From the hour of my birth, you are my guardian; since I left my mother's womb, you are my God! Do not leave me now, when I have none to help me.

My enemies ring me round, packed close as a herd of oxen, strong as bulls from Bashan; so might a lion threaten me with its jaws, roaring for its prey. I am spent as spilt water, all my bones are out of joint, my heart turned to molten wax within me; **parched is my throat, like clay in the baking, and my tongue sticks fast in my mouth;** you have laid me in the dust, to die. Prowling about me like a pack of dogs, their

the place of death, and that his body did not see corruption'
(Acts 2, 25-31). This can only mean that the Holy Spirit put
words into David's mouth which had a meaning beyond what
that king could possibly understand of his own person.

JESUS' PRAYER ON THE CROSS

ABANDONMENT, INSULTS, AND SUFFERINGS. David wrote
many psalms expressing his anguish of soul, especially during
his flight from Saul and the revolt of his son Absalom. Either
of these situations could have put him in the mood to write
this psalm; but on this occasion, the Holy Spirit raised David's
thoughts beyond his own trials, so that he expressed the feelings and sentiments of his Son, the suffering Messiah, on the
cross at Calvary.

As our Lord hung on the cross with gathering darkness
about him, his soul was filled with gloom. As in the garden of
Gethsemani, 'He grew sorrowful and bewildered and dis-
mayed: "My soul," he said, "is ready to die with sorrow." '
As a victim for the sins of mankind, he experienced the
heaped-up enormity of sin; he felt a wall of separation between himself and his Father, as though he were a criminal
abandoned by God.

Added to this interior desolation was the mockery of the
crowd standing around the cross; instead of sympathy and
pity they poured out only scorn, ridicule, and insult: 'The
passers-by blasphemed against him, tossing their heads;
"Come now," they said, "rescue yourself; come down from
that cross if you are the Son of God." The chief priests, with
the scribes and elders, mocked him in the same way. "He
saved others," they said, "he cannot save himself. He trusted
in God; let God, if he favours him, succour him now." Even

wicked conspiracy hedges me in; **they have torn holes in my hands and feet; I can count my bones one by one;** and they stand there watching me, gazing at me in triumph. They **divide my spoils among them, cast lots for my garments.** Then, Lord, do not stand at a distance; if you would aid me, come speedily to my side. Only life is left me; save that from the sword, from the power of these dogs; rescue me from the very mouth of the lion, the very horns of the wild oxen that have brought me thus low.

Then I will proclaim your renown to my brethren; where your people gather, I will join in singing your praise, 'Praise the Lord, all you that are his worshippers; honour to him from the sons of Jacob, reverence to him from Israel's race! He has not scorned or slighted the appeal of the friendless, nor turned his face away from me; my cry for help did not go unheeded.' Take what I owe you, my song of praise before a great assembly. I will pay my vows to the Lord in the sight of his worshippers; **the poor shall eat now, and have their fill,** those who look for the Lord will cry out in praise of him, 'Refreshed be your hearts eternally!'

The furthest dwellers on earth will bethink themselves of the Lord, and come back to him; all the races of the heathen will worship before him; to the Lord royalty belongs, the whole world's homage is his due. Him shall they worship, him only, that are laid to rest in the earth, even from their dust they shall adore.

I, too, shall live on in his presence, and beget children to

the thieves who were crucified with him uttered the same taunts' (Mt. 27, 39-44).

The third element in the picture is physical sufferings. Three details are recorded as fulfilled on Calvary: our Lord's thirst, the wounds in his hands and feet, and the division of his garments by the soldiers. Crucifixion brings on a raging thirst because of the continual pain and loss of blood; our Lord's only complaint on the cross was that he was thirsty. This psalm is so vivid that it seems more like history than prophecy; it is surpassed in the Old Testament only by Isaias 53.

THE FRUITS OF REDEMPTION. At this point in the psalm there is a sudden change of outlook, from sadness to joy. It is no longer the crucified Jesus who is speaking, but the risen Saviour who joins his Church in praising God for listening to his prayer in time of need.

The imagery of the first few verses is from the custom of offering a sacrifice of thanksgiving for favours received. The sacrifice Jesus offers to his Eternal Father is the Blessed Eucharist: 'The poor eat now, and have their fill.' The Church, the true Israel of God, joins with the risen Master in thanking God through the sacrifice of the Mass for the great favour of redemption.

All the heathen nations join with Israel in bowing down to worship God. The conversion of the Gentiles, and the consequent universality (catholicity) of the Church, is the most familiar note of Messianic times. Even those who no longer live on this earth shall join in this adoration of God, whether they be in heaven or purgatory.

The gaze of the risen Master goes out into the future; he sees his life with God in heaven blessed with children down

serve him; these to a later age shall speak of the Lord's name; these to a race that must yet be born shall tell the story of his faithfulness, 'Hear what the Lord did.'

PSALM 30

To you, O Lord, I look for refuge, never let me be ashamed of my trust; in your faithful care, deliver me. Grant me audience, and make haste to rescue me; my hill-fastness, my stronghold of defence, to save me from peril. You strengthen and defend me; you, for your own honour, guide and escort me; by you protected, I shall escape from the snare that lies hidden in my path. **Into your hands I commend my spirit;** you, God ever faithful, will claim me for yourself. I will triumph and exult in your mercy; it was you who pitied my weakness, and saved me when I was hard bestead; before the enemy's toils could close around me, the open plain lay at my feet.

And now, Lord, have compassion on my distress; vexation has dimmed my eyes, frets me away, soul and body. My life is all grief, my years are but sighs; for very misery, my strength ebbs away, my frame is wasted. Openly my foes deride me; even to my neighbours I am a thing of utter scorn; my friends are adread, and the passer-by shuns my contact; I am lost to memory, like a dead man, discarded like a broken pitcher. **On every side their busy whispering comes to my ears; peril all around, so powerful the conspiracy that threatens my life. And still, Lord, my trust in you is not shaken; still I cry, 'You are my God,' my fate is in your hand;** save me from the enemy's power, save me from my pursuers! Smile on your servant once more, and deliver me in your mercy; Lord, do not let me plead in vain.

the ages (this is his Mystical Body); these children shall tell
the story of the crucified Saviour and his redemptive act to
those still unborn.

FATHER, INTO YOUR HANDS

FILIAL CONFIDENCE OF JESUS. During the course of his long
life, David had lots of trouble; but two incidents stand out
above the rest. First of all, he spent several years of his early
manhood as an outlaw, hunted day and night by king Saul;
then, later in his kingship, he fled from Jerusalem to Transjordan, a fugitive from the revolt of his son Absalom. It is difficult to decide which of these two episodes was the occasion
of this psalm. In his commentary St. Robert Bellarmine expresses the opinion that the details best fit David's flight from
Absalom.

The psalm is composed of three parts. In the first and last
paragraph, the external dangers of pursuit from an enemy are
visualized; the psalmist looks to God as a fortress, a sanctuary
to which he can escape from the enemy on his heels. A sec-
ondary idea, at the end of the first paragraph, is escape into
an open plain, when the enemy has him shut up in a narrow
defile.

The second paragraph expresses the state of mind of the
psalmist, his anguish and sadness at the derision of all his
companions. This fits the Absalom revolt (2 Kg. 15-18) better than the flight from Saul.

Only one verse of this psalm is quoted in the gospels. As
our Lord hung dying on the cross, with his last breath he
spoke these words: 'Father, into your hands I commend my
spirit.' But it is quite likely that he had been praying to his
Father in the words of this psalm during the three hours on

What treasures of loving-kindness, Lord, do you store up for the men who fear you, rewarding their confidence for all the world to see! Your presence is a sanctuary, to hide them away from the world's malice; your tabernacle a refuge from its noisy debate. Blessed be the Lord; so wondrous is his mercy, so strong the wall of his protection. **I thought, bewildered, that your watchful care had lost sight of me; but I cried out to you, and thereupon you listened to my plea.**

PSALM 39

Patiently I waited for the Lord's help, and at last he turned his look towards me; he listened to my plea, drew me up out of a deadly pit, where the mire had settled deep, and gave me a foothold on the rock, with firm ground to tread. He has framed a new music on my lips, a song of praise to our God, to fill all that stand by with reverence, and with trust in the Lord. Happy is the man whose trust is there bestowed, who shuns the rites of strange gods, the lure of lies. O Lord my God, how long is the story of your marvellous deeds! Was ever care like yours? How should I tell the tale of those mercies, past all numbering?

No sacrifice, no offering was your demand; enough that you have given me an ear ready to listen. You have not found any pleasure in burnt-sacrifices, in sacrifices for sin. 'See then,' I said, 'I am coming to fulfil what is written of me, where the book lies unrolled; to do your will, O my God, is all my desire, to carry out that law of yours which is written in my heart.' And I told the story of your just dealings before a great throng; be witness, Lord, that I do not seal my lips.

the cross, just as he had been making use of Psalm 21 in the same way. Certainly the whole psalm aptly describes his Passion.

The word 'Father' is an addition to the psalm; it expresses the close relationship between our Lord, the only-begotten Son of God, and his Father in heaven. It shows how we too can Christianize the psalms and make them our own prayers in all our needs. These last words of Jesus have been quoted down the ages by many holy men and women on their death-bed.

THE OBEDIENCE OF CHRIST

INCARNATION AND REDEMPTION. This psalm begins with the picture of David held fast in the mud at the bottom of a deep well. It is a vivid metaphor for some disaster or sickness in the past which brought him close to death. Delivered from this danger by the Lord, David now wants to compose a new song of praise for his Deliverer. Usually it was some animal sacrifice that a grateful Hebrew would offer to God in thanksgiving. But David remembered the Lord's words to Saul: 'The Lord loves obedience better than any sacrifice, the attentive ear better than the fat of rams' (1 Kg. 15, 22). What the Lord wanted was an obedient man, one to carry out his will.

In the Epistle to the Hebrews (10, 5-12) St. Paul puts these words on the human lips of the Second Person of the Trinity: our Lord began his life with an act of obedience to the will of his Father; he continued throughout his life on earth always obedient to the divine will and finally accomplished his supreme act of obedience by his death on the cross. It was this subjection of his own will to the Father's

Your just dealings are no secret hidden away in my heart; I boast of your faithful protection, proclaim that mercy, that faithfulness of yours for all to hear it.

Lord, do not withhold your pity from me; let your mercy and faithfulness be now, as ever, my shield. I am beset with evils past numbering, overtaken by my sins; they fill my prospect, countless as the hairs on my head; my courage fails me. Deign, Lord, to set me free; Lord, give heed and help.

Disappointment and shame be theirs, who lay plots against my life; may they slink away covered with confusion, who now rejoice over my downfall. Joy, joy! is their cry; dumb-stricken let them stand, their hopes belied.

Rejoicing and triumph for all the souls that look to you; 'Praise to the Lord,' will ever be their song, who now long for your aid. **I, so helpless and destitute, and the Lord is concerned for me!** You are my champion and my refuge; do not linger, my God, do not linger on the way.

PSALM 40; 54

Lord have mercy on me, is my prayer; bring healing to a soul that has sinned against you. Bitterly my enemies taunt me: 'How long,' they ask, 'ere he will die, and his name be forgotten?' When one comes to visit me, he comes with smooth words, his heart full of malice, ready to go out and plot against me. Smooth as butter his looks, when his heart is all hatred; soft as oil his speech, yet never was drawn sword so deadly.

There they stand, my enemies, talking of me in whispers, devising hurt. **Why, the very man I trusted most, my own**

that was the essential redemptive act of Jesus' life; in entering into the world he accepted his death on the cross (Phil. 2, 8). By his obedience to the divine will Jesus atoned for Adam's disobedience.

An Appeal for Help from the Cross.   The atmosphere of this second part of the psalm is that of Psalms 21 and 30. Our Lord is now the innocent sufferer for the sins of others (that is the meaning of 'my sins'): 'It was for our sins he was wounded, it was guilt of ours crushed him down. God laid on his shoulders our guilt, the guilt of us all' (Is. 53, 5-6). It was this thought which was the main cause of our Lord's agony in the garden of Gethsemani; it best explains the feeling of helplessness and abandonment expressed in this psalm.

On Good Friday the liturgy uses the sentence, 'May they slink away covered with confusion, who now rejoice over my downfall.' It is an appeal to God that the enemies of the suffering Messiah, mocking him on the cross, may not have a lasting victory. Our Lord commends his cause to God, who is ready at his side to help him.

THE TRAITOR, JUDAS

Achitophel Foreshadows Judas.   The mind behind the conspiracy and revolt of David's son Absalom was that of David's own close personal friend and adviser: 'Men followed Achitophel's advice then as if it were God himself they had consulted; so it was all the time he was David's counsellor, and all the time he was Absalom's' (II Kg. 16, 23). David could bear up under the hatred of his sworn enemies, but not under the betrayal of such an intimate friend. Eventually Achitophel fell from Absalom's favour; in despair he went and hanged himself (17, 23).

intimate friend, who shared my bread, has lifted his heel to trip me up. Had some enemy decried me, I could have borne it patiently; some open ill-wisher, I could have sheltered myself from his attack. But you, my second self, my familiar friend! How pleasant was the companionship we shared, you and I; how lovingly we walked as fellow pilgrims in the house of God!

Lord have mercy on me. Proof of your favour, my enemies are baulked of their triumph; you befriend my innocence; nevermore will you banish me from your presence.

PSALM 68

O God, save me; see how the waters close about me, shoulder-high! I am like one who sticks fast in deep mire, with no ground under his feet, one who has ventured out into mid-ocean, to be drowned by the storm. Hoarse my throat with crying wearily for help; my eyes ache with looking up for mercy to my God. **Countless as the hairs on my head are my wanton enemies,** I am no match for the oppressors that wrong me. Should I make amends to them, I, that never robbed them?

Master, Lord of hosts, shall ill fortune of mine bring shame to those who trust in you, make men repent of looking for aid to you, the God of Israel? It is for your sake that I have met with reproach, that I have so often blushed with confusion, an outcast among my brethren, a stranger to my own mother's children. **Was it not jealousy for the honour of your house that consumed me; was it not uttered against you, the reproach I bore?**

What more could I do? I humbled myself before them by fasting; and that, too, was a matter for finding fault; I dressed

St. Paul refers to Holy Thursday as 'the night when he was being betrayed' (I Cor. 11, 23); and without doubt Judas' betrayal was prominent in our Lord's mind. After he had washed his apostles' feet, he remarked: 'You are clean now; only, not all of you.' This was directed at Judas, sitting among the rest of the apostles at the Last Supper. And our Lord went on to quote Psalm 40 as being fulfilled in Judas' betrayal: 'I am telling you this now, before it happens, so that when it happens you may believe it was written of me' (Jn. 13, 19).

THE ENEMIES OF CHRIST

A CRY FOR HELP. Rain water was caught and stored in underground tanks cut from the limestone rock; these cisterns were a feature common to each house in Palestine in David's time. That is why he pictures himself up to the neck in water, with his feet stuck in the mud at the bottom of the cistern. It expresses David's feeling of helplessness in face of intense and unrelenting attack from his wanton, unmerciful enemies.

That he was writing of the Messiah to come, and not only of himself, is proved from the quotation of a verse from this psalm in John 2, 17. The occasion was the cleansing of the temple by Jesus early in his public ministry. St. John records our Lord's words: 'Take these things hence, and make not the house of my Father a house of traffic.' He sees in this attitude of mind the outlook of the speaker in Psalm 68: 'And his disciples remembered how it is written, "I am consumed with jealousy for the honour of your house." ' The disciples probably did not recall Psalm 68 at the moment of the cleansing; it was not till after his resurrection that our Lord ex-

in sackcloth, and they made a by-word of me. Idlers in the market-place taunt me; the drunkards make a song of me over their wine.

To you, Lord, I make my prayer; never man more needed your good will. Listen to me, O God, full of mercy as you are, faithful as you are to your promise of aid. Save me from sinking in the mire, rescue me from my enemies, from the deep waters that surround me; let me not sink under the flood, swallowed up in its depths, and the well's mouth close above me. Listen to me, Lord, of your gracious mercy, look down upon me in the abundance of your pity; do not turn your face away from your servant in this time of trouble, give a speedy answer to my prayer. Draw near in my distress, and grant deliverance; relieve me, so hard pressed by my enemies. Lord, you know how they reproach me, how I blush with shame; you see how many are my persecutors. Heart-broken with that shame, I pine away, looking round for pity, where pity is none, for comfort, where there is no comfort to be found. **They gave me gall to eat, and when I was thirsty they gave me vinegar to drink.**

Let their feast be turned into a trap, a net to catch them and theirs, ever the blind eye be theirs, ever the halting loin. Pour out your anger upon them, let them be overtaken by the tide of your vengeance; **let their dwelling-place be deserted, their tents for ever uninhabited.** Who is it they persecute? A man already afflicted by you; hard was my hurt to bear, and these have added to it. Do you add guilt to guilt in their reckoning; let them never claim your acquittal; let their names be blotted out from the record of the living, and never written among the just.

See how friendless I am, and how distressed! Let your help,

plained all the Old Testament prophecies concerning himself (Lk. 24, 27).

A CURSE UPON ENEMIES. The cistern imagery of a man drowning is continued in this paragraph. The attacks of David's enemies grow fiercer. The atmosphere resembles that of Psalms 21 and 30; we are back on Calvary again, with Jesus calling on his Father in the moment of his dereliction and persecution.

The sentence 'when I was thirsty they gave me vinegar to drink' is usually applied to our Lord's thirst on the cross. Three times he was offered a drink; the first time, a drugged drink (myrrh or gall) to relieve the pain of crucifixion; the second time, 'The soldiers, too, mocked him when they came and offered him vinegar to drink, by saying, "If you are the king of the Jews save yourself" ' (Lk. 23, 36-37). The third time was when one soldier gave him a drink on hearing him call out that he was thirsty. The first and third occasions were acts of charity; this psalm seems to refer to the second.

The psalmist then breaks out into terrible curses on his enemies. In justification it is necessary to recall that the law of 'an eye for an eye and a tooth for a tooth' was in force in the Old Testament. Also many of the details are poetic and not meant to be taken strictly literally. And, most important of all, it is God's cause that the psalmist has at heart, not his own personal revenge; so that the enemies cursed are really opposing God himself. It is lawful to wish that they be destroyed, and so cease offending the divine Majesty.

St. Peter applies one verse of the cursing portion of this psalm (and a verse of another cursing psalm, 108, 8: 'Let his office be entrusted to another') to Judas Iscariot in Acts 1, 20.

O God, sustain me. I will sing in praise of God's name, herald it gratefully; a more acceptable sacrifice, this, to the Lord than any young bullock, for all its promise of horn and hoof. Here is a sight to make the afflicted rejoice; to cheer men's spirits in their quest for God.

PSALM 108

God that guards my renown, do not leave me unbefriended; there are malicious lips, treacherous lips, that decry me; whispering against me, hedging me about with a conspiracy of hatred, in unprovoked attack. **On their side, all calumny in return for love, on mine all prayer; kindness is repaid with injury, love with ill will.**

Do you, my Lord and Master, take my part, to defend your own honour; no mercy is so tender as yours. Deliver me in my helpless need; my heart is pierced through with anguish. Like a tapering shadow I depart, swept away like a locust on the wing. My knees are weak with fasting, my strength pines away unnourished. **They make a laughing-stock of me, toss their heads in derision as they pass by.** Help me, O Lord my God; deliver me in your mercy; prove to them that my woes are a visitation from you, sent by no hand but yours. Bless me, you, and let them curse as they will; disappoint my adversaries, and grant your servant relief. Let these, my accusers, be covered with shame, wrapped in the mantle of their own confusion. Loudly will I give the Lord thanks, praise him before multitudes that listen; the Lord who has stood at the right hand of the friendless, brought redress to an innocent soul misjudged.

If the whole psalm is to be put into the mouth of Christ, these words of cursing are best understood as a prayer of the Mystical Body for God's intervention against his enemies. Actually in the Litany of the Saints we still pray that God will hear our prayer to bring low the enemies of the Church.

AN INNOCENT SOUL MISJUDGED

CHRIST'S LOVE FOR HIS ENEMIES. A new element in this psalm is our Lord's love for those who hate him. When he was being crucified on Calvary, he kept on saying over and over again, 'Father, forgive them; they do not know what it is they are doing' (Lk. 23, 34).

Our Lord's innocence is also expressly declared in the final sentence of this psalm. This fact is repeated again and again during the Roman trial; despite all the charges brought against Jesus, Pilate judged the prisoner innocent: 'I cannot discover any fault in this man.'

The atmosphere of this psalm is the same as that of the more famous Passion psalms (21, 30, 68). The psalmist has two vivid images to express the extremity of his anguish. He compares himself to a lengthening shadow in late evening, a shadow that will soon disappear and cease to exist; and he likens his helplessness to that of locusts swept off their course of flight by a sudden gust of wind.

The Messianic character of this psalm is proved from the quotation of verse 8 by St. Peter in Acts 1, 20: 'Let another take over his office.' I have omitted this verse, along with the rest of the cursing portion of the psalm (verses 6-20); they have already been discussed in the commentary on Psalm 68.

CONTENTS: Chapter 3

Am. 5, 16-20;		
8, 4-10	The Day of the Lord	56
Am. 9, 7-15;		
5, 24	Blessings of Messianic Times	58
Os. 1—3	God's Love for Israel	60
Os. 14, 2-9; 11, 4;		
13, 14	The Triumph of Divine Love	64
Ps. 44	Christ the Royal Bridegroom	66
Is. 1, 24-27;		
2, 1-5	The Church Visible and Universal	68
Is. 3, 16—4, 6	Divine Protection of Purified Sion	68
Is. 7, 10-25;		
8, 5-10	Virgin Mother of God	72
Is. 8, 16—9, 7	The Prince of Peace	74
Is. 10, 12, 17-23	A Remnant will return	78
Is. 11, 1—12, 6	The Seven Gifts of the Holy Ghost	78
Is. 13—33	The Day of the Lord	82
Is. 19, 1, 16-25	The Gentile World Converted	86
Is. 24—35	The City of God	88
Mich. 4, 1-8; 2,		
12-13; 7, 11-14	The Church Visible and Universal	102
Mich. 5, 2-14	Born at Bethlehem	104
Ps. 71	A Just and Peaceful King	106
Pss. 46; 66; 67; 86	The Universal Church	108

3. The Divided Kingdom

THE kingdom of Israel remained united only for the reign of three kings, Saul, David, and Solomon; on the death of Solomon it split into two, the northern (called Israel) and the southern (called Juda). Solomon is known mainly for his building of the temple in Jerusalem, which had the effect of centralizing the worship of God in that city; Jerusalem became the religious as well as the political centre of Jewish life. This did away with local shrines, arousing the hatred of their priests. Solomon's high living, his despotism, his exemption of Juda from taxes (he was of the tribe of Juda) aggravated the age-old rivalry between Juda and Joseph (the northern tribes). The Schism resulted, destroying the essential political and religious unity of the Sinaitic covenant and leaving both sides too weak to resist outside enemies. Within two hundred years the northern kingdom had nine different dynasties; in 721 B. C. it fell under the onslaught of the Assyrian conqueror.

To keep the Messianic hope alive, and to preserve Israel from idolatry and from foreign domination, God raised up a long line of prophets. The first and most famous was Elias (he appears with Moses at the Transfiguration); he went about preaching the Lord's message during the reign of Achab and Jezabel. Many others followed him; seventeen have left inspired excerpts from their sermons and writings. Selections are given in this chapter from four of these writing prophets, Amos, Osee, Isaias, and Micheas, as well as six psalms composed at this period.

The troubled times in which these four prophets lived are manifest in their writings. The danger of idolatry, of following the ways of the Assyrian overlords and worshipping their gods, became more acute; so that to a great extent the prophets' message from the Lord is a warning against this danger. Their purpose was to keep Israel aware of her great destiny under the rule of the Messiah to come. Isaias has much new revelation on Christ the Prince of peace, endowed with all the gifts of the Holy Ghost and born of a virgin mother in Bethlehem (Micheas).

AMOS 5,16-20; 8, 4-10

This doom he utters, he, the Lord of hosts, he, our Master: 'Market-place or street is none but shall echo with wailing and cries of woe; country-folk, and such as are skilled in mourning, they shall call in to make dirge and dole; dirge, too, the vineyards shall sing; all this, when I make my way through your midst,' the Lord says.

'Fools, that wait eagerly for the day of the Lord's coming! Think you it shall serve your turn? **Nay, it is the Lord's day of triumph, not yours; dawn it must, but in darkness, not in light.** Speeds he well, that shuns lion and meets bear? Has he joy of his home-coming, that leans hand on wall, and all at once is bitten by a viper? And for you, that day brings darkness, not the light you craved for; no radiance haunts about it, only gloom.'

Here is word for you, oppressors of the poor, that bring ruin on your fellow-citizens in their need; you that long for new moon and sabbath to be at an end, for trading to begin and granary to be opened, so you may be at your shifts again, the scant measure, the high price, the false weights! You that for a debt, though it were but the price of a pair of shoes, will make slaves of poor, honest folk; you that sell refuse for wheat! By Jacob's ancient renown the Lord swears it, crimes of yours shall remain for ever unforgotten. Well may the earth quake over such doings, to the hurt of all that dwell in it; everywhere mount up, and shift, and sink, like Egypt's river in flood.

'Day of doom,' says the Lord God, 'when there shall be sunset at noon, and earth shall be overshadowed under the full light! All your feasting turned to lament, all your songs

THE DAY OF THE LORD

A PROPHECY OF DOOM. Amos was a shepherd from the rugged desert country to the east of Bethlehem. As he was herding his sheep, the Lord called him to go and prophesy in Bethel, a town twenty miles to the north. Bethel was one of the sanctuaries in the northern kingdom where king Jeroboam I had set up a golden calf for the Israelites to worship (3 Kg. 12, 26-33). More than 150 years had elapsed since Bethel was set up as a shrine; it was now the reign of Jeroboam II. The opposition between the northern and southern kingdoms had grown even more intense with the passage of time. So Amos, the southerner, went with some eagerness to pronounce God's sentence of disaster on the north. He met with a cold reception from the king and high priest at Bethel; but he delivered his message from the Lord and went back again to his flock in the desert.

This is the first time that the phrase 'the day of the Lord's coming' (in Hebrew, Yom Yahweh) is found in the Old Testament. The Israelites referred to any visible divine intervention as Yom Yahweh. God's intervention during the Exodus from Egypt was the most spectacular in their history. The Hebrews thought of it mainly as God's means of destroying the pagan nations opposing his chosen people. And that is what they were looking for again at this time. But Amos tells them that the day of the Lord will be a day of punishment for SINNERS, whether Jew or Gentile. Their idolatry and social injustices will be punished by the justice of God.

In actual fact Yom Yahweh is still to come. It is the final intervention of God at the end of time, when Christ shall come a second time to judge the living and the dead. In the

to dirge and dole; not a loin but goes clad in sackcloth, not a head but is shaved bald; never was such mourning made, though it were for an only son; bitter the day, bitter its ending.'

AMOS 9, 7-15; 5, 24

'Ethiop or Israelite, what care I?' the Lord says. 'God that brought you here from Egypt was God that brought the Philistines from Caphtor, brought the Syrians from Kir! Divine regard that watches ever this kingdom, marks ever its guilt; I will blot it out, believe me, from the face of the earth.'

And blot out the name of Jacob altogether? 'Nay, not that,' the Lord says. 'At my command, the whole world shall be a sieve, to sift the race of Israel as corn is sifted in the riddle, and never a grain cast out loose on the bare ground; at the sword's point they shall die, all the guilty that are found among my people; the guilty, who now flatter themselves that evil shall never come next or nigh them. **Then I mean to rebuild the fallen dwelling-place of David, all its breaches made good, all its ruins restored; it shall stand once more as it stood long ago; empire it shall have over the Edomites, and all the Gentile folk I claim for my own.**

'A time is coming,' the Lord says, 'when ploughman shall tread on the heels of reaper, sower's task begin ere vintager's is ended; never a mountain-side but shall run with sweet wine, never a hill but its rugged nature shall be tamed. **And like waters rolling in full tide, like a perennial stream, right and justice shall abound.**

'And I will bring back my people of Israel from its exile, to rebuild ruined cities and dwell there, plant vineyards and drink of them, till gardens and eat the fruits of them. Firm

course of time other prophets will make known more specific details; but none of them, not even our Lord, will make known the TIME of the Second Coming.

BLESSINGS OF MESSIANIC TIMES

DAVID'S HOUSE REBUILT. Within fifty years of Amos' words of doom, the people to whom he was speaking would be punished by the Lord with exile; many would be killed by the sword, the leaders of the nation with great numbers of the common people led off into captivity by the Assyrian conquerors. Exiled from the promised land, far away from the Lord's presence in the temple at Jerusalem, they would be punished for their idolatry and evil lives. This temporal punishment was a foreshadowing of eternal punishment for sin when the Last Judgment came; it was a partial fulfilment of the Day of the Lord.

Their favoured position as God's chosen people would not save them from punishment for their sins. But God had promised David that his house would last forever. Exile must eventually pass, and the race of Israel be restored to their own land under the leadership of the Davidic dynasty. At this point the prophet's thought goes beyond the temporal rule of the royal house of Israel to the eternal rule of Christ the King; he it is who will give permanence to David's house. The mention of Gentiles being incorporated into the kingdom is always a sign of Messianic times; and that is how the apostle James interprets this passage at the Council of Jerusalem (Acts 15, 16).

The spiritual blessings of Christ's kingdom are presented under the imagery of material prosperity, as in Genesis 49,

root they shall take in their native soil, never again to be torn away from the home I have given them,' says the Lord, your own God.

OSEE 1—3

When first the divine voice made itself heard through Osee, this was the command given him: 'Wanton wed you, wantons breed you; in a wanton land you dwell, that keeps troth with its Lord never.' So it was he came to marry Gomer, a daughter of Debelaim. When he got her with child, and she bore him a son, 'This one,' the Lord told him, 'you are to call Jezrahel; at Jezrahel the blood was spilt for which, ere long, Jehu's line must be punished, and Israel have kings no more; in Jezrahel valley, my doom is, bow of Israel shall be broken.' And next, she was brought to bed of a daughter; of whom the Lord said, 'Unbefriended call her, in token that I will befriend Israel no longer.' Unbefriended, then, was the name of her; and after she was weaned, once more Gomer conceived, and had a son. This time the command was, 'Call him Strange-folk; no longer shall you be my people, or I be your God.'

Measureless the race of Israel shall be and countless as the sand by the sea shore. In the very place where once the doom was uttered, 'You are but strangers to me,' they shall be welcomed as sons of the living God. As one people, Juda and Israel shall be rallied, under a leader of their common choice; and they shall come flocking from every corner of the land; such great doings there shall be at Jezrahel. God's-folk and Befriended, these are the names they should have by rights, brother and sister of yours.

10. This is based on the picture of the Garden of Eden (Gen. 2), where fertility of the earth is a symbol of sanctifying grace; crop will follow crop with such prolific growth that work will be continuous; even the barren hillsides will be covered with vineyards.

GOD'S LOVE FOR ISRAEL

OSEE'S WIFE AND CHILDREN. It is no easy task to be a prophet of the Lord, particularly when asked to act out that prophecy. Osee was commanded to take as wife a woman from the streets; she symbolized Israel, the spouse of the Lord, always running after false gods, untrue to her husband. By this marriage Osee was a living reminder to the people of their abandonment of God.

The three children of Osee all had symbolical names; they signified the doom that was soon to come on the chosen people; this was the punishment of exile into Assyria. The first son was called Jezrahel, which was the name of a town on the plain of Esdraelon. This was the scene of terrible bloodshed by Jehu, the founder of the reigning dynasty in Israel (4 Kg. 9-10); punishment will come to Israel in the same place and with like bloodshed by the Assyrian invaders. The two other children's names symbolize God's changed attitude to Israel; formerly bound to him by the closest ties of friendship, his own chosen people, they are no longer objects of his love, but complete strangers to the Lord.

Suddenly the picture changes; doom is followed by complete restoration. They shall come back from exile, the northern and southern kingdoms united again; Israel (the name is almost identical with Jezrahel) united to the Lord in the fulness of Messianic times.

The Lord's word came to me: 'To wife that will have gallants a-courting her, show yourself a lover yet. The Lord is yet Israel's lover, that has no eyes but for alien gods, leaves grape for husk.'

So buy her back to me I must, fifteen pieces of silver paying for her ransom, and a core and a half of barley. 'A long time you must wait for me,' I told her, 'your wantonness leaving, yet still unwed; and I will wait for you as faithfully.'

A long time the sons of Israel must wait, neither king nor prince to rule them, neither sacrifice nor shrine to worship at, neither sacred mantle nor their own images to consult. **Then they will come back, and to the Lord, their own God, betake them, and to David that is their true king; the Lord, and the Lord's goodness, holds them spellbound at last.**

'It is but love's stratagem, thus to lead her out into the wilderness; once there, it shall be all words of comfort. Clad in vineyards that wilderness shall be, that vale of sad memory a passage-way of hope; and a song shall be on her lips, the very music of her youth, when I rescued her from Egypt long ago. Husband she calls me now,' the Lord says, 'Master no longer; that name I stifle on her lips; master-gods of the countryside must all be forgotten. Beast and bird and creeping thing to peace pledge I; bow and sword and war's alarms break I; all shall sleep safe abed, the folk that dwell in her.

'**Everlastingly I will betroth you to myself, favour and redress and mercy of mine your dowry; by the keeping of his troth you shall learn to know the Lord.** When that day comes, heaven shall win answer,' the Lord says, 'answer from me; and from heaven, earth; and from earth, the corn and wine and oil it nourishes; and from these, the people of my sowing. **Deep, deep I will sow them in the land I love; a friend, now, to her that was Unbefriended; to a people that**

THE WANTON WIFE RETURNS.   Amos and Osee spoke to the same audience; they both threatened Israel with the punishment of exile for her abandonment of the Lord. But their approach was entirely different. Amos was from the southern kingdom of Juda; he preached to the schismatic and hated northern kingdom of Israel. His theme was the justice of God: Israel had broken the covenant with the Lord and must suffer for it.

Osee belonged to the north; he was a member of the people he was addressing; emotionally he was deeply moved by the disaster soon to overtake Israel. He saw his people as a person, an erring wife unfaithful to her husband; it was God's love, not his justice, that was the theme of his preaching. He might be called the prophet of divine love in the Old Testament; his approach is similar to our Lord's in the parable of the Prodigal Son (Lk. 15).

Instead of the father-son relationship, Osee has that of husband and wife. The prodigal wife has left her husband for other lovers; she has sunk so low that she is now a concubine slave. Osee is ordered to buy her back for thirty shekels (a core and a half of barley was worth fifteen shekels), the price of a slave (Ex. 21, 32). This is a reference to Israel's exile in Assyria, away from the Lord her husband who still loves her: 'All at once my heart misgives me, and from its embers pity revives' (11, 8).

From the wilderness of exile, Israel comes back repentant to the Lord. Now that she is bound to him by bonds of love, with the true Messianic king David to rule over her, the desert blooms once again, like the Garden of Eden. Love, not servitude, is the bond that binds Israel to her God; the word 'Master' (in Hebrew, Baal) is forbidden because of its association with pagan gods.

was none of mine I will say, "You are my people," and they to me, "You are our God." '

OSEE 14, 2-9; 11, 4; 13, 14

Come back, Israel, to the Lord your God; it is sin that has caused your overthrow. Come back, men of Israel, with a plea ready on your lips: 'Pardon all our guilt, and take the best we have in return; the praises we utter shall be our victims now. No longer we will find refuge in Assyrian help, mount our men on horses from Egypt; no longer will we give the name of gods to the things our own hands have made; you are the friend of the friendless who trust in you.'

'Sons of Adam,' the Lord says, 'they should be drawn with leading-strings of love. **I will bring healing to their crushed spirits; in free mercy I will give them back my love; my vengeance has passed them by.** From the grave's power to rescue them, from death to ransom them; I, death's mortal enemy, I, corruption's undoing!

'I will be morning dew, to make Israel grow as the lilies grow, strike roots deep as the forest of Lebanon. Those branches shall spread, it shall become fair as the olive, fragrant as Lebanon cedar. **None that dwells under the protection of that name but shall come back to me;** corn shall be theirs in plenty, and they will grow like one of their own vineyards, famed as the vintage of Lebanon itself. The false gods of Ephraim are forgotten; mine to answer his prayer and tend him, ever-green as a fir-tree; from me all your increase comes.'

The names of the three children now express the new relationship with the Lord. Jezrahel means 'the Lord has sown'; it stands for Israel (the two names even sound alike). It no longer signifies bloodshed, but a crop of God's own planting, basking in the Lord's favour.

THE TRIUMPH OF DIVINE LOVE

REPENTANCE AND RESTORATION OF ISRAEL. Man must be sorry for his sins before God will forgive him. The two main causes of Israel's exile were the sin of idolatry and their want of trust in God's power. They had worshipped false gods, and even set up an idol of the Lord in the form of a golden calf at Bethel. Instead of looking to the Lord for help, when in danger from foreign enemies, they had relied on political alliances, now with Assyria, now with Egypt; Assyrian exile was the punishment.

In exile they had come back to God; divine grace had moved them to repent of their past. So God would bring them back from exile and settle them once more peacefully in their own land. This restoration goes beyond a merely temporal return to Palestine; it extends into Christian times when the chosen people became the Church, ransomed by the blood of Christ and closely united to him by the bonds of divine love.

This life of sanctifying grace, as we have seen, is commonly presented to the people of the Old Testament under the imagery of material prosperity. Here, the trees, flowers and crops of the famous fertile slopes of the Lebanon Mountains are symbolical of the spiritual blessings of Messianic times. The Lord himself will be the dew that falls by night, the source of grace that makes the Christian full of vitality and fruitful in good works.

PSALM 44

Joyful the thoughts that well up from my heart, the King's honour for my theme; my tongue flows readily as the pen of a swift writer.

Yours is more than mortal beauty, your lips overflow with gracious utterance; the blessings God has granted you can never fail. Gird on your sword at your side, great warrior, gird yourself with all your majesty and all your beauty; ride on triumphant, in the name of faithfulness and justice. Dread counsel your own might shall give you; so sharp are your arrows, subduing nations to your will, daunting the hearts of the king's enemies. **Your throne, O God, endures for ever and ever, the sceptre of your royalty is a rod that rules true;** you have been a friend to right, an enemy to wrong, and God, your own God, has given you an unction to bring you pride beyond any of your fellows. Your garments are scented with myrrh, and aloes, and cassia; from ivory palaces there are harps sounding in your honour. Daughters of kings come out to meet you; at your right hand stands the queen, in Ophir gold arrayed.

(Listen, my daughter, and consider my words attentively; you are to forget, henceforward, your own nation, and the house of your father; your beauty, now, is all for the king's delight; he is your Lord, and worship belongs to him.) The people of Tyre, too, will have its presents to bring; the noblest of its citizens will be courting your favour. **She comes, the princess, all fair to see, her robe of golden cloth, a robe of rich embroidery, to meet the King.** The maidens of her court follow her into your presence, all rejoicing, all triumphant, as they enter the king's palace!

CHRIST THE ROYAL BRIDEGROOM

THE WEDDING-DAY PROCESSION.   The prophet Osee is usually credited with being the first to emphasize God's love for Israel, and Christ's love for the Church, as a relation of husband and wife. Psalm 44 takes up the same theme; later, the Song of Songs will develop the idea more fully; and the final stage comes in St. Paul: 'The man is the head to which the woman's body is united, just as Christ is the head of the Church, he the Saviour on whom the safety of his body depends' (Eph. 5, 23-32).

Psalm 44 proceeds like the account of a wedding in true oriental style, as described in our Lord's parable of the Ten Virgins (Mt. 25, 1-13). The material for the imagination of the author may have been provided by some actual royal wedding, such as that of Solomon and his Egyptian princess (3 Kg. 3, 1). It begins with a description of the bridegroom—his beauty, strength, justice, wealth, and magnificence; the perfumed garments and music indicate the joy and grandeur of the occasion. As he comes to bring his bride to the wedding, a few words of advice (written within brackets) are given to her by the psalmist. The richness of presents is indicated by the word 'Tyre,' noted for its wealth. The wedding-dress of the bride is described as she waits for the royal bridegroom.

John the Baptist called our Lord the bridegroom (Jn. 3, 29), and Jesus also so described himself (Mk. 2, 19-20). That he is the bridegroom of Psalm 44 is proved from Hebrews 1, 8-9, where St. Paul quotes two verses to prove the divinity of Christ: 'Your throne, O God, endures for ever and ever' could be written of no man but Christ.

The woman is primarily the Church, but she also stands for

You shall have sons worthy of your own fathers, and divide a world between them for their domains. While time lasts, mine it is to keep your name in remembrance; age after age, nations will do you honour.

ISAIAS 1, 24-27; 2, 1-5

This is a message which was revealed to Isaias, the son of Amos, about Juda and Jerusalem. What, then, does the Lord proclaim; he, the God of hosts, he, the Prince of Israel? 'Out upon it, I will rid myself of these rebels, my enemies shall have their deserts. And then I will take you in hand again, smelting you till you are free from dross, purging away all that base alloy. Once more I will give you judges like the judges of old, counsellors like the counsellors of past days, and you shall be called the home of right, the faithful city.'

Right and justice shall be done, when Sion is redeemed, when her exiles return. **The mountain where the Lord dwells will be lifted high above the mountain tops, looking down over the hills, and all nations will flock there together.** A multitude of peoples will make their way to it, crying, 'Come, let us climb up to the Lord's mountain peak, to the house where the God of Jacob dwells; he shall teach us the right way, we will walk in the paths he has chosen.'

The Lord's commands shall go out from Sion, his word from Jerusalem, and he will sit in judgment on the nations, giving his award to a multitude of peoples. They will melt down their swords into ploughshares, their spears into pruning-hooks, nation levying war against nation and training itself for battle no longer. 'Come you too,' they will say,

Mary. 'Your beauty now is all for the king's delight' recalls Gabriel's 'Hail, full of grace; the Lord is with you' (Lk. 1, 28). The shining gold wedding-dress is almost identical with the sunlit raiment of the 'woman that wore the sun for her mantle' (Apoc. 12, 1).

THE CHURCH VISIBLE AND UNIVERSAL

THE PRE-EMINENCE OF JERUSALEM. Isaias began his ministry at the time when Osee was finishing his, about twenty years before the fall of the northern kingdom. Unlike Osee and Amos (this prophet was not Isaias' father), Isaias prophesied only in the southern kingdom, at Jerusalem. He has the same message of punishment for idolatry; this would mainly take the form of exile, from which the Lord's former rebels and enemies would return purified.

Sion is only another name for Jerusalem; this city, with its house of God, the temple, as its central feature, would be headquarters for the restored Israel of God: 'And I saw that holy city which is the new Jerusalem, being sent down by God from heaven' (Apoc. 21, 2). Isaias pictures it as visible to all the world: 'A city cannot be hidden if it is built on a mountain-top' (Mt. 5, 14). It will not be the material city of stone, but a rallying-point and a source of light and life to all the nations of the world. This quality of catholicity or universality is always a sign of Messianic times.

Instead of nation warring against nation, there will be 'peace on earth to men that are God's friends' (Mt. 2, 14). This will result from the pursuit of love and justice by peoples who follow the commands of the Lord as their rule of life. Where such conditions exist there will be no longer need of weapons of war. This is what our Lord promised: 'Peace is my

'children of Jacob, let us walk together in the path where the Lord shows us light.'

ISAIAS 3, 16—4, 6

This, too, the Lord says: 'See what airs they put on, the women-folk of Sion, walk head in air, look about them with glancing eyes, click the trappings on their feet with mincing steps.' Ay, but the Lord has his doom ready for them; bald of head and bare of temple the women of Sion shall know it. In one day the Lord will sweep away all their finery, the shoes with the rest; locket, and collar, necklace and bracelet and veil; hair-pin, ankle-ring, chain, scent-box, pendant, signet-ring and nose-ring; gala dress and gown and scarf, bodkin and mirror and shawl and riband and kerchief. There will be new fashions then; stench for scent, hempen rope for waist-band, baldness for curls, and hair shirt for stomacher.

Of the men-folk, too, all that is fairest shall fall by the sword, all that is bravest, slain in battle. See where she sits on the ground desolate, every gateway of hers full of sorrow and lament! Day of desolation! Here are seven women catching hold of one man, and promising, 'We will earn our bread, find ourselves in clothing; only let us bear your name, and be saved from the reproach of barrenness!'

When that day comes, bud and fruit there shall be, of the Lord's fostering; burgeoning of glory made manifest, harvest of our soil, the trophy of Israel's gleanings. **Set apart for him, all that dwell in Sion now, all that survive the city's purging;** none else will be left alive in Jerusalem, when the Lord sweeps away the guilt of Sion's women-folk, washes Jerusalem clean from the blood that stains her, with the searing breath of his judgment. **And over mount Sion, the shrine of his**

bequest to you, and the peace which I will give you is mine to give' (Jn. 14, 27).

DIVINE PROTECTION OF PURIFIED SION

CHASTISEMENT OF THE WOMEN OF JERUSALEM. The Lord himself accused the whole of Israel of infidelity: 'Ox recognizes its owner, ass knows the way to its master's crib; and I? I go unacknowledged; my people of Israel gives me never a thought' (Is. 1, 13). Not only was the civil authority corrupt (3, 1-15), but even the usually devout element, the women, gave no thought to God. In the capital city of Jerusalem, where Isaias prophesied, they dressed up in all their finery, resplendent with jewellery; vanity and pride was the whole purpose of their lives.

Their pride will be humbled when they go into exile; in place of joy there will be mourning; they will exchange their fine clothing for the garb of a slave. So many of their men will be slain in war that it will be almost impossible to find a husband (unmarried women were the most wretched class in ancient society); they will go to any lengths to get the protection of a man's name.

As Isaias describes this sudden reversal of fortune, he suddenly changes his line of thought. The women fade away, and in their place sits Jerusalem (the women symbolizing the city), the queen of cities, mourning the disaster of exile, a punishment from God for sinful living.

But a day of redemption will come; God's heart is moved to pity at the sight of suffering. Three elements of Messianic times are noted: (1) The fertility of the land symbolizing spiritual blessings of divine grace. (2) The holiness of a purified remnant that comes back from exile converted from their

name, cloud shall hang by day, glowing haze by night, a veil
for glory. Canopy they shall have, to shade them from the
day's heat, a refuge to give them shelter from storm and rain.

ISAIAS 7, 10-25; 8, 5-10

The Lord sent this message to Achaz, 'Ask the Lord your
God to give you a sign, in the depths beneath you, or in the
height above you.'

But Achaz said, 'Nay, I will not ask for a sign; I will not
put the Lord to the test.'

'Why then,' said Isaias, 'listen to me, you that are of
David's race. Cannot you be content with trying the patience
of men? Must you try my God's patience too? Sign you ask
none, but sign the Lord will give you. **Maid shall be with
child, and shall bear a son, that shall be called Emmanuel.
On butter and honey shall be his thriving, till he is of age to
know good from harm; already, before he can tell this from
that, the land shall be abandoned.** Whereas you are in fear
before two kings, the Lord means to bring upon you, and
your people, and your father's house such days of trouble as
have not been seen since Ephraim parted from Juda, with the
coming of the king of Assyria.'

Days when the Lord will whistle up those plagues of his,
yonder flies that hatch by the last rivers of Egypt; yonder
bees, that hive in the land of Assur. Invading swarms, that
settle even upon mountain, gully and rock, cavern; thicket is
none, nor underground pit, shall be safe from them. Hard
times, when the Lord will be hiring mercenaries from beyond
Euphrates, the king of Assyria's men, and will leave you quite
bare, hair of head and legs shaved close with this hired rasor

evil ways by suffering: 'Crimson-dyed be your guilt, it shall turn snow-white; like wool new-washed yonder scarlet stain' (1, 8). (3) God's loving care for his Church symbolized by the Shekinah, the luminous cloud of the Exodus wanderings that guided and protected the chosen people (Ex. 40, 34-38).

VIRGIN MOTHER OF GOD

EMMANUEL: GOD WITH US. King Achaz of Juda had been approached by Israel and Syria to join with them in a revolt against Assyria, then the dominant power in the Middle East. When he refused, Israel and Syria marched on Jerusalem. At this point Isaias was sent by the Lord with a guarantee of divine protection; but Achaz had already decided to appeal to Assyria for help. Such a course of action was a denial of the Sinaitic Covenant by which the chosen people agreed to trust in God and not in political alliances: 'Then I will make you my own people, and will be your God.' Achaz took as his slogan: 'Assyria-with-us'; it should have been 'God-with-us.'

The alliance with Assyria was to have disastrous consequences for the chosen people. Achaz inaugurated a state of affairs that would affect the Davidic dynasty: the Messiah (Emmanuel) would be born in lowly state, not in royal splendour, amid hardship and privation. This seems to be the meaning of 'butter and honey' in this context; it signifies a state of drought and famine, when no crops are sown or land cultivated: 'Hard times, when one heifer and a pair of sheep are all the stock a man has.'

Achaz's infidelity to the Lord did not prevent the coming of the Messiah, but it did determine the circumstances of his birth—in a stable instead of a palace. As a punishment of the Davidic dynasty, Christ would not be born into a reigning Jewish family.

Waiting for Christ

of his, and the beard too! Hard times, when one heifer and a pair of sheep are all the stock a man has; milk plentiful, so that he has butter to eat; of butter and honey the survivors will have no lack; but where once a thousand vines grew, each worth a silver piece, all will be thorns and brushwood. Covert of thorns and brushwood, where men go armed with bow and arrows; only the hillsides, that have felt the hoe, shall be free from the terrors of the covert, and these the cattle shall graze, the sheep trample under foot.

And the Lord went on to say to me, 'This people of mine has cut itself off from the gently-flowing waters of Siloe; and now the Lord will bring the waters of Euphrates upon it, in full flood; I mean the king of the Assyrians, in all his greatness. This flood will fill up all the channels of the river, overflow all its banks, till it pours over Juda, overwhelming her and reaching up to her very neck. **Wings spread out wide, till they cover the whole breadth of your own land, Emmanuel, the God who is with us!'**

Muster, then, you peoples, to your own overthrow; obey the call, distant lands, in vain; summon up your valour, arm yourselves in vain! All your scheming baffled, all your boasts belied; God is with us!

ISAIAS 8, 16—9, 7

Now to guard the prophetic record close, now to seal up these instructions, in the keeping of my disciples! What though the Lord hide his face from the men of Israel? To him will I look, and wait patiently for him; here stand I, and

Jesus would be born of a virgin mother. Isaias used the Hebrew word 'ALMAH,' maiden, and that is how St. Matthew, under the inspiration of the same Holy Spirit who had inspired Isaias to utter the words, tells us that they are fulfilled in Mary and her virginity (Mt. 1, 23).

In the light of the Incarnation, Emmauel takes on a deeper meaning than it had for Isaias; God is not only with us to save us but is now present on this earth in the person of Jesus Christ our Lord.

THE LAND OF EMMANUEL. Palestine is the promised land. It is only because Jesus was to be born and live there that it occupies such an important place in this prophecy. God's plan to save his people in the past, present, and future is based on the Messiah to come; without him Israel's history has no meaning. That is why the prophets are not concerned over the time element: Christ is always present as the saving force of his people.

In this paragraph the imagery is taken from the river Euphrates (one of the main rivers of Assyria), in flood, inundating Palestine, 'reaching up to her very neck' (Jerusalem). This is a punishment for abandoning the Lord, symbolized under 'the gently-flowing waters of Siloe' (the Jerusalem water-supply).

THE PRINCE OF PEACE

THE DAWN OF BETTER TIMES. In a private session with his disciples, Isaias warns them not to look to wizard and diviner for information about the outcome of the Assyrian invasion; it is the Lord alone who can tell them what is to happen in

these children the Lord has given me, a portent, a warning sent to Israel by the Lord of hosts, who dwells on mount Sion. Men will bid you consult wizard and diviner, that talk in ghostly voices over their enchantments: 'Who doubts,' they will say, 'God will send his own people answer, an oracle from the dead to the living?' By these instructions rather abide, this record of prophecy; who follows other inspiration, shall not see the dawn.

Land of Zabulon and Nephthali, its burden at first how lightly borne! but afterwards affliction weighed on it, Galilee, by the sea road where the Gentiles dwell west of Jordan. **And now the people that went about in darkness has seen a great light; for men abiding in a land where death overshadowed them, light has dawned.** Their number you increased, but gave them no joy of it; now, they shall rejoice in your presence, as men rejoice when the harvest is in, as men triumph when victory is won, and booty taken, and they fall to dividing up the spoils. Yoke that fixed the burden, shaft that galled the shoulder, rod of the tyrant, all lie broken now, as they did long ago, when Madian fell. All the trophies of the old tumultuous forays, all the panoply stained with blood, will be burnt up now, will go to feed the flames.

For our sakes a child is born, to our race a son is given, whose shoulder will bear the sceptre of princely power. What name shall be given him? Peerless among counsellors, the mighty God, Father of the world to come, the Prince of peace. Ever wider shall his dominion spread, endlessly at peace; he will sit on David's kingly throne, to give it lasting foundations of justice and right; so tenderly he loves us, the Lord of hosts.

the future. At that time Assyria had already occupied the area around the lake of Galilee, the territory of the tribes of Zabulon and Nephthali. The Lord now reveals to Isaias that it will be in this very place that salvation will dawn for Israel. This was fulfilled to the letter when our Lord came and settled at Capharnaum, by the shores of the lake of Galilee (Mt. 4, 13-16).

The preaching of our Lord, with his headquarters by the lakeside, is vividly presented as light shining in darkness: the light of truth dissipating the darkness of ignorance and error. In ancient times there was no adequate artificial lighting, so that the rising of the sun meant the return of light and warmth; it is a frequent biblical metaphor. Three other metaphors, signifying the joy of Messianic times, follow the light-darkness imagery. Men will be happy like those at the celebrations marking the end of a successful harvest; they will rejoice like soldiers returning from a battle they have won, with much booty taken from the enemy; the state of slavery and subjection, under the imagery of the hard lot of beasts of burden, will no longer gall the shoulders of the chosen people.

This state of peace, justice, and right is pictured as actually existing with the birth of the Messiah prince. This absence of time perspective (it would be more than seven hundred years till the birth of Christ) is common in Hebrew prophecy. Four qualities of the Messiah are listed: He will be wise, powerful, paternal, and peaceful. That he would be the omnipotent Lord himself ('mighty God') would not be clear to Isaias; but in the light of the Incarnation it is clear to us that these titles have a deeper meaning: God himself became Man (Jn. 1, 14).

ISAIAS 10, 12, 17-23

Wait we, till the Lord has carried out all his designs upon
mount Sion and Jerusalem. Then he means to reckon with
the boastful ambition of Sennacherib, with the proud glance
of those scornful eyes. He who is our light will turn into a
fire, the Holy One of Israel will be a flame, that will burn up
suddenly; in one day those thorn-bushes, that dry brushwood
shall be consumed. Like a proud forest, or a garden plot, he
shall be eaten up, body and soul; see where he flies in terror!
Of all the trees in that forest so few shall be left, a child
might count them.

And when that day comes, the remnant of Israel, the survivors of Jacob's line, will learn to trust, not in the staff that
turns into rod to smite them, but in the Lord, the Holy One
of Israel; here he shall find loyalty. **A remnant will turn back,
only a remnant of Jacob, to God, the Mighty One. Countless
though Israel be as the sea sand, only a remnant of it will return;** there must be a sharp reckoning first, before we are
restored, abundantly, to his favour. Short and sharp is the
reckoning the Lord, the God of hosts, will make, with the
whole world for the scene of it.

ISAIAS 11, 1—12, 6

**From the stock of Jesse a scion shall burgeon yet; out of his
roots a sapling shall spring. One shall be born, on whom the
spirit of the Lord will rest; a spirit wise and discerning, a
spirit prudent and strong, a spirit of knowledge and of piety,
and ever fear of the Lord shall fill his heart.** Not his to judge
by appearances, listen to rumours when he makes award; here

A REMNANT WILL RETURN

GOD WILL DESTROY SENNACHERIB. King Achaz of Jerusalem called in the Assyrians to help him against the attacks of the northern kingdom and Syria. Thirty years later, the Assyrians under King Sennacherib besieged Jerusalem; they failed to take the city only because 'an angel of the Lord smote down 185,000 men in the Assyrian camp' (3 Kg. 19, 35). Isaias pictures this divine intervention as a forest fire sent by the Lord to destroy the might of the enemy. The chosen people should have learnt their lesson from this incident: They must not trust in political alliances, but in the Lord alone.

This dramatic deliverance was still years off when Isaias delivered the message contained in this paragraph. Would the extermination of the Assyrian bring all the Jews back to the service of the Lord? By no means; only a handful would be converted from their sinful ways. It will be the same story when the Messiah himself comes to win back men from sin. Of the millions of Jews living at the time of Christ's coming only a small percentage will accept the Redeemer (Rom. 9, 27). It was a small body of twelve apostles that became the universal Church.

THE SEVEN GIFTS OF THE HOLY GHOST

A WISE AND PEACEFUL RULER. No matter how low the chosen people may be brought, the Messiah will rise from this devastated and despoiled nation like a new shoot springing from the stump of a felled tree.

He is presented as a wise ruler, like Solomon. His human nature will be perfected by seven (only six in the Hebrew

is judgment will give the poor redress, here is award will right the wrongs of the defenceless. Word of him shall smite the earth like a rod, breath of him destroy the ill-doer; love of right shall be the baldric he wears, faithfulness the strength that girds him.

Wolf shall live at peace with lamb, leopard take its ease with kid; calf and lion and fatling in one dwelling-place, with a little child to herd them! Cattle and bears all at pasture, their young ones lying down together, lion eating straw like ox; child new-weaned, fresh from its mother's arms, playing by asp's hole, putting hand in viper's den! All over this mountain, no life taken. **Deep as the waters that hide the sea-floor, knowledge of the Lord overspreading the world!**

There he stands, fresh root from Jesse's stem, signal beckoning to the peoples all around; the Gentiles will come to pay their homage, where he rests in glory.

Then, once again, the Lord's hand at work! From Assyria, from Egypt, Pathros and Ethiopia, from Elam and Sennaar, from Emath, from the islands out at sea, his people, a scattered remnant, shall return. High lifted, for a world to see it, the standard that shall call Israel home, gather in the exiled sons of Juda from the four corners of the earth.

Gone, Ephraim's envious looks, vanished away Juda's enemies; Ephraim shall hate Juda, Juda harry Ephraim, no more. Together they will sweep down on Philistia's neck, there by the western sea; plunder the children of the east, Edom and Moab in their grasp, the sons of Ammon pliant to their will.

And the Lord will make a desert out of the tongue of sea that flanks Egypt; with the blast of his breath he will threaten Euphrates, dividing it into seven streams, that a man can cross

text; 'piety' may be an inspired addition in LXX) gifts which dispose him to be always attentive to divine guidance: 'An attentive ear the Lord has given me; not mine to withstand him; not mine to shrink from the task' (Is. 50, 5). In our Lord's life this concern for the will of God is his outstanding characteristic: 'It is the will of him who sent me, not my own will, that I have come down from heaven to do' (Jn. 6, 38).

The result of a wise and just rule is peace. This is pictured as a return to the idyllic state of the Garden of Eden. It is not to be taken literally; the animals are symbols of the different classes of men. Christian peace removes national hatred and enmity between men by bringing in the knowledge of God and his holy law as the basis for all human conduct.

UNITY OF THE KINGDOM OF CHRIST. Our Lord himself was the 'signal,' the green light to the Gentiles, who were to be united in the one Mystical Body with the Jews: 'He is our bond of peace; he has made the two nations one, breaking down the wall that was a barrier between us, the enmity there was between us, in his own mortal nature' (Eph. 2, 14). His death removed all national barriers.

Among the chosen people themselves there was the long-standing feud between the northern (Ephraim, the leading tribe of this federation) and southern (Juda) kingdoms. They had quarreled and fought ever since their first settlement in the promised land under Joshua. This enmity will cease in the Church of Christ; men will return to God in that close union of sanctifying grace; they will love one another because of their love of God.

Of the four paragraphs in this section, the second and fourth are devoted to the return of exiles to their homeland, Palestine. Wherever they may be scattered, God will bring

dry-shod. And so the remnant of my people which is left among the Assyrians will find a path made for it, as a path was made for it when it came up out of Egypt, long ago.

'Angry with me, Lord?' you will say, when that day comes; 'ay, you were angry with me, but now, praised be your name, the storm has passed; **all is consolation. God is here to deliver me;** I will go forward confidently, and not be afraid; source of my strength, theme of my praise, the Lord has made himself my protector.'

So, rejoicing, you shall drink deep from the fountain of deliverance; singing, when that day comes, 'Praise the Lord, and call upon his name, tell the story of his doings among all the nations, keep the majesty of his name in grateful remembrance. Sing in honour of the great deeds the Lord has done, make them known for all the world to hear. Cry aloud in praise, people of Sion; great is the Holy One of Israel, that dwells among you.'

ISAIAS 13—33

Cry aloud, for the day of the Lord is coming; his the dominion, his the doom. No hand now but will hang useless, no heart but will be fainting with dismay; tortures and pangs will seize them, throes as of a woman in travail; each man looks at his neighbour in bewilderment, their faces ashy pale.

Yes, the day of the Lord is coming, pitiless, full of vengeance and bitter retribution, ready to turn earth into a wilderness, ridding it of its sinful brood. Poor earth, polluted by

them back; not all of them, but a remnant only, from Egypt, Assyria, Babylonia and wherever else they may have been taken by conquerors. God will make their path home secure by his protection; they will cross the Euphrates as easily as they crossed the Red Sea.

THE EXILES' HYMN OF PRAISE. St. John presents a great choir of the redeemed, 144,000 of them, singing a song of thanksgiving to the Lord: 'These have come here out of the great affliction; they have washed their robes white in the blood of the Lamb' (Apoc. 7, 14). That is the reality about which the Isaian exiles were singing, though they did not fully understand it in those days of the Assyrian invasion.

Sometimes it is the Messiah, a human descendant of David, who is to bring salvation to his people; here it is the Lord God himself who is responsible for their delivery from exile. In the fulness of time God became Man, and so fulfilled both these aspects of salvation as portrayed in the Old Testament prophets.

THE DAY OF THE LORD

PUNISHMENT OF A SINFUL WORLD. In the midst of comforting words of promise about the Messiah and his kingdom, Isaias breaks into denunciation of guilty and sinful men. Like Amos, who first used the phrase 'the day of the Lord,' he has as his purpose to warn his hearers of the terrible consequences of abandoning the Lord by worshipping idols.

The immediate consequence of Israel's infidelity to God was the devastation of their land by the Assyrian invader. This

the men that dwell on it; they have broken God's law, traversed the decree he made for them, violated his eternal covenant with men; cankered it lies by a curse, peopled with guilty men, only a frantic remnant left of its inhabitants. **The stars of heaven, its glittering constellations, will shed no ray; sunrise will be darkness, and the moon refuse her light.**

'I will punish the world's guilt, and tax the wicked with their misdoings, stilling the rebel's pride, crushing the haughtiness of tyrants, till a man is a rarer sight than gold, and a slave cannot be bought with all the treasure of Ophir. **So terribly will I shake the heavens, and move earth from its place, to show that the Lord of hosts will be patient no longer, and the hour of his bitter vengeance has come.'**

See where the majesty of the Lord comes from far away; his anger is aflame, and there is no withstanding it! There is menace on his lips, his tongue is like a consuming fire, and his breath like a mountain stream that floods over till it is neck-deep. He will sweep away whole nations into oblivion, sweep away the bridle of false fears that curbed his peoples till now. The Lord will make his dread voice heard, will lay bare his terrible arm, volleying out his anger in flashes of devouring fire, laying all low with his whirlwind, with his hailstones; and Assur will shrink in fear from the Lord's voice, and will feel his rod. In these times a new Topheth has been made ready; this, too, made ready by a king. **It is deep and wide, fed with flaming brands in abundance; and the breath of the Lord comes down like a stream of brimstone, to kindle it. Who**

was a punishment and a means of purification; Israel must learn by bitter experience that the Lord will not tolerate sin among his people. Each historical visitation of divine anger is a partial anticipation of that final day, the Second Coming of Christ, when the whole world will be brought to account for its sins.

The imagery of darkness and earthquake was also used by Amos (8, 8-9), and will be found on the lips of our Lord when he is describing the fall of Jerusalem and the end of the world: 'Immediately after the distress of those days, the sun will be darkened, and the moon will refuse her light, and the stars will fall from heaven, and the powers of heaven will rock' (Mt. 24, 29). This is not meant to be an actual description of things that will happen; it is merely traditional imagery for disaster that comes from the hand of God and is beyond man's control.

DIVINE JUDGMENT ON ASSYRIA.   The Lord used Assyria as an instrument to chastise Israel. It was no matter for Assyria to boast of; once its purpose was accomplished, the divine judgment would descend on Assyria too; she would experience God's punishing hand.

The main imagery used here to express the divine judgment is that of fire; it emphasizes the fierceness and power of God's wrath. It has local colour from the place of burning (Topheth) in the valley of Hinnom (New Testament Gehenna) to the south of Jerusalem. Here sacrifices were offered to Moloch (king), the god of the Assyrians. The divine King has his own burning-place to punish evil-doers; it is the eternal fires of hell (Gehenna). Though Isaias did not know of the fires of hell, the Holy Spirit might have inspired him to

shall survive this devouring flame, the near presence of fires that burn unceasingly?

But, you, that night, will be singing for joy, as if it were the night when a solemn feast begins; your hearts will be light, as men's hearts are light when they go up, with the flutes playing about them, to the mountain of the Lord, where he dwells, the strong God of Israel. And now the Lord will have pity on Jacob; on the sons of Israel, his chosen people of old. Sion never rested in the Lord so surely; here be friendless folk that trust in him. **Mercy and faithfulness return; a throne set up in David's dwelling-place, for a judge that loves right and gives redress speedily! Then at last man will turn to his Maker, will look towards the holy one of Israel.** He will turn no longer towards altars of his own designing, have eyes no longer for pillar and shrine of his own fashioning.

ISAIAS 19, 1, 16-25

What burden for Egypt? See where the Lord comes into Egypt, with the cloud-drift for his chariot, and all the false gods of Egypt tremble, the very heart of Egypt melts away! Weak as a woman Egypt shall be, when that day comes, dazed and terrified, to see the Lord of hosts lift his hand so threateningly. Upon Juda Egypt must needs look with awe; fear is in the very name of it, as they scan the future; what means the Lord of hosts now? Cities five there shall be in the land of Egypt that talk with the speech of Chanaan, and take oaths in the name of the Lord of hosts; one shall be called the City of Justice.

use words that would aptly express the eternal torments of hell in the light of later revelation and teaching (Mk. 9, 42-48).

THE CHOSEN PEOPLE RETURN TO GOD. The hand of the Lord will not remain forever raised to punish; once Sion has been purified by suffering, and the enemy, Assyria, destroyed, the divine mercy will be poured out on his beloved children. Isaias pictures them going up to the solemn feast of the pasch at Jerusalem singing psalms as they prepare to eat the lamb at nightfall.

Israel will now be a holy people, dedicated to the service of God, no longer worshipping idols of their own making. In Jerusalem, a descendant of David, the royal Messiah, will reign as king, ruling his people wisely and justly. And that is what happened: In the fulness of time Jesus was raised on the cross at Jerusalem to begin his reign over the hearts and minds of men.

THE GENTILE WORLD CONVERTED

THE SPIRITUAL CONQUEST OF EGYPT. The chosen people never forgot their long sojourn in Egypt, and the oppression they endured there, until Moses led them out from bondage into the promised land. And even after the Exodus, they had not very happy relations with the Egyptians; it was Egyptian intrigue that caused Juda to revolt from Assyria in the time of Isaias. So Egypt was looked on as the proverbial enemy of Israel.

In presenting the conversion of the Gentile world to the true worship of the Lord in Messianic times, Isaias here pictures a military invasion of Egypt similar to that when Joshua

There will be an altar set up to the Lord for all Egypt to
see, and at its frontier a pillar dedicated to him, a trophy,
there, in Egypt, bringing the Lord of hosts to mind. **Cry they
out to him, when they suffer oppression, he will give them a
saviour, a champion, to deliver them. Thus the Lord will
reveal himself to Egypt; the Egyptians, when that day comes,
will acknowledge him, doing him worship with sacrifices
and offerings, will make vows to the Lord and perform them.**

First calamity, then healing; when they come back to the
Lord, he will relent and restore. There will be a high-road,
then, between Egypt and the Assyrians; either shall visit
other, and Egypt with Assyrian will worship God. And with
these a third people shall be matched; who but **Israel, source
of the whole world's happiness?** Such blessings the Lord of
hosts has pronounced upon it, 'Blessed be my people in
Egypt, and the home I have made for the Assyrian to dwell
in; but Israel is the land of my choice.'

ISAIAS 24—35

In the midst of the wide earth, among these many peoples,
what shall be left? A remnant, **the last olives that are shaken
from the tree, the gleanings that remain when vintage-time
is over.** Few only, but they shall lift up their voices in praise;
God's honour vindicated, their rejoicing shall be heard across
the sea, 'Lord, you are our God; we extol you and praise your
name for your wonderful doings; for your designs, so long
prepared, so faithfully executed. **Stronghold you are of the
poor, stronghold of the helpless in their affliction, refuge
from the storm, shade in the noonday sun;** against that wall
the rage of tyrants blusters in vain.'

When that day comes, the Lord will hold a reckoning with

led the chosen people into the promised land. As the Lord's army advances, guided by the luminous cloud (the Shekinah), the enemy feels an inexplicable terror and lays down its arms in surrender. It is a repetition of Joshua's conquest of the five cities (Jos. 10, 3), one of which was Jerusalem, the city of justice.

As a sign of subjugation, the Egyptians will speak the language of their conquerors ('the speech of Chanaan' is Hebrew); they will call on the name of the Lord, the God of the Hebrews, and will embrace the true religion by setting up altars to the one true God. Worship of God will not be confined to the temple of Jerusalem but will be world-wide, as Malachy will later foretell (1, 10-11). In this new Christian Church, embracing both Jew and Gentile, there will be no enmity; Assyria, Egypt, and Israel will be united as one people. In time of persecution, the Lord will raise up defenders of the faith to deliver them as in the time of the Judges.

THE CITY OF GOD

The Remnant on Mount Sion. The background for the next eight sections remains constant: the devastation of Palestine and exile for many of its inhabitants. From this purifying process only a few, the remnant, will remain true to the Lord. The Assyrian invader will be destroyed, and a new Jerusalem will emerge, more glorious than ever. So I have included all eight sections under one general heading, THE CITY OF GOD, a title St. Augustine borrowed from St. Paul to describe Christ's kingdom: 'Looking forward all the while to that city which has true foundations, which is God's design and God's fashioning' (Heb. 11, 10). The fulfilment of these prophecies is the Christian Church, built on the foun-

the hosts of heaven, there above, with the kings of the earth, here on earth; huddled together, as captives are huddled together in a dungeon, they shall remain prisoners; so, at last, the reckoning will be held. **And then the Lord of hosts will reign at Jerusalem, on mount Sion; and the moon will be put to shame, and the sun hide his face, before the glory in which he will appear,** with the elders of his people about him.

A time is coming when the Lord of hosts will prepare a banquet on this mountain of ours; no meat so tender, no wine so mellow, meat that drips with fat, wine well strained. Gone the chains in which he has bound the peoples, the veil that covered the nations hitherto; on the mountain-side, all these will be engulfed; death, too, shall be engulfed for ever. No furrowed cheek but the Lord God will wipe away its tears; gone the contempt his people endured in a whole world's eyes; the Lord has promised it.

When that day comes, men will be saying, 'He is here, the God to whom we looked for help, the Lord for whom we waited so patiently; ours to rejoice, ours to triumph in the victory he has sent us.' On yonder mountain the divine deliverance shall rest, and by his power the enemy shall be crushed, like straw ground in the chaff-cutter; the enemy shall stretch out his hands, like a man swimming, and low shall his pride fall when they crash down to earth! Down they must come, the battlements that crown those walls, lie inglorious in the dust.

But in the land of Juda, when that day comes, what shall their song be? 'Sion is ours, an impregnable fortress; divine protection it has for wall and breastwork; wide let its gates be opened, to welcome true hearts that still keep troth with

dations of the twelve apostles: 'Israel has missed the mark; only this chosen remnant has attained it' (Rom. 11, 7).

Isaias uses two images in this section; the first from an olive grove, the second from the Shekinah, that bright, shining cloud of the Exodus which symbolized God's presence. The illumination of divine grace will be so splendid in the Church that it will outshine all natural glory such as sun and moon (Apoc. 21, 23).

THE MESSIANIC BANQUET. The convivial picture of a group sitting down to a festive meal remained one of the most popular among the Jews to express the joyfulness of the coming of the Messiah. Our Lord himself built a famous parable on this same idea: 'Here is an image of the kingdom of heaven; there was once a king, who held a marriage feast for his son, and sent out his servants with a summons to all those whom he had invited to the wedding' (Mt. 22, 1-14). It is God the Father who prepares the feast for his Son, our Lord Jesus Christ. And at the Last Supper, our Lord gave deeper significance to the banquet image when he took bread and wine and changed them into his own body and blood; the Blessed Eucharist then became the food of the Church.

With a series of expressions Isaias emphasizes the happiness of Messianic times: No more chains, no veil (God's revelation hidden from the Gentiles in Old Testament times), death removed (1 Cor. 15, 54), and no more tears (Apoc. 21, 4). Such will be the change brought about by God's grace through the redemption of Christ.

The banquet is held on a mountain, which signifies the fortress citadel Jerusalem, the centre and capital of the Messianic kingdom in Jewish prophecy. Our Lord developed this same metaphor in describing his Church: 'It is upon this

him. **Our thoughts wayward no longer, you will maintain us in peace, peace that comes surely to those who trust in you.'** Yours to trust in the Lord continually, the Lord that is evermore your protection. Mountain-dwellers he can bring low, towering city walls he can level, level them with the ground, drag them down to the dust. There they lie, trodden under foot; poor folk trample on them now, the disinherited spurn them as they pass.

Hard and heavy and strong that sword is which the Lord carries; shall he not wreak his vengeance, in due time, upon the monstrous serpent that bars the gate, and the monstrous serpent that coils up yonder; shall he not deal death to the great beast of the sea? And the praise of his doings shall be sung by his own vineyard, a vineyard rich in wine.

'I, the Lord, am the keeper of this vineyard; I come soon to water it. Day by day I watch over it, to shield it from attack, nor any grudge my heart bears it. Would I were an enemy as relentless as thorns and briars are! Then I would trample it down and make a bonfire of it. But now, see how it clings to my protection! Ay, it shall have peace, it shall make its peace with me.' Israel shall flourish and put forth shoots, multitudes that shall be added to the number of Jacob; with its offspring the wide face of earth shall be peopled.

So should the race of Jacob find pardon for its sins. Cleansed now from guilt, to bear fruit in full abundance; ground fine as chalk the altar-stones, pillar and shrine raised up no more! A time is coming, when the Lord will beat the fruit from his trees, as far away as the bed of Euphrates and the river of Egypt, and you, sons of Israel, shall be gathered in one by one. That day, a call will be sounded on a great trumpet, and men long lost will come from Assyria, and

rock that I will build my Church; and the gates of hell shall
not prevail against it' (Mt. 16, 18). Isaias continues this
same metaphor of a fortress attacked by hostile forces (Assyria); but the power and pride of the whole city of God's
enemies will be humiliated. The gates will then be thrown
wide open to all who trust in the Lord; men will no longer
need the implements of war when they live together in true
peace.

THE VINEYARD OF THE LORD. Archaeologists discovered a
library of ancient documents dating back to the time of
Moses; they are known as the Ras Shamra Tablets from the
place on the Syrian coast where they were found. They were
translated and published between 1930 and 1940. In them
the three mythical monsters, here mentioned by Isaias, are
presented as symbols of Chaos that reigned before the creation of the world. Isaias takes these figures and makes them
symbols of the powers hostile to God and his chosen people;
they probably represent Assyria, Babylon, and Egypt, as the
context suggests.

All over Palestine the terraced hillsides are covered with
vineyards. In chapter 5, Isaias describes the making of a vineyard: 'He fenced it in, and cleared it of stones, and planted a
choice vine there; built a tower, too, in the middle, and set
up a wine-press in it . . . It is the house of Israel that the Lord
called his vineyard.' And that is the image he considers in
this paragraph; it will be made immortal later by our Lord in
a similar parable (Mt. 21, 33-41). Protected by the Lord himself, the vineyard will be fruitful and will spread over the face
of the entire earth. Both Jew and Gentile will become fruit-
bearing plants in the Church.

In the perspective of Isaias, the chosen people must first be
purified from their idolatry by exile; then they will return

exiles from Egypt, to worship the Lord on his holy mountain, in Jerusalem.

The Lord has his own people still left him; to these he shall be a crown to boast of, a garland of pride; his the justice that inspires them when they sit in judgment; his the courage that rallies them when they fall back, fighting, to the gates.

Short the time shall be, and quickly fled, ere Lebanon forest shall be fruitful as Carmel, ere land fruitful now shall be reckoned as forest. Then this book will have a message for deaf ears to hear, for blind eyes to see through the mist that darkens them; **restless hearts will attain true knowledge then, and the murmurers learn wisdom.** Humble folk shall yet learn to rejoice in the Lord, poor clods of earth triumph in the Holy One of Israel. Vanquished, the triumphant foe, scornful incredulity is silenced; where are they now, that spent themselves on wrong-doing, watching a man's words to convict him of guilt, defrauding him of justice at the city gate, setting aside, with a quibble, the plea of the innocent?

Here is a message to the race of Jacob from the Lord, that was Abraham's deliverer: 'No longer shall Jacob be disappointed, no longer put to the blush. He shall see children of his, my gift, doing honour publicly to my name; honour to the Holy One of Jacob, homage to the God of Israel! **See, I am laying a stone in the foundations of Sion that has been tested and found true, a corner-stone, a stone of worth, built into the foundations themselves.'**

What if the Lord waits his time before he will have mercy on you? The more glorious, when it comes, his deliverance.

from Assyria, Babylon, and Egypt, and worship the Lord once more in Jerusalem; from then on God alone will be their pride and glory. Isaias vividly presents them as summoned by the loud blast of a trumpet. Our Lord has the same imagery for the call of the Gentiles into the Church from the four corners of the earth (Mt. 24, 31), and St. Paul for the Last Day (1 Cor. 15, 52).

CHRIST THE CORNER-STONE. This paragraph consists of five different aspects of the Messianic kingdom; there is no close connection between them. (1) Spiritual blessings are presented under the usual form of material prosperity: Carmel and Lebanon were two of the finest wooded areas of the Middle East. (2) The lowliest and most unfortunate members of the city of God will have true knowledge of God and his revelation; they will be as happy as the wise and powerful. (3) Justice will be practised among the members of the kingdom in all their dealings with each other. (4) The Christian world will publicly honour and worship the Lord. (5) Faith and trust in the Lord will be the foundation of the life of the whole Church.

St. Peter quotes the last sentence (Is. 28, 16) as being fulfilled in Christ (1 Pet. 2, 6). In the light of the Incarnation, faith in God means relying on Jesus, the source of grace and the author of redemption. Our Lord also used the corner-stone image of himself (Mt. 21, 42). This stone was essential to the stability of a building; it was cut with great care and precision and was fitted as one single stone into the foundation of the building where two walls met; the whole house rested on it.

TRUE CITIZENS OF SION. God always holds the initiative in all his dealings with his creatures; the first step in the re-

The Lord is a God who makes award justly, blessed they shall be that wait for him. **In Jerusalem they only will be left, true citizens of Sion.** And you, Jerusalem, tears shall have none to shed; mercy is none he shall withhold. Soon as he hears you crying out to him, the answer will come. They shall no longer hide away in corners, the men he gives you for your teachers; always you will have a true counsellor in sight, always hear his voice in your ear as he warns you, 'This is the true path, follow it; no swerving to right or left!' Silver leaf on your graven images defaced now, defaced the sheaths of gold; you will cast all away, as a woman casts away defiled clouts of hers, and bid it begone.

And thereupon, sow where you will all over the land, rain shall be granted to your crops; rich and full shall be your harvest of wheat; you shall have pasture, then, for lambs to browse in at liberty. Ox and ass on your farm shall have mixed feed, pure grain fresh winnowed on the threshing-floor; never a mountain-top, never a high hill, but will flow with torrents of water, when that day comes. The dead shall lie in heaps that day, and towers come crashing down; **moon's light will be like the light of the sun, and the sun will shine in sevenfold strength, as if the light of seven days were joined in one, when the time comes for the Lord to bind up his people's hurt, and heal their grievous wound.**

But first the hail-storm must do its work, forest be laid low, city levelled with ground. All this, until the spirit is poured out on us from above; fruitful as Carmel then the wilderness, to make your well-tilled lands seem but waste. **Alike desert and fruitful field the home, now, of innocence, the abode of loyalty; loyalty, that has peace for its crown, tranquillity for its harvest, repose for ever undisturbed.** In quiet homes this people of mine shall live, in dwelling-places

habilitation of his people comes from his divine mercy. The sufferings of exile were but a process of purification in God's plan to re-establish his own city of Jerusalem. This city of God will be inhabited only by true citizens; these will be men dedicated to the true worship of God, living lives of holiness.

The city of God, the Church of Christ, will have an infallible voice in guiding its members; revelation will come to men in a more perfect form through Christ. This will be in contrast to the Old Testament system, where it was often difficult to distinguish the true from the false prophet and where revelation was only partial and fragmentary. True citizens of the New Testament Sion will find it easier to walk in the path of holiness when their footsteps are guided by an authoritative voice that never errs and cannot deceive with false advice.

The great abundance of blessings, which will be a characteristic of Messianic times, is symbolized under the familiar picture of material prosperity. Food will be so plentiful the whole year long that even animals will be able to pasture on the choicest food, usually reserved for mankind alone. The fulfilment of this detail is surely the Blessed Eucharist, the universal nourishment of the Christian Church. The grandeur and glory of the Church is symbolized by the increased light and warmth of the sun and moon.

THE SECURITY OF DIVINE PROTECTION. A familiar refrain throughout the Old Testament is: 'At ease you shall sit, each of you with his own vine, his own fig tree to give him shade, and none to raise the alarm.' Such freedom from fear was an essential condition for peaceful and contented living. It is indicated in the first sentence of this paragraph; the Assyrian devastation of the holy land is signified under the image of a hail storm.

that fear no attack; all shall be ease and plenty. Ah, blessed race, their seed sowing, their oxen and asses driving, by every stream that flows!

As parent bird hovers over nest, so will the Lord of hosts protect Jerusalem; protect her and bring her safe through, grant signal deliverance. Come back, sons of Israel, that have hidden yourselves away so deep. Time, then, for each man to cast away his idols of gold and silver, idols your guilty hands have made.

Listen then, you that live far off, to the story of my doings; and you, who dwell close to me, learn the lesson of my power. In Sion itself there be guilty folk that tremble, false hearts full of dismay; who shall survive this devouring flame, the near presence of fires that burn unceasingly? He only, that follows the path of innocence, tells truth, ill-gotten gain refuses, flings back the bribe; his ears shut to murderous counsels, his eyes from every harmful sight turned away.

On the heights his dwelling shall be, his eyrie among the fastnesses of the rocks, bread shall be his for the asking, water from an unfailing spring. No more shall they cry out on their helpless plight, these, your fellow-citizens; **none dwells there now but is assoiled of his guilt. Those eyes shall look on the king in his royal beauty, have sight of a land whose frontiers are far away.**

Of those old fears, how you will recall the memory! Where are they now, the notaries, the men who weighed out tribute, that counted the captives? No longer will you see before you a barbarous people, all talk that passes your comprehension, stammering in a tongue that you cannot understand.

Look around you at Sion, goal of our pilgrimage, see where

Two other conditions need fulfilment for men to live in security: the citizens of the city of God must live holy lives, following out all that the law of God demands. The final condition is that the Lord extends his protecting hand over his people; without his guidance all human attempts will prove vain and useless. This is expressed under the homely figure of a parent bird, reminiscent of our Lord's words: 'Jerusalem, Jerusalem, how often have I been ready to gather your children together, as a hen gathers her chickens under her wings' (Mt. 23, 37).

THE KING IN HIS ROYAL BEAUTY. When the angel Gabriel announced to Mary that her Son would be the Messiah, he spoke of him as a king: 'The Lord God will give him the throne of his father David, and he shall reign over the house of Jacob eternally' (Lk. 1, 32). It is the same scion of David's line that Isaias here foretells, as he did earlier: 'There he stands, fresh root from Jesse's stem.' (Jesse was the name of David's father.) The Lord God himself is also spoken of by Isaias in this paragraph as king of Jerusalem. There is no contradiction, because Jesus was both God and Man, so fulfilling both these aspects of Messianic deliverance.

Two conditions have to be fulfilled before the Davidic king can take possession of his throne: Israel's guilt must be pardoned and the Assyrian oppressor vanquished. Isaias mentions the first condition when he foretells the acquittal ('assoiled') of the citizens of Sion, the city of God. The second condition is considered when he refers to the removal of notaries, the Assyrians weighing out tribute (there were no coins in those days) and counting those who were to be taken into captivity. There will be no longer the sound of foreign tongue in Israel.

Jerusalem lies, an undisturbed dwelling-place; here is tent securely fixed, its pegs immoveable, its ropes never to be broken. Here, as nowhere else, our Lord reigns in majesty; a place of rivers, of wide, open streams, yet no ship's oar will disturb it, no huge galleon pass by; **the Lord our judge, the Lord our law-giver, the Lord our king, will himself be our deliverance.** Now, your tackle hangs loose and unserviceable, too weak your mast is to display your pennon; then, you will have the spoil of many forays to divide, even lame folk shall carry plunder away.

Thrills the barren desert with rejoicing; the wilderness takes heart, and blossoms, fair as the lily. Blossom on blossom, it will rejoice and sing for joy; all the majesty of Lebanon is bestowed on it, all the grace of Carmel and of Sharon. Stiffen, then, the sinews of drooping hand and flagging knee; give word to the faint-hearted, 'Take courage, and have no fear; **see where your Lord is bringing redress for your wrongs, God himself, coming to deliver you!'**

Then the eyes of the blind shall be opened, and deaf ears unsealed; the lame man, then, shall leap as the deer leap, the speechless tongue cry aloud. **All alike shall see the glory of the Lord, the majesty of our God.** Springs will gush out in the wilderness, streams flow through the desert; ground that was dried up will give place to pools, barren land to wells of clear water; where the jackal had its lair once, reed and bulrush will show their green.

A high road will stretch across it, by divine proclamation kept holy; none that is defiled may travel on it; and there you shall find a straight path lying before you, wayfarer is

The results of redemption are threefold. (1) Israel will be a holy people, innocent, truthful, honest (refusing bribes), their 'eyes from every harmful sight turned away.' (2) The security of life in Sion is pictured under the imagery of a tent, a shelter that will stand up against any storm of wind that blows; 'the gates of hell shall not prevail against it.' (3) Freedom from fear of conquest. Isaias presents the blessings of Messianic times under the symbol of water, 'wide, open streams' of the irrigation ditches. So broad will they be that navies could sail on them; but no vessel of an invading force will be able to take advantage of these streams of divine grace; the Church must always be victorious.

GOD HIMSELF COMING TO DELIVER YOU. Isaias here bursts into song at the thought of the Lord breaking the power of the Assyrian oppressor and restoring Jerusalem to its rightful position as the centre of the Messianic kingdom. But in the light of the Incarnation, his words take on a deeper meaning. God truly did come to redeem his people and the whole world; the Messiah king was really the Second Person of the Trinity made Man. Actually our Lord quoted from this passage to prove to John the Baptist his claim to be the Messiah: 'The blind see, and the lame walk, and the deaf hear' (Mt. 11, 5).

There will be joy and happiness on earth when the Lord comes to redeem mankind (Phil. 4, 4). The blessings brought by Christ are presented under the imagery of a wilderness blossoming in spring; this is the promised land, now as fertile as the three famous regions of Lebanon, Carmel, and Sharon. A second image is that of the familiar streams of water irrigating the holy land; this is sanctifying grace, the gift of the Holy Spirit (Jn. 7, 37-38).

none so foolish he can go astray. No lions shall molest it,
no beasts of prey venture on it. Free men shall walk on it,
coming home again to Sion, and praising the Lord for their
ransoming. **Eternal happiness crowns them, joy and happiness
in their grasp now, sorrow and sighing fled far away.**

MICHEAS 4, 1-8; 2, 12-13; 7, 11-14

The temple hill! One day it shall stand there, highest of all
the mountain heights, overtopping the peaks of them, and
the nations will flock there together. A multitude of people
will make their way to it, crying, 'Come, let us climb up to
the Lord's mountain peak, to the house where the God of
Jacob dwells; he shall teach us the right way, we will walk in
the paths he has chosen.'
**The Lord's command shall go out from Sion, his word
from Jerusalem;** over thronging peoples he shall sit in judgment, give award to great nations from far away. Sword they
will fashion into ploughshare and spear into pruning-hook;
no room there shall be for nation to levy war against nation,
and train itself in arms. **At ease you shall sit, each of you with
his own vine, his own fig-tree to give him shade, and none to
raise the alarm:** such blessing the Lord of hosts pronounces
on you. Let other nations go their own way, each with the
name of its own god to rally it; ours to march under his
divine name, who is our God for ever and for evermore!

'When that time comes,' the Lord says, 'I will gather them
in again and take them to myself, **flock of mine that go limp-**

A third image is that of a highroad through the holy land along which pilgrims can approach the temple at Jerusalem, God's dwelling-place among his people. Free from oppression and sin, men can now approach God. This is the narrow road spoken of by our Lord, the path of virtue that men follow by walking in his footsteps; the end of the road is eternal happiness.

THE CHURCH VISIBLE AND UNIVERSAL

THE TEMPLE HILL. Micheas not only lived and prophesied at the same time as Isaias, he also expressed the same ideas. They were probably associated in the work of preaching to the people of Jerusalem at the time of the Assyrian oppression. His prophecy reads almost like an abridged edition of Isaias.

This paragraph is the same as that of Isaias 2, 1-5. The key Isaian idea of Sion as the centre of the Messianic kingdom is here echoed by Micheas. The temple at Jerusalem is the divine dwelling-place from which all mankind will learn the truths of revelation; it is the Church set high on a hill for all men to see and enter.

As in Isaias, peace is the main product of the Messianic reign. Micheas expresses this spiritual peace of Christ's Church under two material images: weapons of war shall be fashioned into agricultural tools, and every man can sit peacefully in his garden without fearing to hear a call to arms from a nearby hill, announcing the approach of an enemy bent on plunder.

THE FLOCK OF THE LORD. From the very beginning of their history the Hebrews were shepherds; the patriarch Abraham

ing and straggling, ever since I brought calamity on them; lame shall yet be a stock to breed from, and wayworn shall grow into a sturdy race; here in Sion they shall dwell, and the Lord be king over them, for ever henceforward. And you, the watchtower of that flock, cloud-capped fastness where the lady Sion reigns, power shall come back to you as of old, once more Jerusalem shall be queen. **Trust me, Jacob, I mean to assemble you in full strength, rally all that is left of Israel in one place, thronging like sheep in fold, like herd in byre,** hum of voices echoing all around; where the breach has been made ready for them, break they out and pass on their way, sally forth with a king to lead them with the Lord at their head.'

Day of pell-mell disorder it shall be, the day of your wall's rebuilding; a day when folk shall resort to you from all the lands that lie between Assyria and the towns of Egypt, between sea and sea, mountain-range and mountain-range. **With that staff of yours gather your people in, the flock that is your very own, scattered now in the forest glades, with rich plenty all around them;** Bashan and Gilead for their pasture-grounds, as in the days of old.

MICHEAS 5, 2-14

Bethlehem-Ephrata! Least do they reckon you among all the clans of Juda? Nay, it is from you I look to find a prince that shall rule over Israel. Whence comes he? From the first beginning, from ages untold!

Marvel not, then, if the Lord abandons his people for a time, until she who is in travail has brought forth her child; others there are, brethren of his, that must be restored to the

wandered about Palestine with his flocks and herds. With no fences and no sheep dogs, the shepherd himself had to live with his sheep, guiding them to pasture and defending them from wild animals. This brought about a close personal bond between shepherd and sheep which has been immortalized by our Lord in the parable of the Good Shepherd (Jn. 10). There are also two famous shepherd passages in the Old Testament, Ezechiel 34, 23-31 and Psalm 22. In John and Ezechiel the Good Shepherd is the Messiah; in Psalm 22 he is the Lord God.

The background of these shepherd excerpts from Micheas is the Assyrian exile; the sheep of the Lord's flock have been carried off into foreign lands. Micheas assures the chosen people that their divine Shepherd has not forgotten them. He puts before them the confident hope expressed in Psalm 22: 'The Lord is my shepherd; how can I lack anything? Dark be the valley about my path, but I fear none while he is with me.'

The thought of Jerusalem, the city of God, is never far from the minds of Isaias and Micheas; that is why Micheas mixes the imagery of Sion with that of the flock in this paragraph. The rebuilding of the walls of Jerusalem was the first essential to the security of its people.

BORN AT BETHLEHEM

THE PRINCE, THE PEOPLE, THE LAND. When the wise men came to Jerusalem asking to see the new-born king of the Jews, king Herod assembled his learned men and enquired of them where it was that the Messiah would be born. They told him, 'At Bethlehem in Juda' (Ephrata is only the name of the district); to prove their claim, the Jewish scribes quoted this passage from Micheas (Mt. 2, 6).

citizenship of Israel. **Enabled by the Lord his God, confident in that mighty protection, stands he, our shepherd, and safely folds his flock;** fame of him now reaches to the world's end; who else should be its hope of recovery? What though the Assyrian invade our country, trample down our strongholds? Seven leaders of men we shall find to marshal us, and an eighth yet in reserve; sword in hand, they shall herd the men of Assyria, naked steel for the land of Nemrod! Invade they, trample they as they will, he shall be our deliverance.

Poor remnant of Jacob, lost among that multitude of peoples! Yet thrive it shall; does not the grass thrive, with dew and shower from the Lord to water it, nor looks for man's tending, unbeholden to your human toil? Poor remnant of Jacob, among those heathen multitudes lost! Yet lion amid the forest herds, lion's whelp amid flock of sheep, finds not easier passage, brings not down more inexorably his prey. High triumph you shall have over your enemies; perish all that bear you ill-will!

'All other help,' the Lord says, 'shall then be denied you; gone, horse and chariot of yours, the cities lost, ruined the strongholds. Sorcery you shall have none to trust in, nor divinings; gone idol and sacred pillar of yours, nor any of your own imaginings left you; uprooted the woods of your false worship, fallen the cities. Only then shall my fierce anger find its scope, only then fall my vengeance upon the nations that defied me.'

PSALM 71

Grant to the king, O God, your own skill in judgment; the inheritor of a throne, may he be just, as you are just; may he give your people right awards, and to your poor, redress.

Although Bethlehem was David's birthplace, the capital of
his kingdom was Jerusalem. The fact that the Messiah was
to be born in an insignificant village, not the royal palace,
shows that the Davidic line would not be reigning in Palestine at the time of his birth. (Herod was an Edomite, not a
Jew.) There is an immense contrast between the lowly origin
of Christ as man and his divine origin from all eternity ('the
first beginning').

As in Genesis 3, 15 and Isaias 7, 14, Mother and Child are
linked in the work of salvation. It is the Assyrian invasion
and oppression of the Jewish people that Micheas visualizes
as the background against which the Messiah appears; Assyria
represents the forces of evil from which only the prince born
of a virgin mother can deliver his people; he is the shepherd
of the flock that conquers through the power of the Lord.

With a victorious prince at their head, the people of God
(the Church) must be victorious too. Micheas expresses this
by means of two illustrations: The 'seven leaders . . . and an
eighth' signify a plentiful supply of heroes in time of danger.
The second picture is that of a lion easily subduing its prey.

The land is described in the familiar terms of adequate
water-supply to make the grass grow; this is a material image
of divine grace. God alone shall be their protection; all dependence on weapons of war ('horse and chariot') shall be
unnecessary in the Church of God.

A JUST AND PEACEFUL KING

UNIVERSALITY AND ETERNITY OF HIS RULE. This psalm
describes the reign of Christ the King. It does not present him
as a victorious warrior, as David did in Psalms 2 and 109; the

Such the harvest his subjects shall reap, peace on every mountain, justice on every hillside. Watch and ward he will keep over the friendless, protect the children of the poor, and crush the oppressor. Ageless as sun or moon he shall endure; kindly as the rain that drops on the meadow grass, as showers that water the earth. **Justice in his days shall thrive, and the blessings of peace; and may those days last till the moon shines no more.**

From sea to sea, from the great river to the ends of earth, his sway shall reach. In his presence rebels shall bend the knee, all his enemies will be humbled in the dust; gifts shall flow in from the lords of Tharsis and the islanders, tribute from the kings of Arabia and Sheba; all kings must needs bring their homage, all nations serve him.

He will give the poor redress when they cry to him, destitute folk, with none to befriend them; in their need and helplessness, they shall have his compassion. Their lives he will take into his keeping, set them free from the power of wrong and oppression, dearly avenge their blood.

Long life shall be his, and gold from Arabia shall be given him; men will pray for him continually, bless his name evermore. The land shall have good store of corn, high up the hillsides, rustling like the woods of Lebanon; shall multiply its citizens like grass on the ground. **For ever let his name be used in blessing, a name to endure while the sun gives light; in him all the tribes of the earth shall be enriched, all the nations shall extol him.**

PSALMS 46; 66; 67; 86

Clap your hands, all you nations, in applause; acclaim your God with cries of rejoicing. The Lord is high above us, and

picture is rather that of Isaias' Prince of Peace (Is. 9-11). The Messianic king is more after the style of Solomon than of David; it is likely that its author based many of the details of this psalm on the wise and peaceful reign of Solomon.

When our Lord was born at Bethlehem, thousands upon thousands of angels appeared in the fields nearby singing their song of praise: 'Glory to God in high heaven, and peace on earth to men that are God's friends' (Lk. 2, 14). This note of peace is one of the characteristics of Christ's kingdom; it is the re-establishment of friendship between God and mankind, the restoration of that peaceful state that existed before the fall of Adam.

That our Lord was a just as well as a peaceful ruler is seen from his championing of the poor and oppressed; he preached the gospel to publicans and sinners. It was the good of others he had at heart, and he did not fear to make enemies of the rich and powerful.

The eternity of his reign is clearly shown by a comparison with the sun and moon; as long as these two luminaries shine in the vault of the sky, so shall the reign of Christ the King endure. The familiar note of universality is also presented under a twofold image: a geographical description of his rule, 'from sea to sea' (Mediterranean Sea to Persian Gulf), and tribute from the nations of the world.

The idea that the wise men who came to worship the Christ-child (Mt. 2) were kings is derived from this psalm; the three kings of Tharsis (a city in Spain), Arabia, and Sheba bring gifts, one of which is gold.

THE UNIVERSAL CHURCH

GOD IS KING OF ALL THE EARTH. These four psalms were written at the time of the Assyrian invasion, from which Jeru-

worthy of dread; he is the sovereign ruler of all the earth; he has tamed the nations to our will, bowed the Gentiles at our feet, claimed us for his portion, Jacob the fair, the well beloved.

God goes up, loud are the cries of victory; the Lord goes up, loudly the trumpets peal. A psalm, a psalm for our God, a psalm, a psalm for our King! **God is King of all the earth; sound the hymn of praise! God reigns over the heathen, God sits enthroned in holiness.** The rulers of the nations throw in their lot with us, that worship Abraham's God; a God so high, he has all earth's princes for his vassals.

May God be merciful to us, and bless us; may he grant us the favour of his smile. **Make known your will, O God, wide as earth; make known among all nations your saving power.** Honour to you, O God, from the nations, honour from all the nations!

The Gentiles, too, may rejoice and be glad; a whole world abides your judgment, and the Gentiles, too, obey on earth your sovereignty. Honour to you, O God, from the nations, honour from all the nations!

The land has yielded its harvest; such bounty God, our own God, affords. God grant us ever his blessing, and may earth, far and wide, do him reverence.

Show your power, O God, show your Divine power, perfect your own achievement for us; **to honour your temple at Jerusalem, kings shall bring gifts before you.** Tame the wild beasts of the marshes, fierce bulls that lord it over the peaceful herd of nations; down fall they, bringing silver pieces for their ran-

salem was delivered by the direct intervention of the Lord
God himself (4 Kg. 19, 35).

The imagery of this first psalm is taken from the customary
victory procession after a battle; with great clapping and
shouting and loud peals of trumpets, the people marched to
the Lord's house, the temple, there to proclaim his universal
sovereignty.

The psalmist's thoughts go beyond the present to that great
day in the future when all nations will submit to the Lord;
this will not come to pass until Messianic times when Jew and
Gentile will form one Church: 'So there will be one fold, and
one shepherd' (Jn. 10, 16).

HONOUR TO GOD FROM THE NATIONS. This psalm was written probably on the occasion of one of the feasts, such as
Pentecost, when the people offered thanks for the harvest.
God's bounty in granting Israel his blessing by a fruitful
harvest turns the thoughts of the psalmist to that final blessing when the harvest will not be wheat and barley but the
souls of all men, both Jew and Gentile.

This was fulfilled at the feast of Pentecost following our
Lord's death, when the Holy Ghost made the apostles speak
in foreign tongues, indicating that God would be praised from
now on, not in Hebrew only, but in the languages of all men
on the face of the earth.

KINGS SHALL BRING GIFTS. This paragraph is the last seven
verses of Psalm 67, another processional psalm that cele-
brates the Exodus from Egypt to Jerusalem; it was composed
possibly when the ark was carried into the temple after the
slaughter of the Assyrians. Egypt and Ethiopia are symbols of

som. Scatter the nations that delight in war, till Egypt sends hither her princes, till Ethiopia makes her peace with God.

Kingdoms of the earth, raise your voices in God's honour, sing a psalm to the Lord; a psalm to God, who mounts the heavens, the immemorial heavens, and utters his word in a voice of thunder. Pay honour to God, the God whose splendour rests over Israel, who holds dominion high among the clouds. Awe dwells about him in his holy place! The God of Israel gives his people strength and courage; blessed be God!

His own building amidst the inviolate hills, dearer to the Lord are Sion walls than any other home in Israel. How high a boast, city of God, is made for you, 'Mine it is to reckon the folk of Egypt, of Babylon, too, among my citizens!' Philistines, Tyrians, Ethiopians, all must claim Sion as their birthplace; **'None was ever born,'** the proverb shall run, **'that did not take his birth from her';** it was the most High, none other, that founded her. 'This was their birthplace,' the Lord shall write over the muster-roll of the nations; nor any but shall tell her praises with song and dance, each claiming from her its only origin.

the enemies of the chosen people (a detail from the times of the Exodus). Egypt is indicated in 'the wild beasts of the marshes,' the crocodile and hippopotamus that lived in the reeds of the Nile.

The psalmist again looks forward to the birthday of the universal Church, an era of peace, when all nations will show their obedience to God by bringing their gifts, the tribute of their minds and wills. The Lord Almighty is pictured enthroned in majesty (our Lord at the right hand of his Father in heaven) while all the kingdoms of the world bow down in worship.

OUR MOTHER, THE HEAVENLY JERUSALEM. In the Jewish picture of the Messianic kingdom, Sion was the capital; all the blessings that would come to the members of the universal kingdom were based solely on citizenship in Jerusalem. This idea depends partly on the role played by Jerusalem in David's kingdom, but mainly on the fact that it was the place where God dwelt on earth among his people, in his holy temple.

In the New Testament fulfilment, the Church is called the heavenly Jerusalem (Gal. 4, 26). All peoples become members of the Church by baptism; this makes them citizens with access to all the divine treasures.

CONTENTS: Chapter 4

SOPH. 1, 7-18	The Day of the Lord	116
SOPH. 3, 8-20	The Church One and Holy	118
JER. 3, 11-21; 16, 19; 12, 16	The Old Covenant Abrogated	120
JER. 23, 1-8; 33, 6-26	Redemption and Sanctification	122
JER. 30—31	The New Covenant	128
BAR. 4, 30—5, 9	The Splendour of the Church	132
EZECH. 17; 21, 25-27	A King of David's House	134
EZECH. 34; 37, 15-28	One Flock and One Shepherd	138
EZECH. 36	The New Christian Spirit	144
EZECH. 38—39	Antichrist, Champion of Wickedness	146
EZECH. 40, 1-4; 43, 1-7; 44, 2	Holiness of the Church	150
EZECH. 47, 1-12	Sanctifying Grace	152
PSS. 88; 131; 89	The Eternal Kingship of Christ	154
IS. 40—52; 45 15-26	Deliverance and Salvation	158
IS. 42; 49; 50; 53	The Servant of the Lord	164
IS. 54—66	The Glory of the Church	174
TOB. 13, 11-23	The New Jerusalem	182

4. The Babylonian Captivity

PALESTINE was of strategic importance to the world powers of the Nile delta (Egypt) and the Tigris-Euphrates basin (Assyria, Babylon); it was the bridge between them. The southern kingdom (Juda) survived the Assyrian onslaught, in which the northern kingdom (Israel) fell. Within a century Babylon had supplanted Assyria as the dominant nation in the Middle East. After much intrigue and several unsatisfactory alliances with Egypt and her allies, Juda eventually fell to the Babylonian armies. The capital city, Jerusalem, was captured, the temple was burnt to the ground, and the elite of the population were carried off into exile to Babylon; this was in 587 B. C.

The prophets saw in this disaster a punishment from the Lord for national apostasy; the chosen people had abandoned their covenant with God and idolatrously worshipped the false gods of the heathen. To meet this danger to their national existence God raised up his greatest array of prophets; Jeremias, Ezechiel, Daniel, and Second Isaias (the four major prophets) all lived at this time. Jeremias prophesied in Jerusalem and was present at the capture of the city; he has immortalized it in his Lamentations. The other three all lived in exile and prophesied to the chosen people in captivity. I have left the prophecy of Daniel till the next chapter, because it seems that an inspired writer in Machabean times substantially rewrote it to suit the conditions of his own time.

Jewish rejection of the Lord by idolatry led Jeremias to proclaim that God would make a New Covenant to replace the Old (Jer. 31). The sad plight of the flock of Israel scattered in exile was the basis of Ezechiel's great foretelling of the coming of the Good Shepherd (Ezech. 34; 37). The sufferings of the Jews and their experience of the hardships of exile away from their own land prepared them for the greatest of all Messianic revelations: the four Servant Songs of Isaias, which come to their climax with the death of the innocent Christ as a victim for the sins of all mankind (Is. 52, 13—53, 12).

SOPHONIAS 1, 7-18

Silence, there, to greet the Lord! Here is day of his appoint-
ing, here is great sacrifice of his preparing; all his guests
bidden, all their cleansing done. The Lord's sacrifice! 'A day
of reckoning it shall be, king and prince I will call to account,
all that go clad in foreign bravery, all that spurn yonder
threshold, and fill the house of the Lord their God with
deeds of treachery and wrong. What an outcry that day,' the
Lord says, 'from the Fishmongers' Gate, what lamenting from
the New Town! How the hillsides will echo to the noise of
your ruin! Ay, lament indeed, you that dwell in Mortar Valley; of the merchant folk no more is heard; here is an end of
all that trafficked in silver.

'Time, then, to call for lamps, and search Jerusalem
through! Trust me, I will find them out, spoiled natures, like
wine that has settled on its lees, the men who think to themselves, "From the Lord nothing is to hope, nothing to fear."
Ransacked their wealth shall be, and their homes ruined;
houses they build they shall never dwell in, vineyards they
plant they shall drink of never.'

Nearer, nearer comes the great day of the Lord's reckoning,
ay, and soon; bitter the bruit of its coming; here is peril to
cow the bravest heart. Day of vengeance, day of strain and
stress, day of ransack and ruin; dim and dark, overcast with
cloud and storm! City is none so well fortified, pinnacle is
none so high in air, but shall hear braying of trumpets and
the battle-cry. Guilty wretches, they shall grope in the dark,
flesh and blood of them cheap as dust and dung; silver and
gold of them powerless to buy off the Lord's present vengeance. **Burns through the land the fire of his slighted love;
takes full toll, and speedily, of all that dwell there.**

THE DAY OF THE LORD

THE FIRE OF GOD'S SLIGHTED LOVE.   Almost a hundred years had passed since Isaias and Micheas preached repentance to the Jewish people. In their time King Ezechias had carried out a sweeping reform both in the temple worship and in the moral life of the people. Now, in the time of Sophonias, king Josias found it necessary to institute another reform; Israel had fallen back into its evil ways and had gone again after false gods. Sophonias seems to have been the prophet assigned by God to this task of preparing the chosen people for the reform of Josias, which began in 627 B.C.

As in Amos and Isaias, the day of the Lord is presented, not as the destruction of the pagan enemies of Israel, but as a day of punishment on the guilty members of the chosen people of God. In this opening sermon of Sophonias, the Lord is pictured coming to the temple of Jerusalem at the time of the daily sacrifice. Instead of sitting down peacefully to eat the sacrificial food with the temple worshippers, the Lord calls them to account for their 'deeds of treachery and wrong.' There will not be a single house in the city of Jerusalem that he will not scrutinize closely with a lighted lamp. (In ancient times, with no adequate window lighting, a lamp was needed even in the daytime, Luke 15, 8.)

The result of this divine investigation will be a decree of destruction for the capital city, Jerusalem. This is the day of the Lord's vengeance that will fill all the inhabitants with fear and dread. In actual fact it would come within forty years; Jerusalem was destroyed in 587 B.C. Like the second destruction of the city in 70 A.D., this was a foreshadowing, a rehearsal of that great final day of reckoning, when the Lord comes at the end of time to judge and punish all wrong-doing.

SOPHONIAS 3, 8-20

'Hope, then, is none,' the Lord says, 'till the day, long
hence, when I will stand revealed; what gathering, then, of
the nations, all kingdoms joined in one! And upon these, my
doom is, vengeance shall fall, fierce anger of mine shall fall;
**the whole earth shall be consumed with the fire of my
slighted love.** And after that, all the peoples of the world
shall have pure lips, invoking one and all the Lord's name,
straining at a single yoke in the Lord's service. From far
away, beyond Ethiop rivers, my suppliants shall come to me,
sons of my exiled people the bloodless offering shall bring.

'No need, then, to blush for wayward thoughts that defied
me; gone from your midst the high-sounding boast; no room,
in that mountain sanctuary of mine, for pride henceforward;
a poor folk and a friendless I will leave in your confines, but
one that puts its trust in the Lord's name. **The remnant of
Israel, strangers now to treachery and wrong, the true word
ever on their lips!** Yonder flock may graze and lie down to
rest, none to dismay it.'

Break into song, fair Sion, all Israel cry aloud; here is joy
and triumph, Jerusalem, for your royal heart. Your doom
the Lord has revoked, your enemy repulsed; the Lord, there
in the midst of you, Israel's king! Peril for you henceforth is
none. Such is the message yonder day shall bring to Jerusalem: 'Courage, Sion! What means it, the unnerved hand?
You have one in the midst of you, the Lord your God, whose
strength shall deliver you. **Joy and pride of his you shall be
henceforward; silent till now in his love for you, he will greet
you with cries of gladness.**'

THE CHURCH ONE AND HOLY

GOD'S ANGER IS A PURIFYING FIRE. God cannot tolerate sin; Israel, as well as the pagan nations, must atone for their guilt by suffering. This is the day of the Lord, the day of doom and vengeance of a God whose love has been slighted. For the Jews that day, soon to come, would be the destruction of Jerusalem and the Babylonian captivity; for the nations it would be defeat at the hands of invading armies. Then God's love would triumph, and a purified people would worship him in his holy temple; no more enmity and falsehood, no division and war between countries, no pride and arrogance, but all united in a common purpose of divine service. Jerusalem would be a sanctuary, on the mountain dedicated to the Lord.

The terminology and the ideas are all Old Testament; but the reality was realized only in the New Testament. It was the Church that Sophonias was describing; the remnant that remained true was the small group of twelve apostles; they were the foundation members of this new society, a united and holy people.

STRAYED SHEEP BROUGHT HOME. In true oriental imagery, God's loving care for his people is expressed under the image of a shepherd and his flock. On the part of God there is personal interest and divine protection; the flock is his pride and joy. As for the sheep, the shepherd's care ensures them peace and security; if one strays, the shepherd leaves all to search for it (Lk. 15, 4-6); if one is sick or lame, the shepherd looks after it with all the care of a loving mother.

The situation that Sophonias has in mind seems to be the return of the chosen people from Babylonian exile. The sen-

'Truants that were lost to the covenant I will reclaim,' the Lord says; 'of your company they are, you shall be taunted with them no longer; only for your persecutors that hour shall be the hour of doom. **Lame sheep medicined, and strayed sheep brought home!** Lands that despised them shall hear name and fame of them now. Name and fame you shall have, all the world over, when I call you back and gather you in; when you see the fortunes of Israel retrieved at last.'

JEREMIAS 3, 11-21; 16, 19; 12, 16

And the Lord told me: 'Better than Juda's treachery, the apostasy of Israel deserves to be acquitted. Carry this message of yours to the north country: "Come back to me, apostate Israel," the Lord says, "and there shall be no frown of mine awaiting you; I am merciful," the Lord says, "and vengeance shall not last for ever. Only acknowledge your fault," he tells you, "in deserting the Lord your God and betaking yourself to the bowers of strange lovers, deaf to my call.

' "Must I ever be offering you sonship, and a land so fair that all the peoples of the world might envy you its possession? Must I ever be pleading with you to acknowledge me as your father, and forsake my guidance no more? Hitherto," the Lord says, "nothing could I win from Israel but a false jade's contempt." '

Now from yonder hill-passes, another cry is heard; a cry of mourning and lament from the sons of Israel, over the wrong path they have chosen in forgetting the Lord their God. Wandering hearts, the Lord bids you come back to him, and renew your troth; by ones and twos, from this city and that, from this clan or that, he will claim you for his

tence of punishment now revoked, and the power of Babylon destroyed, the Jews may express their joy by shouting and singing; they are returning to the home of the Lord in his temple at Jerusalem.

This home-coming is the birthday of the Church, a day of gladness and rejoicing because it is God's great intervention in human affairs. Founded by the Lord God, the name and fame of the new restored Israel will become world-wide; it will be a universal Church.

THE OLD COVENANT ABROGATED

DIVINE ENTREATY TO ISRAEL. Jeremias prophesied in the city of Jerusalem, a century later than Isaias. By this time the political situation had changed completely: Babylon had taken over the dominant role in the Middle East in place of Assyria. Jeremias was a young man in his early twenties when the Lord called him to begin his prophetic office; he went on making known the Lord's commands for forty years, until after the fall of Jerusalem in 587 B.C. Some authorities think that Jeremias was cleansed from original sin in his mother's womb; this is based on God's words to him in 1, 5: 'I claimed you for my own before ever I fashioned you in your mother's womb.' But the context suggests rather that God is referring to Jeremias' vocation as a prophet; God destined him for this office before he was born (Ecclus. 49, 9).

That this initial prophecy is Messianic can be demonstrated from internal evidence. From the words 'wandering hearts' there is a change from punishment to restoration, so common in Messianic prophecies. Also four qualities characteristic of Messianic times are found in this passage. (1) Sion as the centre of Christ's kingdom. (2) Good shepherds to guard and

own and bring you back to Sion; and you shall have shepherds of his own choice to guide you well and prudently.

'After that,' the Lord says, 'when all is growth and fertility, **no longer shall you have the Ark of the Lord's Covenant for your rallying-cry; from thought and memory it will have passed away, nor any care shall be bestowed on the fashioning of it.** It is Jerusalem men will speak of as the Lord's throne; there at Jerusalem all the nations of the world will meet in the Lord's name, the false aims of their perverse hearts forgotten. When that time comes, Juda and Israel will be united; together they will come back from the north country to the land I gave your fathers for their home.'

Strength and stronghold, Lord, refuge in time of peril, shall not the Gentiles themselves come to you from the ends of the earth, confessing that all their patrimony is but a heritage of lies, that their idols cannot avail them? And this message came from the Lord: 'If they will but learn the traditions of my own people, and take their oaths by the Lord, the living God, as they once taught my people to take oaths by Baal, their fortunes shall be founded anew in the midst of Juda.'

JEREMIAS 23, 1-8; 33, 6-26

'Out upon them,' the Lord says, 'the shepherds who ravage and disperse my flock, sheep of my own pasturing!' This is the Lord's word to the shepherds that guide his people: 'You are the men who have dispersed my flock, driven it to and fro, and made no account of it; account you must give it me,' says the Lord, Israel's God, 'for all you have done amiss. Then

guide Israel, in place of their present evil rulers. (3) All nations, not Jews only, included in the kingdom of Christ. (4) The union of Juda and Israel, northern and southern kingdoms, so long at enmity.

What is new in Messianic revelation is the Lord's repudiation of the treaty he made with the people of Israel at Sinai. This covenant, written on two stone tablets and placed in the ark of the covenant, was kept in the holy of holies in the temple. Because of their rejection of God, primarily by their idolatry, the covenant will be annulled, and a new covenant made by Christ when he sheds his blood on Calvary. This is formally stated in 31, 31: 'A time is coming, the Lord says, when I mean to ratify A NEW COVENANT with the people of Israel.'

When Nabuchodonosor, king of Babylon, destroyed the city of Jerusalem and its temple, the ark of the covenant was either burnt or else taken to Babylon by the conquerors. It has never been recovered, and it was absent from the new temple built by the exiles in 516 B.C. A legend recorded in 2 Machabees 2, 4-8 that Jeremias hid the ark in a cave in Transjordan can hardly be true, seeing that he was imprisoned at the time (Jer. 38, 28). Machabees records the incident without vouching for its accuracy.

REDEMPTION AND SANCTIFICATION

A FAITHFUL SCION OF DAVID'S STOCK. This prophecy was spoken by Jeremias shortly before the fall of Jerusalem. Sedecias, the last of the Jewish kings, was reigning at the time. Like practically all the royal rulers (David, Ezechiel, and Josias excepted) he had refused to listen to the message from the Lord delivered by the prophets; instead of being a

will I reassemble all that is left of my flock, scattered over so many lands, and restore them to their old pasture-ground, to increase and grow numerous there; shepherds I mean to give them that will do shepherd's work; fears and alarms shall be none to daunt them, and none shall be missing from their full count,' the Lord says.

'Nay, a time is coming,' the Lord says, 'when **I will raise up, from the stock of David, a faithful scion at last.** The land shall have a king to reign over it, and reign over it wisely, giving just sentence and due award. When that time comes, Juda shall find deliverance, none shall disturb Israel's rest; **and the name given to this king shall be, "The Lord vindicates us."**

'In those days to come,' says the divine message, 'the living Lord men swear by will no longer be the God who rescued Israel from Egypt; the living God will be one who rescued Israel and brought them home from the north country, and from all the places of exile he had once designed for them, to live in their own land again.'

Jeremias was still confined to his prison in the court when the word of the Lord came to him a second time. It ran: 'Closed and cured those wounds shall be; I myself will heal them, grant them peace and safety to their heart's content. The fortunes of Juda and Jerusalem I will reverse, and they shall be established as firmly as ever; **all the guilt that offends me purged away, all the wrong and despite they did me forgiven.** My pride and prize, my renown and triumph, to be their benefactor, so that all the world shall hear of it; everywhere the tale of my bounty and my blessing shall strike awe and dread into men's hearts.

'Where all seems to your eyes but a desert, man nor beast

true shepherd of his people, he had sold them into exile and slavery.

The next king to reign over the chosen people would be the promised Messiah. This long gap of six hundred years is passed over by Jeremias; all he is interested in is a comparison and a contrast between Christ and Sedecias. This is not clear until it is understood that the key phrase 'The Lord vindicates us' (Yahweh-Zideqenu) is only another way of writing the name of Sedecias (Zidequi-Yahu).

The two successive kings, Sedecias and Jesus, have the same name, symbolizing the office God entrusted to them. Sedecias was untrue to his office; Christ carried out his perfectly. He was the Good Shepherd of his flock when he laid down his life for them on the cross; by his sacrificial death he won for men acquittal from their sins and access to all divine graces and blessings. In this way he was the champion of the new Israel, vindicating his people from the dominion of sin. This new deliverance far surpasses the first Exodus from Egypt; this time the exiles return from sin to the promised land of holiness.

GOD'S MERCY TO JUDA AND JERUSALEM. For almost forty years Jeremias had preached repentance to the people of Jerusalem; as a prophet of the Lord he had delivered the divine message that would have brought them peace and happiness. The climax of his missionary career was total rejection and imprisonment: 'They thought to compass my death by their clamour; to all my warnings would pay heed no longer' (Jer. 18, 18). His life more closely resembles our Lord's than does that of any other person in the Old Testament; both made known 'the ways that can bring peace' (Lk. 19, 42), and both foretold the destruction of Jerusalem as a punishment for Jewish rejection of God.

left in the townships of Juda and in Jerusalem, empty street, empty house, empty byre, there,' says the Lord, 'you shall hear cries of joy and mirth, voice of bridegroom and voice of bride. There you shall hear men singing, **"Give thanks to the Lord, the Lord is gracious, his mercy endures for ever,"** as they bring to his temple the offerings they have vowed. Your country's doom shall be reversed,' says the divine promise, 'and all shall be as of old.

'Juda and all its townships a desert, no living thing to dwell there? Nay,' says the Lord of hosts, 'once again it shall be the abode of shepherds, a resting-place for their flocks. By hill and plain and the uplands of the south, all over Benjamin and round about Jerusalem, all through the cities of Juda, there shall be flocks passing to and fro, and their masters a-counting them,' the Lord says.

'Behold,' he says, 'a time is coming when I will make good my promise to Israel and Juda; **the day will dawn, the time be ripe at last for that faithful scion to bud from David's stock; the land shall have a king to reign over it, giving just sentence and due award.** When that time comes, Juda shall find deliverance, none shall disturb Jerusalem's rest; **and the name given to this city shall be, "The Lord vindicates us."** Never a man wanting of David's line,' the Lord says, 'to sit on Israel's throne; never a lack of priest and Levite to wait upon me, bring me burnt sacrifice and burn the bloodless offering, and slaughter victims, day after day.'

And the word of the Lord came to Jeremias, giving him this message: 'If you can rescind my ordinance of day and

In this section, Jeremias has words of consolation for the people of Jerusalem. His thoughts go into the future when God will forgive his guilty people; once more restored to divine friendship, they will return to the promised land. As is customary with Old Testament writers, this new life of sanctifying grace in the Church of Christ is presented under material imagery. Jerusalem and the cities of Juda will be rebuilt; again they will be populated with men, just as the countryside will have its flocks grazing in peace and security; the temple will once more be the place of divine worship.

There is a marked contrast between the conditions of gloom and sadness when Jeremias wrote (Jerusalem was surrounded by the Babylonian army that was to capture the city), and the picture of joy and happiness when God should have mercy on his people. This complete reversal of fortune would be due entirely to the goodness of the Lord: He would send his Son to redeem mankind.

A FAITHFUL KING IN JERUSALEM. Two paragraphs back, the title 'The Lord vindicates us' (Yahweh-Zideqenu in Hebrew) was applied to the Messianic Son of David; here the same title is given to the city of Jerusalem. It is a symbolical title, like Emmanuel in Isaias 7, 14, not a personal name; it signifies the office or function of the person or place to which it is applied. Jerusalem stands for the Church, and what is said of Christ may be said of his Mystical Body. Christ in his own person brought us redemption from sin; the Church's function is to store up and apply the fruits of redemption to us. She is that heavenly Jerusalem who distributes God's grace to mankind.

THE KING, THE PRIESTS, THE NATION. In most solemn fashion God here guarantees the permanence of a Davidic

night, that there should be day-time and night-time no more, only then will I rescind the privilege granted to my servant David, and there shall be heirs of his throne no more, Levites and priests to wait on me no more. **My servant David, the Levites that wait on me, these shall have a posterity countless as the stars of heaven, measureless as the sea-sand.'**

This message, too, Jeremias had from the Lord: 'Mark well how they declare, the folk among whom you dwell, that there are two families the Lord has chosen, and both he has cast off; so that they despise my own people, and no longer count it a nation. But this is the divine answer: Laws if I have made none for day and night, for heaven and earth no ordinances prescribed, then let it be thought that I mean to cast Israel away, or depose the line of David from its headship over all who spring from Abraham, Isaac, and Jacob. Trust me, their doom shall be reversed, their lot pitied.'

JEREMIAS 30—31

'Now,' the Lord says, 'a voice is heard in Rama, of lamentation and bitter mourning; it is Rachel weeping for her children, and she will not be comforted, because none is left.' But thus he reassures you: 'Sad voice, lament, sad eyes, weep no more. The Lord means to ransom Jacob, to grant deliverance from the tyrant's power. The exiles will return, greeting mount Sion with cries of gladness; thronging to take possession of the Lord's gifts, corn and oil and wine, increase of flock and herd. Revived their spirits shall be, like a garden when the stream flows full; they shall hunger no more. Glad

king to rule his people, a plentiful supply of priests for divine
worship, and the continuance of national existence for Israel.
History excludes any interpretation that restricts this guarantee to the Jewish people as a nation: Sedecias was the last
Davidic king to sit on the throne of Israel, and the Levitical
priests ceased their sacrificial offerings when the temple was
destroyed in 70 A.D.

The true interpretation of the divine promise is to be found
only in the Christian Church: Christ is the king of David's
line who will rule forever (Lk. 1, 32-33), the Levitical priesthood would give way to the Melchisedechian priesthood of
Christ (Heb. 7), and the nation Israel would find its fulfilment in the Church of Christ, 'God's true Israel' (Gal. 6,
16).

If the Jews had accepted our Lord as their Messiah, the
picture might have been different: Jerusalem the capital and
centre of an independent papal state, and the temple the
mother of all Christian churches.

THE NEW COVENANT

SORROW OF EXILE TURNED TO JOY.   It was at Rama, five miles
north of Jerusalem, that the Jewish captives were assembled
after the fall of Jerusalem; from there they were led off into
exile to Babylon. All the mothers are poetically represented
in Rachel, the wife of Jacob, who mourns the sad fate of her
children. The incident is more familiar to us from its quotation in St. Matthew (2, 18) on the occasion of the slaughter
of the Innocents by king Herod the Great in his attempt to
kill the infant Christ. In both cases a great disaster befell
Israel.

the maidens shall dance, gladness there shall be for young and old alike; I will turn all their sorrow into joy, comfort and cheer their hearts. Full-fed my priests shall be with dainties; blessings my people shall have,' the Lord says, 'till they ask no more.

'They shall obey the Lord their God only, and that David-king of theirs whom he will give them. A prince of their own race they shall have, a home-born ruler, singled out by my own call to serve them; that office,' the Lord says, 'none may take on himself unbidden.

'Have you no fear,' the Lord says, 'Jacob, that are my servant still. Jacob shall return, and live at ease, every blessing shall enjoy, and enemies have none to fear; I am at your side to protect you. Then I will heal that scar of yours, cure you of your wounds; too soon they called you a neglected bride, Sion the unwooed! With unchanging love I love you, and now in mercy I have drawn you to myself. Fickle maid, dally no longer. Here is a new order of things the Lord has established on earth: the bride returns to her husband.'

'A time is coming,' the Lord says, 'when I mean to ratify a new covenant with the people of Israel and with the people of Juda. An eternal covenant I will make with them, nor ever cease to speed them; inspire their hearts with the fear of me, that never swerves aside. It will not be like the covenant which I made with their fathers, on the day when I took them by the hand, to rescue them from Egypt; that they should break my covenant, and I should abandon them,' the Lord says. 'No, this is the covenant I will grant the people of Israel,' the Lord says, 'when that time comes. I will implant my law in their innermost thoughts, engrave it in their hearts;

There is a sudden change from exile to return; the atmosphere alters from weeping to rejoicing. As the exiles come within sight of Jerusalem, they will greet that city with loud cries of gladness. Young and old alike will be happy, sacrificial victims will be offered in abundance to the priests (who received a portion of the food presented for sacrifice); the whole nation will be prosperous. This was only partially fulfilled by the return in 538 B.C. The complete realization came only with Christ; he is that 'David-king,' the greatest blessing ever bestowed by God on his chosen people and all mankind.

It was the prophet Osee who popularized the idea of the relationship of the Lord and Israel as that of husband and wife. By her idolatry Israel proved an unfaithful spouse; but now, as the holy and spotless bride of the New Covenant (Eph. 5, 27), the Church is united to Christ in the bonds of perfect love; this is an entirely new order of things. St. Jerome translated the last sentence of this paragraph: 'A woman shall compass a man.' By this he makes the text an explicit reference to the Incarnation; Mary is the woman, Jesus is the man in her womb at Nazareth.

THE NEW AND ETERNAL COVENANT. This prophecy of Jeremias is unique in the Old Testament: it is the only mention of a NEW covenant. Jeremias stands almost halfway between the first covenant which God made with Israel at Sinai more than six hundred years earlier, and the second covenant which he made with the Church on Calvary six hundred years later. Both were treaties between two parties, though they are better known under the names Old and New Testament. The reason for a new covenant was the failure on the part of Israel to live up to her treaty obligations; God abandoned Israel because she first rejected him.

I will be their God, and they shall be my people. One will they shall have, and journey by one way, living evermore in the fear of me, winning for themselves and their sons a blessing. There will be no need for neighbour to teach neighbour, or brother to teach brother, the knowledge of the Lord; all will know me, from the highest to the lowest. **I will pardon their wrong-doing; I will not remember their sins any more.'**

A message from the Lord, from him, the God of hosts, the same who brightens day with the sun's rays, night with the ordered service of moon and star, who can stir up the sea and set its waves a-roaring: 'All these laws of mine will fail me,' he says, 'before the line of Israel fails me; **a people it must remain until the end of time.'** You have the Lord's word for it: 'When you can measure heaven above,' he tells you, 'and search the foundations of earth below, then I will cast away the whole line of Israel, for all its ill deserving.

'Behold,' says the divine promise, 'a time is coming when the city shall be rebuilt in the Lord's honour, from Hananeel's Tower as far as the Corner Gate; nay, in advance of that the limit of its range shall reach, across Gareb hill, to take in Goatha, burial-ground and ash-pit and all the dead soil as far as Kedron brook, and eastward as far as the corner by the Horsemen's Gate; **all shall be consecrated to the Lord;** tree shall not be uprooted there henceforward, nor house overthrown.'

BARUCH 4, 30—5, 9

Yourself, Jerusalem, take courage! He that called you by name brings you comfort. Turn about, and look to the sun's

There is a threefold contrast between the two covenants.
(1) The old was written on tablets of stone, the new is en-
graved on men's hearts (2 Cor. 3, 3). This externalism of the
old and spirituality of the new is best seen in our Lord's
Sermon on the Mount (Mt. 5). (2) The Jews were unfaithful to their obligations; they did not observe the law. The
Church will always be true to God; Christians will receive
grace that will ensure their carrying out of the divine precepts. (3) The old conferred only legal or external sanctifica-
tion; of itself it did not bring men sanctifying grace. The new
unites men to God in perfect friendship by complete and
absolute forgiveness of sins. This quality is treated at length
by St. Paul in Hebrews, where he quotes this passage from
Jeremias (Heb. 8, 8-13; 10, 15-17). Hebrews not only demonstrates that Jeremias' prophecy is Messianic, it also shows the
superiority of the new over the old covenant.

The Old Testament lasted for almost thirteen hundred
years, the New Testament will last forever; it is an eternal
covenant. Our Lord made this clear in his final commission to
his Church: 'And behold I am with you all through the days
that are coming, until the consummation of the world' (Mt.
28, 20). It is the Church of the New Testament that is meant
when Jeremias prophesies that 'a people it must remain until
the end of time.' Likewise his final description of the rebuilding of Jerusalem, a city completely consecrated to the Lord,
is not to be taken literally; it is the heavenly Jerusalem, the
city of God on earth.

THE SPLENDOUR OF THE CHURCH

RESTORATION OF JERUSALEM AS QUEEN. Baruch was secre-
tary to Jeremias, and a disciple of his in the prophetic min-

rising; see what rejoicing the Lord has in store for you; sons of yours, in many lands lost to you, gathered by his call from east to west shall come back again, praising joyfully God's holy will.

Enough, Jerusalem; lay aside now the sad garb of your humiliation, and put on bright robes, befitting the eternal glory God means for you; cloak of divine protection thrown about you, your temples bearing a diadem of renown. **In you God will manifest the splendour of his presence, for the whole world to see;** and the name by which he will call you for ever is, 'Loyalty rewarded, Piety crowned.'

Up, Jerusalem, to the heights! Look to the sun's rising, and see if your sons be not coming to you, gathered from east to west, joyfully acknowledging God's holy will! Afoot they were led off by the enemy; it is the Lord that shall lead them home, borne aloft like royal princes. He will have the ground made level; high mountain must stoop, and immemorial hill, and the valleys be filled up, for Israel's safe passage and God's glory; spinneys of every scented tree shall grow, by his divine command, to give Israel shade. So merciful he is, and so faithful! **In great content, their journey lit by the majesty of his presence, Israel shall come home.**

EZECHIEL 17; 21, 25-27

Word came to me from the Lord: 'A riddle, son of man, a parable for the men of Israel to interpret! This shall be your message from the Lord God: A great eagle there was, strong of wing, long of limb; thick and gay his plumage. And this eagle flew to Lebanon, where he robbed cedar of cedar's very

istry. He remained with Jeremias in Palestine after the fall
of Jerusalem. When some of the Jewish zealots killed the
Babylonian governor Godolias, many of the Jewish people
fled to Egypt from fear of Babylonian retaliation. Jeremias
and Baruch accompanied them; when Jeremias died in Egypt,
it seems that Baruch made his way to Babylon and joined the
exiles there.

Together with Ezechiel and Daniel he preached to the
exiles, and in this paragraph he comforts them with the pre-
diction of return to Palestine and the restoration of Jerusalem.
His words are addressed to Jerusalem the queen, once more
dressed in royal robes. She will be glorious and resplendent
with the bright light of the Lord's presence, the Shekinah of
the Exodus. A second metaphor is that of a level, shady highway leading the exiles from Babylon to Jerusalem. This image
is better known from Isaias 40, 4, quoted about St. John the
Baptist (Lk. 3, 4).

It is not the material city of Jerusalem that is so described;
the bright, shining cloud of God's presence, the Shekinah,
was never again present over that city. It is sanctifying grace
that Baruch is describing, the glory of the Church. Possibly
also the Holy Spirit is foretelling the Incarnation by his emphasis on the divine presence, the Son of God living on earth
among men.

A KING OF DAVID'S HOUSE

CEDAR, VINE, AND TWO EAGLES. Ezechiel went into exile
to Babylon with the second group of captives (there were
three groups all told); this was eleven years before the fall
of Jerusalem. The first twenty-four chapters of his prophecy
are addressed to the exiles during the last six years prior to

pith; tore away its crown of leaves and carried it off to Merchant-land, set it down in Traffic City. Then back he flew to that same country, chose out both seed and seed-ground there; it was on a level lawn by a brimming stream he planted it. When the plant grew, it proved to be a spreading vine, low of stature, and ever branch curled inwards and root struck downwards, yet vine it was, with sprig that burgeoned, shoot that sprang.

'But now, here is a second eagle comes in sight, another great eagle, strong of wing, thick-plumed; and it seems as if the vine, in the garden where it grows, were stretching out its roots, waving its tendrils, to ask this second eagle for water instead. What, when it was planted in ground so fair, by waters so abundant, with such promise of leaf and fruit, a vine so destined to greatness! Will any good come of this?' asks the Lord God. 'Nay, roots shall be plucked up, fruit ravaged, branches left to wither; fade it must, nor is it like to need great strength or many hands for its unearthing. Take root is not thrive; rich soil or none, when the sirocco parches it, the vine must wither.'

And here is a message from the Lord God: **'Pith of the tall cedar I will take and sit it firm, young branch from its crest of branches I will snap off, and plant it on a mountain that stands high above the rest.** High in the hill-country of Israel I will plant it, and there it shall grow into a great cedar-tree; **no bird on the wing but shall find rest under its shade, nestle among its branches;** till all the forest learns its lesson, that I, the Lord, bring high tree low, raise low tree high, wither the burgeoning trunk, give life to the barren.

'And you, perjured wretch that rules Israel, your time has run out; off with headband, off with crown, symbols that honour the base, the noble degrade! I will wrest it this way,

the destruction of Jerusalem; the remainder (the most important part) of his book deals with the situation in Babylon after the fall of Jerusalem. Most of the exiles lived in a settlement not far from the city of Babylon; it was called Tel Aviv (the present capital of Israel is named after it); there Ezechiel delivered most of his prophecies to his fellow exiles.

Ezechiel is noted for his picturesque language, his parables, visions, and symbolical actions; the Hebrews delighted in such oriental forms of speech and conduct. That is why our Lord's parables had such an appeal; these riddles were a challenge to the audience and were easy to remember for later consideration. In this allegory, the cedar stands for the house of David, both because of the majesty of this tree and the fact that David's dwelling in Jerusalem was made of cedar wood from Lebanon. The pith or the topmost shoot of the tree represents king Joachin (Jechonias of Matthew 1, 12), who was taken off into captivity at the same time as Ezechiel. Nabuchodonosor, king of Babylon, is the first eagle; he it was who led Joachin captive to Babylon ('Merchant-land' is the country, 'Traffic City' the metropolis of Babylon).

In place of Joachin, Nabuchodonosor appointed Sedecias, king of Juda; Sedecias is called a vine planted by a stream of water. His kingdom should have prospered; but in fact he allowed himself to be led astray by a second eagle, the Pharao of Egypt. This was contrary to God's plan, as made known by Jeremias, at that time prophesying in Jerusalem. In consequence God determined to destroy the house of Sedecias, the king reigning when Jerusalem was conquered. He it is that is called 'perjured wretch' in the final paragraph; he was the last to wear the crown in Israel; the next king would be Christ our Lord, to whom the crown really belonged by right (Gen. 49, 10). He is that shoot from David's house (through

wrest it that, as it was never wrested yet; **at last one shall come that claims it of right, and to him I will give it.'**

EZECHIEL 34; 37, 15-28

Word came to me from the Lord: 'Now, son of man, prophesy doom to the rulers of Israel, the shepherds of my flock. This be your message from the Lord God: "Out upon Israel's shepherds, that had a flock to feed, and fed none but themselves; the milk drank, the wool wore, the fat lambs slaughtered, but pastured these sheep of mine never at all! The wasted frame went unnourished, the sick unhealed; nor bound they the broken limb, nor brought strayed sheep home, nor lost sheep found; force and constraint were all the governance they knew. So my sheep fell a-wandering, that shepherd had none; every wild beast fell a-preying on them, and they scattered far and wide. All over the mountains they strayed, all over the high hills were scattered, this flock of mine, and no search was made for them, no search at all."

'This doom, then, the Lord pronounces on yonder shepherds: "As I am a living God, I will have a reckoning for sheep of mine carried off, sheep of mine the wild beasts have preyed on, while they went all untended, with shepherds that would not go in search of them, shepherds that no flock would feed, but themselves only."

'A word, shepherds, for your hearing, a message from the Lord God: "Out upon yonder shepherds! I will hold them answerable for the flock entrusted to them, and they shall have charge of it no more, feed themselves out of its revenues no more. From their greedy power I will rescue it; no longer shall it be their prey."

Joachin, Mt. 1, 12) planted on mount Sion; in his Church, the tall tree, all the peoples of the earth will find shelter (Mt. 13, 32).

ONE FLOCK AND ONE SHEPHERD

UNFAITHFUL SHEPHERDS OF ISRAEL. The Hebrews were a pastoral people; from the time of Abraham, when they first settled in Palestine, their lives were taken up with the care of sheep. With no fences and no sheep dogs, the duty of minding the flock, searching out pasture, and guarding from wild animals fell to the shepherd. Each morning he led his sheep out from the fold; he spent the day seeing that none strayed from the selected patch of grass; he cared for the old and sick sheep; at nightfall he brought them home to spend the night in the fold.

The chosen leaders of Israel had proved false to their divine calling; instead of caring for the Lord's flock, they thought only of their own interests. The sheep went untended, preyed on by enemies and finally scattered into lands far from Palestine. These rulers of Israel here condemned by God were of four kinds. (1) The king: the leader of the people in civil affairs, especially in warfare (1 Kg. 8, 20). Of the forty-two kings who reigned from Saul to Sedecias, only three, David, Ezechias, and Josias (Ecclus. 49, 5), were pleasing to God. (2) The priest: the high priest, with his assistant priests and Levites (lesser ministers), was the supreme guide in the worship of God in the temple at Jerusalem. (3) The prophet: a man specially called by God to speak in his name (it is the false prophets, not the true, that God here rebukes). (4) The wise man: one who expounded and interpreted the Mosaic law; they are better known in New Testament times as scribes.

'This is what the Lord God says: "I mean to go looking for this flock of mine, search it out for myself. As a shepherd, when he finds his flock scattered all about him, goes looking for his sheep, so will I go looking for these sheep of mine, rescue them from all the nooks into which they have strayed when the dark mist fell upon them. Rescued from every kingdom, recovered from every land, I will bring them back to their own country; they shall have pasture on the hillsides of Israel, by its water-courses, in the resting-places of their home. Yes, I will lead them out into fair pastures, the high mountains of Israel shall be their feeding-ground, the mountains of Israel, with soft grass for them to rest on, rich feed for them to graze.

'"Food and rest," says the Lord God, "both these I will give to my flock. **The lost sheep I will find, the strayed sheep I will bring home again; bind up the broken limb, nourish the wasted frame, keep the well-fed and the sturdy free from harm; they shall have a true shepherd at last."**

'This is what the Lord God says: **"They shall have a single shepherd to tend all of them now; who should tend them but my servant David? He shall be their shepherd, and I, the Lord, will be their God, now that he rules them on earth; such is my divine promise to them.** Such a covenant I will make as shall grant them security; beasts of prey there shall be none, safe resting, now, in the desert, safe sleeping in the woods; on my hillsides they shall dwell, a blessed people in a blessed home, rain in its season fall on them, and blessings all the while.

'"Wild trees their fruit, the earth its crops shall afford; undisturbed they shall dwell on their own lands, acknowledging my power at last, my power that severed strap of yoke, rescued

THE LORD HIMSELF WILL SHEPHERD ISRAEL. Israel was a theocracy, i.e. ruled directly and personally by God. His care for his flock is described in Psalm 22: 'The Lord is my shepherd; how can I lack anything? He gives me a resting-place where there is green pasture, leads me out to the cool water's brink, refreshed and content. As in honour pledged, by sure paths he leads me; dark be the valley about my path, hurt I fear none while he is with me; your rod, your crook are my comfort.'

What is emphasized in this paragraph is the Lord's concern for his lost sheep of the exile. He will search them out like the shepherd of our Lord's parable (Lk. 15, 4-6); he will take loving care of the sick and wounded; the entire flock will be restored to green pastures in their own land. This was realized fully only in New Testament times, when God himself came down on earth to live in the midst of his flock, to save them from the exile of sin, and to give them his own body and blood as food.

JESUS THE GOOD SHEPHERD. In the previous paragraph Yahweh, the Lord God himself, was presented as the true shepherd of Israel, in contrast to the faithless shepherds, the kings, priests, prophets, and wise men in Israel. Here it is the Messiah who is spoken of under the title 'David.' Ever since God's promise to king David (2 Kg. 7, 11-17) that a son of his would sit on the throne of Israel for ever, the Messiah to come had been known as 'Son of David.' Ezechiel leaves out the word 'son' and speaks of the Messiah directly as 'David.' The reason for this is probably that David himself was a shepherd, and Ezechiel wishes to emphasize that the Messiah will carry on the same role in the guidance of the flock of Israel.

'I am the good shepherd. The good shepherd lays down his

them from the tyrant's hand. Forgotten, the enemies that despoiled, the wild beasts that preyed on them; they will live sheltered from all alarms. Once more their renown shall burgeon; never again the land starve with drought, never the alien's taunt be heard. None shall doubt that I, the Lord their God, am at their side, and they are my own people, the race of Israel," the Lord God says. "Flock of mine," the Lord God says, "flock of my pasturing, you are the sheep of my flock and I am your God." '

And word came to me from the Lord: 'Son of man, take two pieces of wood, and write on one, "For Juda, and the tribes of Israel that take part with him"; on the other, that is the stick of Ephraim, write, "For Joseph, and all the tribes of Israel that take part with him." Then join them together into the form of a single stick, so that they are united in your hand. And when your fellow-countrymen would have you tell them what you mean by all this, give them this message from the Lord: "Here is this stick of Joseph and his confederate tribes, with Ephraim at their head; I mean to join it with Juda's and make one stick of it; one stick now, and in my hand."

'And while you are still holding the inscribed sticks, there in the presence of your fellow-countrymen, say this: "A message from the Lord God! I mean to recall the sons of Israel from their exile among the Gentiles, gather them from every side and restore them to their home. And there, in the hill-country of Israel, **I will make one nation of them, with one king over them all;** no longer shall they be two nations under two crowns. No more shall they be contaminated with idol-worship, and foul rites, and forbidden things a many; I will deliver them from the lands that were once the haunts of

life for his sheep, whereas the hireling abandons the sheep and takes to flight as soon as he sees the wolf coming, and so the wolf harries the sheep and scatters them' (Jn. 10, 11-12). In these words, Jesus identifies himself with the true shepherd of Ezechiel. Protection from enemies is brought out in both Ezechiel and John; this is the security from harm that will be characteristic of the Church of Christ. Ezechiel also mentions prosperity, an abundance of supernatural grace.

SYMBOL OF THE TWO STICKS OF WOOD.   Ezechiel is full of visions and symbolical acts. The oriental mind took great delight in such riddles and spent much time in solving them, seeking for the deeper meaning that lay hidden under the externals taking place before their eyes. They would watch every detail of Ezechiel's performance with the two sticks and would easily understand and appreciate the significance of what he was doing.

The rivalry between the two dominant sons of Israel was deeply rooted in the history of the chosen people. Right from their entry into the promised land, Juda and Joseph stood out as the natural leaders of the people. The tribe of Joseph received a double portion in the allocation of territory in Palestine; each of his sons, Ephraim and Manasses, being give a section of land. The tribes of the north rallied round Ephraim, while the south stood firm by Juda. This jealousy was held in check by David, who was of the tribe of Juda; but in the time of Solomon the division showed up once more. On his death the kingdom split up into two parts, the north and south, with a king ruling over each kingdom.

In the Church of Christ, which is God's restored Israel, there will be no place for rivalry and division; this is sym-

their sinning, and make them clean again; they shall be my people, and I will be their God.

' "They shall have one king over them, a shepherd to tend them all, my servant David; my will they shall follow, my commands remember and obey. And their home shall be the home of your fathers, the land I gave to my servant Jacob; they and their children shall enjoy it, and their children's children, in perpetuity, and ever my servant David shall be their prince. My covenant shall pledge them to prosperity, a covenant that shall never be revoked; I will bless them and give them increase, and set up my sanctuary in their midst for ever. My tabernacle over them; they my people, and I their God; proof to all the world that I, the Lord, have set Israel apart, I that dwell apart in their midst for ever." '

EZECHIEL 36

A promise from the Lord God to every mountain and hill, every upland and valley in the land of Israel! 'Till now,' the Lord God says, 'you have been put to the blush before your neighbours, but now my love and my indignation can contain itself no more. My oath upon it,' the Lord God says, 'these neighbours of yours shall be put to the blush in their turn. But you, mountains of Israel, must burgeon anew, and grow fruit for my own people to enjoy; their home-coming is not far off now. Watch for me, I am coming back to you; soil of you shall be ploughed and sown anew; and men, too, shall thrive on it, Israel's full muster-roll, peopling the cities, restoring the ruins. Full tale you shall have of men and beasts that thrive and multiply; I will make you populous as of old, more than of old my blessings lavish, and you shall not doubt my power.

bolized under the removal of the age-old opposition between Juda and Joseph. Isaias 11, 13 mentions this same unity as a sign of Messianic times, and our Lord himself puts unity in the first place as the outstanding mark of his Church: 'I pray for those who are to find faith in me; that they may all be one; that they too may be one in us, as you Father are in me, and I in you; so that the world may come to believe that it is you who have sent me.' (Jn. 17, 20-21). It is only under the rule of Jesus Christ, the new Davidic king, that the original unity of the kingdom of God can be restored, as it was in king David's time. He will be both king and shepherd; he will gather his sheep from their exile from God's friendship and bring them into one flock under his loving care; his divine authority will guarantee unity.

THE NEW CHRISTIAN SPIRIT

THE RESTORATION OF ISRAEL.   Ezechiel was the prophet of the Jewish exiles in Babylon. In the second half of his prophecy, chapters 33-48, his sole concern is the divine mercy calling a repentant nation back home to Palestine. In the sections just treated (the most important message he had to deliver from the Lord) he gives a picture of Israel as a scattered flock; this is the Babylonian exile where each man was left to his own devices to try to live as a true Jew should. They would achieve unity only through the advent of a new David, king and shepherd, the long-awaited Messiah; he it was who would give security, protection, and prosperity to his flock.

But in all Messianic prophecy the people must return to their homeland, to the land promised to Abraham and his descendants for ever. In this paragraph Ezechiel personifies the promised land, addressing 'every mountain and hill, every

'The very Gentiles will recognize my power,' the Lord God says, 'when I proclaim my majesty in their sight by delivering you. I mean to set you free from the power of the Gentiles, bring you home again from every part of the earth. **And then I will pour cleansing streams over you, to purge you from the taint of your idolatry. I will give you a new heart, and breathe a new spirit into you; I will take away from your breasts those hearts that are hard as stone, and give you human hearts instead. I will make my spirit penetrate you, so that you will follow in the path of my law, remember and carry out my decrees.** So shall you make your home in the land I promised to your fathers; you shall be my people, and I will be your God.

'A time is coming when I will set you free from the guilt which stains you; when I will people your cities, rebuild your ruins; when the deserted land shall be tilled anew. Desolate the passers-by saw it once; now they will say, **"Why, it is a very garden of Eden, the countryside which once lay all uncultivated; the empty towns, all gone to rack and ruin, are walled and populous!"** This boon,' says the Lord God, 'Israel shall yet have of me, as a flock thrives their manhood shall thrive. Yonder empty cities shall be thronged, too, but with men; the proof of my divine power. What the Lord promises, the Lord fulfils.'

EZECHIEL 38—39

Word came to me from the Lord: 'Son of man, turn your regard now towards Gog, of the land of Magog. Prophesy, then, son of man, the doom of Gog: "Have at you, Gog, that has the lordship of Mosoch and Thubal! **Trust me, I will turn you about this way and that, bridle those jaws of yours!**

upland and hill' (the emphasis is on the mountainous nature of Palestine). Though the description is in great part a material restoration, in reality it is imagery for the foundation of the Christian Church.

Before restoration is possible, the enemies standing in the way must be removed from power; then the cities can be rebuilt and peopled once more. This was fulfilled in the Church by the great number of peoples of all nations submitting to the authority of the Church.

Membership in the Church is by the sacrament of Baptism, those 'cleansing streams' that wash away the stain of original sin: 'Believe me, no man can enter into the kingdom of God unless birth comes to him from water, and from the Holy Spirit' (Jn. 3, 5). This removal of guilt makes the Church 'a very garden of Eden'; it is a return to that idyllic state of divine friendship which is symbolized by Eden and its life-giving streams.

As in Jeremias 31, the essential mark of the new covenant is a new spirit. This is an anticipation of what our Lord was to teach in his Sermon on the Mount (Mt. 5-7): holiness is in the will, not in external actions. A Christian must love the Lord with his whole heart; this is the only way in which a man is able to observe all the commandments, laws, and obligations imposed on him by God.

ANTICHRIST, CHAMPION OF WICKEDNESS

Gog makes war on the Church. The setting of this prophecy is in the future, when Israel is restored to her own land; all is peace and security when the hordes from the north march on the promised land. The name Gog means darkness, and Magog is probably an abbreviation of Matgog, the

I will bring you out to battle, with all your army; with horses and mailed cavalry, with a great company that ply spear and shield and sword.

' "Long hence your turn shall come; long years must pass before you march on Israel; a land, now, recovered from its blood-letting; its hills, desolate till now, are repeopled with exiles from many shores, come back to dwell there in security. Storm never rose so suddenly, cloud-wrack never darkened it so fearsomely, as you with that host of yours, those confederate hordes. What thoughts will be in your heart that day," the Lord God says, "what foul design will be a-brewing? Why, you will think to march on a land unfortified, a people dwelling free from all alarms, that walls about them have none, bolt nor bar to shut them in; spoil for your spoiling, plunder for your plundering."

'Prophesy, then, son of man, and make known to Gog this divine message: "None better ware of it than you, when my people of Israel is living at peace, free from alarms! Then it is you will come down from those northern fastnesses, with your hordes about you, your troops of cavalry, a great muster, an army irresistible, sweeping down on my people of Israel like a cloud that overshadows the land. **Offspring of that later age, you shall march on yonder land of mine, so that in Gog's doom my power may be vindicated, and the heathen may learn what I am.**

' "When Gog marches against Israel," the Lord God says, "my indignation will contain itself no longer; jealous love and fierce anger of mine, I swear it, shall throw all the land of Israel into commotion. Fish in sea, bird in air, beast on earth and all the creeping things of earth shall tremble at my presence, and the world of men, too, shall tremble; moun-

land of darkness. It does not seem that this leader of an army is meant to represent any historical figure; he is rather a symbol of those forces of evil that will always be ranged against the Church of Christ. It is possible that Ezechiel borrowed some details, such as the origin of the hostile forces from 'northern fastnesses,' from the invasion of the Scythians, some fifty years earlier; these enemies came from the north, from the region of the Black Sea, roughly modern Russia.

The Old Testament prophets usually present the enemies of Israel as the contemporary nations with whom they are engaged in conflict, such as the Philistines, Assyrians, and Babylonians. Here, for the first time, the enemies of the Church are personified under a symbolical name, Gog. This is the beginning of a series of revelations about Antichrist, whom St. Paul calls 'the champion of wickedness' (2 Thess. 2, 3). Daniel presents the same character under the image of a terrifying beast (Dan. 7, 7), which St. John further develops and identifies by the number 666 (Apoc. 13, 18); this is the emperor Nero.

In the gospels (Mk. 13, 22) and in the epistles of John, Antichrist is shown to be the personification of the forces of evil perpetually at war with Christ and his Church; he is not an individual appearing only at the end of time: 'Now you must know that he is here in the world already' (1 Jn. 4, 3; 2, 18-22; 2 Jn. 7).

THE LORD DESTROYS GOG IN BATTLE.   St. John, in his Apocalypse, refers to this incident from Ezechiel: 'Then, when the thousand years are over, Satan will be let loose from his prison, and will go out to seduce the nations that live at the four corners of the earth—that is the meaning of Gog and Magog—and muster them for battle, countless as the sand by

tains be overthrown, defences totter, walls come toppling to the ground.

' "All through this hill-country of mine my word shall run, 'The sword!' And with that," the Lord says, "friend shall turn his sword against friend; ordeal they shall have of pestilence and of blood-letting, of lashing storm and great hailstones; fire and brimstone I will rain down upon them, all that great army and the hordes that follow it. **My greatness, my holiness, shall then be displayed for a world of nations to see, and they will recognize my power at last.**

' "Among my own people of Israel my renown shall spread, and never more shall my holy name be dragged in the dust; **the heathen shall know what manner of God it is that dwells apart in Israel.** In glory I will reveal myself to the Gentiles; the doom I have executed, the power I have exerted, shall be for all to see; nor shall Israel doubt thenceforward that I, the Lord, am their God. **And I will turn away from them no longer, I, that have poured out my spirit on the whole race of Israel."** '

EZECHIEL 40, 1-4; 43, 1-7; 44, 2

It was the tenth day of the month; the twenty-fifth year of our banishment, and the fourteenth since the fall of the city, was just beginning. This was the precise day upon which the Lord's power came over me, and I fell into a transport; in which transport, so the divine revelation would have it, I was carried off to the country of Israel. There, I found myself on the top of a very high mountain, that seemed to have a city built on it, sloping away towards the south. Into this city I was taken, and there met a man whose look dazzled the eye like bronze; he stood there in the gateway, holding a flaxen

the sea. They came up across the whole breadth of the earth, and beleaguered the encampment of the saints, and the beloved city. But God sent fire from heaven to consume them' (Apoc. 20, 7-9).

The thousand years is a symbol for the long life of the Church on earth between the First and the Second Coming of Christ. Satan will always be on the watch to incite men to hatred of the Church; Gog represents the forces of paganism that will attempt from time to time, during the whole length of the Church's history, to destroy 'the encampment of the saints.' God's victory is spoken of in terms of battle, with all the awe-inspiring imagery of a Palestinian storm. This is traditional language (see Psalm 17) for The Day of the Lord, that day of divine intervention to vindicate his Church and punish wrong-doers. In point of fact it will be a spiritual not a material victory over men; the way God wins the victory is by converting those who oppose him. This is indicated in the text of Ezechiel, when he says that 'a world of nations will recognize my power at last.'

HOLINESS OF THE CHURCH

THE GLORY OF THE LORD IN THE TEMPLE. In this final vision Ezechiel sees the promised land divided up once more among the twelve tribes of Israel; in the city of Jerusalem the Lord will once again take up his dwelling in his holy temple. It is the end of exile in Babylon; the ruin and devastation of Palestine is a thing of the past. As Ezechiel walks about the rebuilt city, he is guided by a dazzling angel who explains the significance of what is shown him and repeats what the Lord speaks.

During the forty years' wandering in the wilderness under

cord and a measuring-rod. 'The open eye, son of man,' said he, 'the open ear, and mark well all I show you! You were brought here to see, and tell the men of Israel what you see.'

Then he took me to the eastern gate; **and all at once, from the sun's rising, the bright presence of the God of Israel made entry there. Like the sound of waters in deep flood his voice was, and earth was lit up with the splendour all around;** down fell I, face to earth. In it came through the eastern gateway, the splendour of the Lord himself; and with that, a transport seized me, carrying me off into the inner court, where already the brightness of the Lord's presence filled the temple.

Thence it was I heard his voice speaking to me; and the man who stood at my side passed on the message: 'Son of man,' he told me, '**here is my throne; here eternally, in the heart of Israel, is my resting-place. Shut this gate must ever be,**' the Lord told me, '**nor open its doors to give man entrance again, since the Lord, the God of Israel, entered by it.**'

EZECHIEL 47, 1-12

And last, he took me to the door of the temple itself, and showed me where a stream of water flowed eastwards from beneath the threshold of it. Eastward the temple looked, and eastward these waters flowed, somewhat to the temple's right, so as to pass by the southern side of the altar. Through the northern gate he led me, and round the walk that passed the outer gate, taking the eastern sun; and here, to the right of the gate, the water gushed out. Eastward then he faced, the man of the measuring-rod; measured a thousand cubits, and led me across a stream that reached my ankles. Another thou-

Moses there was over the tabernacle 'the divine cloud by day, the divine fire by night' (Ex. 40, 32-36). This was called the Shekinah, symbol of God's presence. It also appeared over the temple when Solomon dedicated it (3 Kg. 8, 10-13). This is what Ezechiel sees over the temple in the New Jerusalem: the Lord has taken up his abode for ever in the midst of his people.

In actual fact there was no Shekinah over the temple built by the Hebrews on their return from Babylon. So what Ezechiel describes is the ideal temple, which stands for the kingdom of Christ, the Church. No longer will it be desecrated by idolatry and sin; it will belong entirely to the Lord. It is this quality of HOLINESS that is emphasized in Ezechiel's description: 'It is a holy thing, this temple of God which is nothing other than yourselves. Surely you know that your bodies are the shrines of the Holy Spirit, who dwells in you' (1 Cor. 3, 17; 6, 19). God will never again depart from his chosen people: 'And behold I am with you all through the days that are coming, until the consummation of the world' (Mt. 28, 20).

SANCTIFYING GRACE

THE STREAM FROM THE TEMPLE. Just outside the eastern wall of Jerusalem is the Kedron, a dry water-course separating the city from the mount of Olives. It winds its way south, then swings east to run for twenty miles until it ends at the Dead Sea. Ezechiel is led along by the angel of his vision down the Kedron valley; he crosses and recrosses the stream every five hundred yards (a thousand cubits), the water becoming deeper and more plentiful all the while; within a mile and a half of his starting-place he is unable to walk across this stream.

sand, and when I crossed the stream it reached my knees; another thousand, and it was up to my waist, another thousand, and now it had become a torrent I might not cross any longer, so high the waters had swelled, out of my depth. 'Mark it well, son of man,' said he; and with that he brought me out on to the bank again; when I reached it, I found that there were trees growing thick on either hand.

'This stream,' he told me, 'must flow eastward to the sand dunes, and so fall into the desert; pass into the Dead Sea and beyond it, cleansing those waters by its passage. **Wherever it flows, there shall be teeming life once again;** in the Dead Sea itself there will be shoals of fish, once this stream has reached it, **this stream that heals all things and makes all things live.** Fisher-folk will line the shores of it, and there will be drying of nets all the way from Engaddi to Engallim, and fish there will be in great shoals, varied in kind as the ocean fish are. Only the swamps and marshes about it there is no cleansing; these shall turn into salt-pits. **And on either bank of the stream fruit-trees shall grow of every kind; never leaf lost, never fruit cast; month after month they shall yield a fresh crop, watered by that sanctuary stream; fruit for man's eating, and medicinal leaves.'**

PSALMS 88; 131; 89

Here is a song to put the Lord's mercies on record for ever; ages will pass, and still these words of mine shall proclaim your faithfulness. Long ago, in a vision, you made a promise to your faithful servants. You said: 'I have crowned you a warrior king, chosen out among the common folk a man of

This new river has two startling effects: trees line its banks, and fish abound in its waters. The country between Jerusalem and the Dead Sea is entirely desert, without any vegetation; the Dead Sea itself is lifeless. The presence of orchards and the teeming shoals of fish attract a population that can live in ease and properity; the whole shore of the barren Dead Sea will be lined with fishermen and their nets.

This picture is based on the Hebrew attitude to water: where water is, there is life. In a dry country the soil remains unproductive without water. There is probably an allusion to the four streams that watered the garden of Eden (Gen. 2, 10-14), and possibly a reference to the water from the rock in the wilderness (Ex. 17, 6).

Our Lord identifies this water with sanctifying grace in his talk to the woman at the well: 'The man who drinks the water I give him will not know thirst any more. The water I give him will be a spring of water within him, that flows continually to bring him everlasting life' (Jn. 4, 13-14). And St. John understands Ezechiel's stream in a Christian sense: 'He showed me, too, a river, whose waters give life; it flows, clear as crystal, from the throne of God, from the throne of the Lamb. On either side of the river grows the tree that gives life, and the leaves of this tree bring health to all the nations' (Apoc. 22, 1-2).

THE ETERNAL KINGSHIP OF CHRIST

THE LORD'S PROMISE TO DAVID. Saul was the first king in Israel; because of his disobedience God took the kingdom from him and gave it to David; no son of Saul was to succeed him on the throne. But with David it was a different story: the Lord God himself solemnly guaranteed that there should

honour. Here was my servant David; on him my consecrating oil has been poured. My hand shall never leave him unprotected, my arm shall give him courage. My faithfulness and mercy shall go with him; by my favour he shall rise to preeminence. I will make his power rest on the sea; to the streams of the great river his hand shall reach out.

' "You are my Father," he will cry out to me, "you are my God, my stronghold and my refuge"; **and I will acknowledge him as my first-born, overlord to all the kings of earth.** I will continue my favour towards him for ever, my covenant with him shall remain unbroken; **I will give him a posterity that never fails, a throne enduring as heaven itself. His posterity shall continue for ever, his royalty, too, shall last on in my presence like the sun; like the moon's eternal orb, that bears witness in heaven unalterable.'**

The Lord's choice has fallen upon Sion, this is the dwelling he longed for: 'Here, for ever, is my resting-place, here is my destined home. Trust me, I will bless her with abundant store, the poor shall have bread to their heart's content; I will clothe her priests in the vesture of triumph, cries of rejoicing shall echo among her faithful people. **There the stock of David shall bud, there shall a lamp burn continually for the king I have anointed. I will cover his enemies with confusion; on his brow the crown I gave shall shine untarnished.'**

And now? Now you have only loathing and scorn for us; heavy your hand falls on him you have anointed. Spurned lies the covenant you made with your servant, you have dishonoured his royalty in the dust. You have robbed him of the bright glory that once was his; you have cast down his throne to earth, cut his manhood short before its time; confusion

always be a son of David on the throne of Israel. This divine promise is recorded in 2 Kings 7; the occasion was David's proposal to build the Lord a house (the temple) in Jerusalem, alongside his own royal palace. In God's plan it was David's son, Solomon, who was to build the temple; but the Lord was pleased at David's good will, and promised on his side that David's house (his posterity) should continue on the throne forever. This is the 'vision' that the psalmist recalls here in Psalm 88.

Two details of the psalmist's description of the kingship of David and his successors on the throne can be applied only to the person of the Messiah; they are the eternity of his reign and his rule over all the kings of earth. The angel Gabriel makes reference to this in his message to our Lady at the Annunciation: 'The Lord God will give him the throne of his father David, and he shall reign over the house of Jacob eternally; his kingdom shall never have an end' (Lk. 1, 32-33).

David made Jerusalem (Sion) the capital of his kingdom. From the time of Solomon it also became the site of the temple, the home of God among his people. The combination of these two facts made Sion a prominent feature of the Messianic hope; it would be the centre of the kingdom founded by Christ. He it is who is referred to as 'the stock of David' (Jer. 23, 5) and 'a lamp' that burns eternally in God's presence.

HAS GOD FORGOTTEN HIS PROMISE? The Babylonian exile seemed to invalidate the promise made long ago to David: the Jews were now in exile from their own land; their king Joachin was a prisoner in the hands of the heathen; their holy city Jerusalem and its temple lay in ruins. That is the atmosphere which gave rise to this cry of anguish from the psalmist,

overwhelms him.

Lord, will you always turn your face away so obdurately, will the flame of your anger never be quenched? Lord, where are those mercies of an earlier time, promised so faithfully to David? Remember how a world's taunts assail your people, and this one heart must bear them all; shall they hurl taunts, Lord, these, your enemies, after the man you yourself have anointed?

Relent, Lord; must it be for ever? Be gracious to your servants. **For us your timely mercies, for us abiding happiness and content;** happiness that shall atone for the time when you afflicted us, for the long years of ill fortune. **Let these eyes see your purpose accomplished, to our own sons reveal your glory; the favour of the Lord our God smile on us!** Prosper our doings, Lord, prosper our doings yet.

ISAIAS 40—52

'Take heart again, my people,' says your God, 'take heart again. Speak Jerusalem fair, cry aloud to her that her woes are at an end, her guilt is pardoned; double toll the Lord has taken for all her sins.'

A cry: 'Make way there, out in the wilderness, for the Lord's coming; a straight road for our God through the desert! Bridged every valley must be, every mountain and hill levelled; windings cut straight, and the rough paths paved; the Lord's glory is to be revealed for all mankind to witness; it is his own decree.'

A voice came, bidding me cry aloud; asked I in what words, in these: 'Mortal things are but grass, the glory of them is but grass in flower; grass that withers, a flower that fades, when

who was expressing the thoughts in the minds of the Babylonian exiles.

The audacity of the psalmist's words in seeming to question God's loving care and mercy to his chosen people is based on the Israelite's deep faith in divine omnipotence. He is trying to force the Lord to cut short the exile by reminding him of his promise that the kingdom of David would last forever. A Jew could not visualize the Messianic kingdom unless first the chosen people were restored to their own land and a king of David's line sat on the royal throne in Jerusalem.

The final paragraph, which is from Psalm 89, ends on a note of hope and confidence. The words 'happiness, content, glory, favour' express the conditions of Messianic times, when the Lord will change the present sorrowful exile to the joy and gladness of his divine friendship.

DELIVERANCE AND SALVATION

A HIGHWAY FROM BABYLON TO JERUSALEM. The exile was a divine punishment for idolatry and abandonment of the Lord; but now the time of pardon has come; Israel has done penance for her sinful past. We do not know the name of the prophet who announced this good news; we call him Second Isaias because he collected and edited the prophecies delivered by Isaias (1-35), 150 years earlier, and then, under divine inspiration, added his own message to his fellow exiles (40-66), in which he repeated for their benefit the teachings of the great prophet.

Babylon is five hundred miles due east of Jerusalem; they are separated by a trackless waste, a desert region uninhabited by man. The prophet pictures a broad highway laid down

the Lord's breath blows upon it. The whole people, what is it but grass? Grass that withers, a flower that fades; but the word of our Lord stands for ever.'

Good news for Sion, take your stand, herald, on some high mountain; good news for Jerusalem, proclaim it, herald, aloud; louder still, no cause now for fear; tell the cities of Juda: 'See, your God comes! See, the Lord God is coming, revealed in power, with his own strong arm for warrant; and see, they come with him, they walk before him, the reward of his labour, the achievement of his task, his own flock! Like a shepherd he tends them, gathers up the lambs and carries them in his bosom, helps the ewes in milk forward on their way.'

Thus says the Lord: 'There shall be pasture for my flock by the wayside, feeding-grounds they shall have on all the barren uplands; they will hunger and thirst no more, noonday heat nor sun overpower them; theirs is a merciful shepherd, that will lead them to welling fountains and give them drink. And I will turn all these mountains of mine into a highroad for you; safe through the uplands my path shall lead. See how they come from far away! Exiles from north and west, exiles from the south country return. Ring out, heaven, with praise; let earth keep holiday, and its mountains echo that praise again; the Lord brings consolation to his people, takes pity on their need.'

Welcome, welcome on the mountain heights the messenger that cries, 'All is well!' Good news brings he, deliverance cries he, telling Sion, 'Your God has claimed his throne!' A shout goes up from the watchmen; they are crying out all at once, all at once echoing their praise; their own eyes shall

across this wilderness along which the returning exiles can make their way in comfort and safety. In actual fact they followed the usual route up the Euphrates in a northerly direction, then came down south along the Mediterranean coast. The poetic description of Second Isaias is developed in three scenes. He hears an angelic voice announcing the start of the pilgrimage from Babylon along the new highway; then a second voice tells the prophet to announce to the exiles that Babylon ('the whole people') is only an ephemeral power ('grass'), impotent to prevent the Lord bringing home his chosen people. The third scene is set in Jerusalem itself; a watchman on the walls of the city announces the arrival of the exiles.

The picture of the Lord himself leading his people across the desert reminds the prophet of a shepherd guiding his flock back to the sheepfold. With infinite tenderness he picks up the tired straggling lambs, and takes special care of the mothers of small lambs; he shelters them from the heat of the mid-day sun and always finds them water to quench their thirst. It is a familiar image, beloved by the Israelites, all through their literature both of the Old and New Testaments.

St. Luke (3, 3-6) sees a complete fulfilment of the Isaian highroad image in John the Baptist making the way ready for the coming of our Lord; along this road Jesus walked, leading mankind home to their everlasting abode, which he would open for them by his saving death.

THE LORD HAS PITY ON SION. The previous paragraph was written from the point of view of the exiles coming home from Babylon; this paragraph visualizes the reaction of the inhabitants of ruined Sion at the return of the Lord God at the head of the returning exiles. It is a scene of rejoicing and

witness it, when the Lord brings Sion deliverance. Rejoice, echo all at once with rejoicing, ruined homes of Jerusalem; comfort from the Lord for the Lord's people, Jerusalem redeemed! The Lord bares his holy arm for all the nations to see it; to the remotest corners of earth he, our God, makes known his saving power.

And has the Lord no pity for Sion, left desolate, no pity on her ruined state? **Doubt not he will turn that wilderness into a garden of delight, that loneliness into a paradise;** in her, too, mirth and gladness shall be found, there shall be thanksgiving and songs of praise.

'People of mine, men of a chosen race, give heed and hearing! What, can a woman forget her child that is still unweaned, pity no longer the son she bore in her womb? Let her forget; I will not be forgetful of you. Why, I have cut your image on the palms of my hands; those walls of yours dwell before my eyes continually.

'Henceforth, my law shall be promulgated, my decrees be ratified, for a whole world's enlightening. Soon, now, my salvation will come, even now it is on its way to deliver you. **You heavens, send dew from above, you skies, pour down upon us the rain we long for, God's faithful mercies; may salvation spring from the closed womb of earth, and with it let right order take its being.** My saving power is eternal, my faithfulness lives on from age to age.'

ISAIAS 45, 15-26

Truly, God of Israel, our Saviour, you are a God of hidden ways! All the makers of false gods must needs be disappointed, must go away ashamed and abashed. **Israel has found deliverance in the Lord, eternal deliverance;** while ages last, no shame, no disappointment for you.

gladness; at long last God has redeemed his people from exile and restored the city of Jerusalem to all its former glory and grandeur.

God's love has brought this about; he has never ceased loving Jerusalem all through the long years of her ruin and desolation. How could he, seeing that his love is as tender as that of a mother for her baby son? With a sudden change of imagery, the Lord likens his affection for Sion to that of a worshipper who brands the name of his God on his body like a slave; the Lord is so devoted to Sion that he has her name cut into his hands, a perpetual reminder always before his eyes.

The nature of divine redemption is presented under two images. First, it is a return to that idyllic state of Adam and Eve in the garden of Eden; the delights of that earthly paradise signify the close relationship of man with God in the state of original holiness. The second image is from the dew and rain that fall on the earth to make it produce food for mankind; this fertility of the earth is a symbol of sanctifying grace.

This final paragraph is the Advent hymn, Rorate Coeli. In the Vulgate, St. Jerome wrote 'the Just One' for 'God's faithful mercies,' and 'Saviour' for 'salvation.' By so doing he referred the prophecy directly to the person of Christ, through whom salvation was to come.

WORSHIP OF GOD NOT IDOLS.   This canticle is recited in the breviary at Lauds on Friday. Its theme is God's plan for the human race: all mankind, Jew and Gentile alike, will worship the one true God; no longer will they spend their time on the cult of idols, in Messianic times. This plan is called a 'hidden'

The Lord has pronounced it; the Lord who made the heavens, and the whole frame and fashion of earth, moulded to his will. He did not create it to lie idle, he shaped it to be man's home. And he says, 'It is the Lord that speaks, there is no other to rival me; it was not in secret, not in some dark recess of earth, that my word was spoken. Not in vain I bade the sons of Jacob search for me; I am the Lord, faithful to my promises, truthful in all I proclaim.

'Gather yourselves and come near, flock together to my side, heathen men that have found deliverance; who still, in your ignorance, set up wooden images of your own fashioning, and pray to a god that cannot save. Tell us your thoughts, come, take counsel among yourselves; who was it that proclaimed this from the first, prophesied it long ago? Was it not I, the Lord? There is no God where I am not. Was it not I, the faithful God? There is no other that can save.

'Turn back to me, and win deliverance, all you that dwell in the remotest corners of the earth; I am God, there is no other. **By my own honour I have sworn it, nor shall it echo in vain, this faithful promise I have made, that every knee shall bow before me, and every tongue swear by my name.** Then shall men say of the Lord, that redress and dominion come from him; all those who rebelled against him shall appear in his presence abashed. Through the Lord, the whole race of Israel shall be righted and brought to honour.'

ISAIAS 42; 49; 50; 53

'And now, here is my servant, to whom I grant protection, the man of my choice, greatly beloved. My spirit rests upon him, and he will proclaim right order among the Gentiles.

way, because God acts in a manner so completely different from what men expect. This is seen in his restoration of the chosen people through the instrumentality of a pagan emperor, Cyrus, who was a type of Christ (p. 272). And when the time comes for the salvation of the whole world, he himself will become incarnate at Bethlehem. Such a way of acting is so completely different from our standards of human prudence; but God always acts in such unexpected and simple fashion.

Idol worship was powerfully entrenched in the lives of both heathen and Israelite. The prophets in the Old Testament spent much of their time trying to recall the chosen people to the worship of the Lord. Many of their most famous warnings are devoted to this. The best-known passages are Isaias 44, Jeremias 10, Baruch 6, Psalm 113, and Wisdom 13. The line of argumentation used here by Isaias, and the prophets generally, is that idols have neither power nor knowledge; they are impotent and ignorant. Consider the return from exile, and observe that the idols could not have planned and executed such a restoration; it was the work of the Lord alone.

To conquer the idols God was not content with becoming Man; he even lowered his dignity as man and accepted death on the cross. This, according to St. Paul (Phil. 2, 6-11), was how he brought all mankind back to God. Such was the hidden way planned by God to send the idols tumbling in the dust and bring all nations to the feet of Jesus.

THE SERVANT OF THE LORD

I am Gentle and Humble of Heart. As soon as our Lord began his public ministry by the lake of Galilee great crowds gathered round him: 'And they brought to him all those who

He will not be contentious or a lover of faction; none shall
hear his voice in the streets. He will not snap the staff that
is already crushed, or put out the wick that still smoulders;
but at last he will establish right order unfailingly. Not with
sternness, not with violence; to set up right order on earth,
that is his mission. He has a law to give; in the far-off islands
men wait for it eagerly.'

Thus says the Lord God, he who created the heavens and
spread them out, craftsman of the world and all the world
affords, he who gives being and breath to all that lives and
moves on it: 'True to my purpose, I, the Lord, have summoned you, taking you by the hand and protecting you, **to
make, through you, a covenant with my own people, to shed,
through you, light over the Gentiles: to give sight to blinded
eyes, to set the prisoner free from his captivity, from the
dungeon where he lies in darkness.** I am the Lord, whose
name tells of power; I will not let the boast that is mine
pass to another, to share my renown with graven gods. What
I told you long since, has proved true under your eyes; I tell
you now what is still to be; you shall hear of it before ever it
comes to light.'

Listen, remote islands; pay heed to me, nations from far
away. Ere ever I was born, the Lord sent me his summons,
kept me in mind already, when I lay in my mother's womb.
**The Lord has anointed me, on me his spirit has fallen; he has
sent me to bring good news to men that are humbled, to
heal broken hearts, promising the release of captives, the
opening of prison doors, proclaiming the year of the Lord's
pardon, the day when he, our God, will give us redress.** Word
of mine is sword of his, ready sharpened, under cover of his
hand; arrow he has chosen out carefully, hidden yet in his

were in affliction, distressed with pain and sickness of every sort, the possessed, the lunatics, the palsied; and he healed all their diseases.' In contrast to the contemptuous and domineering ways of the Jewish leaders, who despised the common people, Jesus was kind and friendly. He was as interested in them as a father or brother; he was gentle and sympathetic as a mother; he was willing to pause in his discourse to care for their needs. He was not despotic or demanding; he did not care for publicity. St. Matthew (12, 18-21) sees in this attitude of our Lord the fulfilment of this prophecy of Isaias.

Our Lord came on earth to make known the divine precepts of right living ('right order'); this embraced all the moral laws and dogmatic truths required by man to arrive at his eternal destiny. It was a universal mission to all peoples, both Jew and Gentile. Isaias refers to this twofold aspect of our Lord's mission as a covenant with the Jews and light to the Gentiles. The Jews are also referred to under the image of prisoners in the dungeon of the Babylonian captivity; the Gentiles are referred to as men with blinded eyes, awaiting the divine revelation that was to come through Christ.

OBEDIENCE OF CHRIST TO HIS DIVINE VOCATION. Our Lord preached his first sermon at Nazareth, about four months after the opening of his public ministry. He had just returned from the paschal feast at Jerusalem, where he cleansed the temple. While visiting his home town of Nazareth, on his way to establish headquarters at Capharnaum by the lake of Galilee, he was invited by the Jewish elders of the local synagogue to read the scripture for the day. It was this passage from Isaias beginning 'The Lord has anointed me.' With an air of authority and finality, he shut the book and began to speak to his

quiver. 'You are my servant,' he whispers, 'you are the one I claim for my own.' To me all my labour seemed useless, my strength worn out in vain; his to judge me, he, my God, must reward my work as he would.

But now a new message he sends me; I am his servant, appointed ever since I lay in the womb, to bring Jacob back to him. What if Israel will not answer the summons? None the less, the Lord destines me to honour; none the less, he, my God, protects me. 'Use you I will,' he promises, 'nor with your service be content, when the tribes of Jacob you have summoned, brought back the poor remnant of Israel; nay, **I have appointed you to be the light of the Gentiles, in you I will send out my salvation to the furthest corners of the earth. Before all the world my witness you, a prince and a ruler among the nations.** Summons of yours shall go out to a nation you never knew; peoples that never heard of you shall hasten to your call; such the glory your God, the Holy One of Israel, has bestowed on you.'

A message from the Lord, Israel's ransomer, Israel's Holy One, to the despised one, to him that is abhorred by the nation, to the slave of tyrants: 'Kings, when they see this, shall rise up from their thrones, princes too, and fall down to worship, in honour of the Lord, that keeps his promise so faithfully, the Holy One of Israel, that claims you still.'

Thus says the Lord: **'Here is a time of pardon, when prayer of yours shall be answered, a day of salvation, when I will bring you aid.** I have kept you in readiness, to make, by your means, a covenant with my people. Yours to revive a ruined country, to parcel out the forfeited lands anew, men that are bound in darkness restoring to freedom and to the light.'

hearers: 'This scripture which I have read in your hearing is today fulfilled' (Lk. 4, 14-21). In this dramatic way our Lord proclaimed to the Jews that he was the Messiah, the servant foretold by the prophet Isaias.

His vocation is to the Gentiles as well as the Jews; his kingdom is to be universal, embracing the whole world. This is a feature of Messianic times throughout all the Old Testament prophecies. This twofold aspect of Christ's mission is re-stated several times, in different terms, in this paragraph. It is a true vocation, a call from God the Father to undertake the salvation of the world. It was for this purpose that God the Son became Man; the will of the Father was the very food of his spiritual life. In his final prayer after the Last Supper he said: 'I have exalted your glory on earth, by achieving the task which you gave me to do' (Jn. 17, 4).

Isaias pictures our Lord accomplishing his mission in the face of great difficulties; he suffers the mental torment of knowing that his work of redemption will be useless for so many; he is despised and rejected by his own people ('the nation'). Weighed down by these great humiliations, he is comforted and strengthened for the task by the promise from his Father to bring him aid. These details were fulfilled to the letter in the garden of Gethsemani; on the night before his passion and death, our Lord sweated blood in his struggle against the terrifying prospect of crucifixion; he was comforted by a visit from an angel sent by his heavenly father.

The Hebrew text of 49, 3, and the Greek Septuagint of 42, 1, identify the servant with Israel. If these readings are inspired, Israel stands for the Church: what is said of Christ can be applied to his Mystical Body. This would fit St. Paul's interpretation (Acts 13, 47).

Ever the Lord schools my tongue to utterance that shall refresh the weary; awakes my dull ears, morning after morning, their Master's bidding to heed. **An attentive ear the Lord has given me; not mine to withstand him; not mine to shrink from the task. I offered my body defenceless to the men who would smite me, my cheeks to all who plucked at my beard; I did not turn away my face when they reviled me and spat upon me.**

The Lord God is my helper; and that help cannot play me false; meet them I will, and with a face unmoved as flint; not mine to suffer the shame of defeat; here is One stands by to see right done me. Come, who pleads? Meet me, and try the issue; let him come forward who will, and accuse me. Here is the Lord God ready to aid me; who dares pass sentence on me now? One and all they shall be brought to nothing, like garment the moth has eaten!

Who is here that fears the Lord, listens to his servant's message? Who would make his way through dark places, with no glimmer of light? Let him trust in the name of the Lord, and lean upon his God. For you others, with brand at girdle, that your own fire would make, with fire your own brands have kindled light the path if you can; this is all the gift I have for you, a bed of anguish.

'See, here is my servant, one who will be prudent in all his dealings. To what height he shall be raised, how exalted, how extolled! So many there be that stand gazing in horror; was ever a human form so mishandled, human beauty ever so defaced? Yet this is he that will purify a multitude of nations; kings shall stand dumb in his presence; seen, now, where men had no tidings of him, made known to such as never heard his name.'

'What credence for such news as ours? Whom reaches it,

CONFIDENCE AND CONSTANCY UNDER SUFFERINGS. This is the third of the four Servant Songs; it links up the first two with the fourth. In it we get a preview of what Christ's obedience to his Father's will is going to cost him, to redeem the human race. For the first time the afflictions and persecution that he is to endure are uppermost in the mind of the prophet.

The scene in the Passion of our Lord that most accurately fulfills the prophecy contained in this third song is his imprisonment in the house of Caiphas after questioning by the high priest early on Friday morning: 'The servants who held Jesus prisoner beat him and mocked him and spat in his face; they blindfolded him and fell to buffeting him and smiting him on the cheek, saying as they did so, "Show yourself a prophet, Christ; tell us who it is that smote you."' (Mt. 26, 67). The detail of plucking hairs from his beard is not mentioned in the gospels; it was most painful, and an insulting treatment according to oriental standards.

Our Lord's trust in aid from God shows how close is the relation of Father and Son. All those who are members of his Mystical Body must imitate Jesus by following his example of confidence and constancy; for those who doubt there is nothing but trouble and disaster.

HANDED OVER TO DEATH FOR OUR SINS. It was this passage from Isaias that the Ethiopian courtier was reading as he drove along in his chariot on his way home from Jerusalem; Philip the deacon was sent by an angel to instruct him on its true meaning. 'And the eunuch turned to Philip, and said, "Tell me, about whom does the prophet say this? Himself, or some other man?" Then Philip began speaking, and preached to him about Jesus, taking this passage as his theme' (Acts 8, 34-35).

this new revelation of the Lord's strength? He will watch this servant of his appear among us, unregarded as brush-wood shoot, as a plant in waterless soil; no stateliness here, no majesty, no beauty, as we gaze upon him, to win our hearts. Nay, here is one despised, left out of all human reckoning; bowed with misery, and no stranger to weakness; how should we recognize that face? How should we take any account of him, a man so despised?

'Our weakness, and it was he who carried the weight of it, our miseries, and it was he who bore them. A leper, so we thought of him, a man God had smitten and brought low; and all the while it was for our sins he was wounded, it was guilt of ours crushed him down; on him the punishment fell that brought us peace, by his bruises we were healed. Strayed sheep all of us, each following his own path; and God laid on his shoulders our guilt, the guilt of us all.'

A victim? Yet he himself bows to the stroke; no word comes from him. Sheep led away to the slaughter-house, lamb that stands dumb while it is shorn; no word from him. Imprisoned, brought to judgment, and carried off, whose fate is beyond our caring; numbered among the living no more! Be sure it was for my people's guilt he was smitten. Takes he leave of the rich, the godless, to win but a grave, to win but the gift of death; he, that wrong did never, nor had treason on his lips! Ay, the Lord's will it was, overwhelmed he should be with trouble.

'His life laid down for guilt's atoning, he shall yet be rewarded; father of a long posterity, instrument of the divine purpose; for all his heart's anguish, rewarded in full. The Just One, my servant; many shall he claim for his own, win their acquittal, on his shoulders bearing their guilt. So many lives ransomed, foes so violent baulked of their spoil! Such

It is the classic text on the suffering Messiah, and the high-point of the Old Testament revelation on the redemption of mankind. It is so vivid and real that it seems to have been written at the foot of the cross; it is for this reason that Isaias has been called the fifth evangelist. It is a perfect poem of five stanzas (paragraphs), reaching its climax in the central third paragraph. In the first and fifth paragraphs it is the Lord who is speaking; in the second and third paragraphs the Jewish people narrate the death of Christ; in the fourth paragraph the prophet himself makes his own comments.

In the first paragraph there is a contrast between the pitiable condition of Christ during his passion, and his future glory. Kings and nations will stand, struck dumb with wonder, looking at the wonderful effects of redemption manifest throughout the whole world.

Paragraph 2 gives a picture of the lowly origin of the Messiah; he will be born in poverty and humble circumstances, not in a royal palace. His passion is introduced without any indication of change in time; the brutal beatings he was to receive would mar the beauty of his appearance; he would be an object of contempt.

In paragraph 3 we are told WHY Christ suffered: it was for us. He was an innocent victim atoning for sin: 'Christ never knew sin, and God made him into sin for us, so that in him we might be turned into the holiness of God' (2 Cor. 5, 21). It is only through incorporation in Christ by baptism that we share in the redemptive death of the head of the Mystical Body.

In paragraph 4 the innocence of Christ is explicitly stated; he was not infected by the sins he bore on the cross. It is also stated that he willingly submitted to the Father's will; he was obedient to death.

is his due, that gave himself up to death, and would be
counted among the wrong-doers; bore those many sins, and
made intercession for the guilty.'

ISAIAS 54—66

'Sing with praise, barren city that is childless still; echo
your praise, cry aloud, wife that was never brought to bed;
forsaken, she is to have more children now,' the Lord says,
'than wife whose husband remains with her. Not yours to fear
disappointment, not yours to blush for hopes unfulfilled;
forget, henceforward, the shame of younger days, the reproach
of your widowed state; think upon it no more. **Husband now
you have, and the name of him is the Lord of hosts, your
creator; he, the Holy One of Israel, that will now be called
God of the whole earth, makes you his own.** If I abandoned
you, it was but for a little moment, and now, in my great
compassion, I bring you home again. Hid I my face from you,
it was for a short while, till my anger should be spent; love
that takes pity on you shall be eternal,' says the Lord, your
ransomer. 'Let the mountains be moved, the hills shake; my
compassion towards you stands immovable, my promise still
unshaken,' says the Lord your comforter.

For love of Sion I will no more be silent, for love of Jerusalem I will never rest, until restoration is revealed to her like
the dawn, until her deliverance shines out like a flame. All
the nations, all the kings of the nations, shall see your deliverance and your glory, and a new name shall be given you by
the Lord's own lips. The Lord upholds you, his royal diadem.
No longer shall men call you Forsaken, or your land Desolate;
you shall be called My Beloved, and your land a Wife, now

In the final paragraph the Lord himself speaks again; his theme is the glorious effects of redemption. The chief reward of Christ will be an enduring posterity, the vast numbers that will make up his Mystical Body.

THE GLORY OF THE CHURCH

THE NEW JERUSALEM, BRIDE OF CHRIST. St. Paul quotes the first sentence of this passage as a description of the Christian Church, 'Our mother the heavenly Jerusalem, a city of freedom' (Gal. 4, 26-27). Later on, St. John will describe a vision in the Apocalypse: 'And I, John, saw in my vision that holy city which is the new Jerusalem, being sent down by God from heaven, all clothed in readiness, like a bride who has adorned herself to meet her husband' (Apoc. 21, 2). It is the bride-city imagery that runs throughout this passage from Isaias.

In the first paragraph it is the Lord who is speaking. He describes Israel as a lonely widow and as a divorced wife. The first image refers to the condition of the city of Jerusalem during the period of Babylonian exile: her Lord had departed from her with the destruction of the temple, and all her children were in a foreign land. The second image is another aspect of the exile: God had rejected Israel because of her infidelity in worshipping false gods. This divorce was only temporary; the eternal love of the Lord would soon take her back again; this time the union of Christ and his Church would last forever.

In the second paragraph Isaias shows his confidence in God's promise by foretelling the future glory of the Lord's bride. He has three images: the dawn that dissipates darkness, the giving of a new name to the city and the land, and the

the Lord takes delight in you, now your land is espoused once again. **Gladly as a man takes home the maiden of his choice, so your Builder shall espouse you; gladly the Lord shall greet you, as bridegroom his bride.**

Listen, while I tell again the story of the Lord's mercies, what renown the Lord has won; all the Lord has done for us, all the wealth of blessings his pardoning love, his abounding pity has lavished on the race of Israel. **In love and pity he ransomed them, lifted them in his arms and raised them up, all through the days gone by.**

Banish from your midst oppression, and the finger pointed scornfully, and the plotting of harm, spend yourself giving food to the hungry, relieving the afflicted; then shall light spring up for you in the darkness, and your dusk shall be noonday. Then, suddenly as the dawn, the welcome light shall break on you, in a moment your health shall find a new spring; divine favour shall lead you on your journey, brightness of the Lord's presence close your ranks behind. Then the Lord will listen to you when you call on him; cry out, and he will answer, 'I am here at your side.

'So many athirst; who will not come to the water? So many destitute; who will come and get him food, get wine and milk free, no price to be paid? What, always spending, and no bread to eat, always toiling, and never a full belly? Do but listen, here you shall find content; here are dainties shall ravish your hearts. To my summons give heed and hearing; so your spirits shall revive; **a fresh covenant awaits you, this time eternal; gracious promise of mine to David shall be ratified now.**

Lord as the husband-builder. The conferring of a name was an important act for a Jew: it symbolized the new status and official function of a person or thing. God only changed the name of a person who had some important office to perform in his name; such were Abraham and Jacob in the Old Testament and Peter in the New.

A NEW AND ETERNAL COVENANT. It was not anything the exiles did that won their return from Babylon; the mercy of God was the ultimate reason for their restoration. This had been the source of all Israel's blessings down through their long history; and now his pardoning love moved him to have pity on them, restore them to their own land, and redeem them through Christ.

They must remember that the Lord is holiness itself, and that he demands that his people be holy too; morality in daily life is an essential condition, for divine grace to come and dwell in them. Sin is the great evil; if they banish it from their midst, then God will illumine their minds with the clarity of the rising sun; he will move their wills to choose and act in accordance with the divine will, and so prosper all their doings.

The itinerant water-seller is a familiar sight in most oriental cities. The Lord is pictured by Isaias as walking the city streets with all the treasures of divine grace; he will give freely, without payment, to all who come to him; and not only water, but food as well, and even milk and wine. These are material images for spiritual things, just as our Lord spoke of grace under the symbolism of water: 'The man who drinks the water I give him will not know thirst any more' (Jn. 4, 13).

The idyllic state of abundance of grace will come only

'This covenant I will make with them,' the Lord says: 'Spirit of mine that dwells in you, words of mine entrusted to your lips, on your lips shall dwell, on the lips of your children and your children's children, henceforth and for ever.'

Thus says the Lord: 'Heaven is my throne, earth the footstool under my feet. So ready I to answer, and ask they will not; so easy to be found, and search for me is none! A people that will not call on my name; else my own voice should whisper, "I am here, I am close at hand."

'Peace,' the Lord says, 'peace to those who are far away, and to those who are near at hand. **Claimed my house shall be, for a house of prayer, by all the nations.** Peace shall flow through her like a river, the wealth of the nations shall pour into her like a torrent in flood; this shall be the milk you drain, like children carried at the breast, fondled on a mother's lap. **You shall go out where men never heard of my name, never saw my glory yet, to reveal that glory among the nations.**'

This, too, he promises: 'See where I create new heavens and a new earth; old things shall be remembered no longer, have no place in men's thoughts. Enduring your race and name shall be as the new heavens, the new earth I fashion, to stand continually in my presence.'

Who is this that comes stained with red, with garments more deep-dyed than a vintager's? Who is this, so gaily clad, marching so valiantly?

'I am one who is faithful to his promises, a champion bringing deliverance.'

through the Son of David, Jesus Christ our Lord. He will make a new covenant with mankind by his death on the cross. The Church, which is the Mystical Body of Christ, will be indwelt by the Holy Spirit. She will speak in the name of, and with the authority of, God himself: 'He who listens to you, listens to me' (Lk. 10, 16).

THE CONVERSION OF THE GENTILES. The universality of salvation is a consistent characteristic of Messianic times; God, who rules in heaven above, has an interest in all his creatures. In Old Testament times the Jews were a people apart, with little zeal for winning Gentiles to their way of life; a man had to be born a Jew; there was no such thing as conversion. In New Testament times the apostles will roam the world in search of converts; they will win the Gentile world to the peace that comes from membership in the Church of Christ. All nations will have the right to worship God; his temple will be wide open to men of every race under heaven.

The Church will be such a wonder of divine making that it can be called a new creation; God's creative power will be so manifest that it could be called a second beginning of the human race. St. John in the Apocalypse (21, 2) echoes Isaias' words, and St. Paul uses the same bold imagery: 'When a man is in Christ Jesus, there has been a new creation' (Gal. 6, 15).

A CHAMPION BRINGING DELIVERANCE. This poem is in the form of a dialogue between Sion and the Lord. Watchers in Jerusalem see a figure approaching, clothed in a military tunic all covered in blood. He identifies himself as the Lord; the bloodstains come from the enemies he has just slaughtered.

And why are your garments stained with red? Why do you go clad like the men who tread out the wine-press?

'None other has trodden the wine-press but I only; out of all the nations, no champion came to stand by my side. I have been treading them down in my anger, trampling on them, full of vengeance; their blood has been sprinkled on the clothes about me; I come in garments deep-dyed.

'My heart told me the time had come for vengeance, this was my destined year of ransom; looked I around, there was none to help me; vainly I called for aid. My own arm should bring the deliverance I intended; my own indignation uphold me. I have trampled the peoples down in my anger, stunned them with my fury, brought down their strength to the dust.'

Rise up, Jerusalem, and shine forth; your dawn has come, breaks the glory of the Lord upon you! What though darkness envelop the earth, though all the nations lie in gloom? Upon you the Lord shall dawn, over you his splendour shall be revealed. Those rays of yours shall light the Gentiles on their path; kings shall walk in the splendour of your sunrise.

Lift up your eyes and look about you; who are these that come flocking to you? Sons of yours, daughters of yours, come from far away, or rising up close at hand. Heart of you shall overflow with wonder and gratitude, to see all the riches of ocean, all the treasure of the Gentiles pouring into you!

A stream of camels thronging about you, dromedaries from Madian and Epha, bringing all the men of Sheba with their gifts of gold and incense, their cry of praise to the Lord! Into you all the herds of Kedar shall be driven, the rams of Nabaioth shall be your victims; gifts at my altar accepted, to make the fame of my temple more famous yet.

Who are these that come, swift as the cloud-wrack, as doves flying home to the dove-cot? These, too, are your sons;

He describes his conquest as treading out grapes in the wine-press; it expresses the completeness of his victory and accounts for the red stains on his clothing. It is a picture of the Lord's deliverance of his chosen people from Babylonian exile: He alone was responsible for the removal of all forces opposed to Israel and Israel's restoration to Sion.

The enemy Christ came to conquer was sin; he accomplished this by his passion and death. This scene from Isaias foreshadows two aspects of his struggle: his loneliness in Gethsemani ('vainly I called for aid') and his garments stained with blood from the brutal scourging inflicted at the order of Pilate. It shows how much he suffered to restore us to the friendship of God.

SION, RELIGIOUS CENTRE OF THE WORLD. Brought back from exile by the power of the Lord, the chosen people can rebuild the temple and the city of Jerusalem, the capital of the Messianic kingdom. It is a picture of the Church: the City of God embracing all nations and bringing peace and security to the world.

The first image of light shining in darkness is taken partly from sunrise (a daily wonder to people living without any adequate artificial light) and partly from the Shekinah, that luminous cloud of God's presence during the Exodus. The image was completed and perfected by the Incarnation, when Jesus Christ the Son of God became the light of the world; the light of divine revelation made known to mankind by the teaching of the Church will guide men to walk in God's ways.

In the second paragraph the Jews are pictured returning from Babylon like sheep returning to the fold, just as their forefathers came out of Egypt under the leadership of Moses. They are laden with all the treasures acquired during the exile. Jews were first to enter the Church in apostolic times.

long since, the islands and the ocean-going ships have awaited my signal, when I would bring them home from far away, their silver and their gold with them, for the honour of the Lord your God, the Holy One of Israel, that has bestowed this glory on you.

Your gates shall stand open continually, no need to shut them day or night; make way for the wealth of the nations that shall flow into you, for the kings with their escorts! See how they come bending low before you, how the men that once despised you worship the ground you have trodden, calling you 'The City of the Lord, Sion, dear to the Holy One of Israel.' You, the desolate, you, the unbefriended, a place unvisited by man, shall be the pride of ages, the joy of succeeding generations. **No longer will you have the sun to shine by day, or the moon's beam to enlighten you; the Lord shall be your everlasting light, your God shall be all your splendour.**

TOBIAS 13, 11-23

Jerusalem, city of God, what divine punishments your own ill deeds have brought on you! Yet thank the Lord for the blessings that are yours, praise him, the eternal God. **So may he rebuild your dwelling-place, recall your exiles, give you joy that shall last forever. You shall yet shine with dazzling brightness, for all the ends of the world to worship you.** From far away, nations shall come bringing their gifts, to worship the Lord within those walls of yours; shall reckon your soil holy ground, so great the name they shall invoke within you. Cursed shall they be that blaspheme you, blessed shall they be that build you again. What joy will you have of your chil-

In the third paragraph the first Gentiles are presented arriving from the East, bringing their wealth with them for the worship of the true God. This passage is used for the Feast of the Epiphany when the wise men arrived on their camels with gifts of gold, frankincense, and myrrh to worship the new-born king at Bethlehem.

In the fourth paragraph men come in ships from the West, from Spain and the countries of the Mediterranean Sea ('the islands'); they too come to worship the Lord as members of the universal Church.

In the final paragraph the nations who destroyed Jerusalem will come to rebuild the city and stay there in peace and security forever. No enemy will prevail against the Church; the gates will stand open continually. The Church is indestructible because the Lord dwells within her as the source of all her splendour: 'Behold I am with you all through the days that are coming, until the consummation of the world' (Mt. 28, 20).

THE NEW JERUSALEM

A VISION OF RESTORED JERUSALEM. The Book of Tobias is the story of a young man living in Niniveh after the exile of the northern kingdom in 721 B. C. Both he and his father have the same name. The vision here recorded is presented as seen by the elder Tobias. In it Jerusalem is already in ruins; Tobias (otherwise Tobit) sees it restored to a grandeur surpassing that of the destroyed temple. It is possible that Tobias did have a prophetic vision both of the destruction and the future restoration of the temple, to take place more than a hundred years later (it was not destroyed till 587 B. C.) But it is more likely that this particular vision is a later addition,

dren, a blessed race, gathered in the Lord's fold anew! A blessing on all that love you, on all that welcome your good news!

Give thanks, my soul, to the Lord, the Lord our God who has delivered Jerusalem, his own city, from all the afflictions she endured; happy I count myself, if any posterity of mine is left to see Jerusalem in her splendour. **Sapphire and emerald Jerusalem's gates shall be, of precious stones the wall that rings her round; shining white and clean the pavement of her streets; no quarter of her but shall echo the Alleluia-chant of praise.** Blessed be the Lord, that has set her on the heights; may he reign there for ever, reign for ever as her king. Amen.

written about the same time that Second Isaias prophesied the same things in Babylon. Actually many modern authors think the whole story was composed after the Babylonian exile, and that only the main framework of Tobias' long journey is historical.

Jerusalem, the City of God, stands for the Church, the splendour of Messianic times. The Lord reigns there in the midst of his returned exiles, with all the nations of the world joined in common worship of God. It is an ideal picture based on the unique position of Jerusalem in the life of the chosen people ever since the time of David. The imagery of precious stones shows the beauty and glory of the Church, as in Apocalypse 21.

CONTENTS: Chapter 5

SONG OF SONGS	A Dialogue of Divine Love	188
AG. 2, 2-10	The Lord in his Temple	194
ZACH. 2; 8	Divine Protection of Church	194
ZACH. 3, 1-10; 6, 9-15	Christ the Branch of David	200
ZACH. 9, 1-10	Palm Sunday	202
ZACH. 11–13	The True Shepherd put to Death	204
ZACH. 14	King over all the Earth	208
MAL. 1, 6-11	The Sacrifice of the Mass	210
MAL. 2, 17–3,5; 4, 1-5	The Lord visits his Temple	212
JOEL 2, 12–3, 21	The Coming of the Holy Spirit	214
ABD. 1, 15–18, 21	The Day of the Lord	218
DAN. 2, 1-3, 26-45	The Empire of Christ	220
DAN. 7, 1-27	The Son of Man	224
DAN. 9, 1-6, 16-27	Seventy Weeks of Years	228
Pss. 84; 125; 149	Deliverance from Bondage	232
Pss. 95; 96; 97; 98	The Lord reigns as King	236
Pss. 116; 117	Christ the Corner-stone	242
Ps. 129	Forgiveness of Sins	244
PROV. 8; SIRACH 24; WISDOM 7	Christ the Wisdom of God	246
WIS. 2, 1, 10-20; 4, 20-25, 5	Christ's Passion and Death	252
2 MACH. 7, 1, 7-19	Resurrection of the Body	256
2 MACH. 12, 38-46	Prayers for the Dead	258

5. The Restoration

IN 538 B. C. the Persian King Cyrus issued a written decree permitting the return of the exiled Jews to their homeland (I Esd. 1, 1); the captivity in Babylon had at last come to an end. About 42,000 of the estimated 80,000 Jews in exile returned to Jerusalem in triumph, to be met by those 40,000 who had remained in Palestine after the fall of Jerusalem in 587 B. C. The excitement and enthusiasm of the first group of returning exiles is apparent from the opening chapter (40) of Second Isaias: he pictures them returning along a highway, the Lord himself leading his people back to Jerusalem. This was the inauguration of a new era for the chosen people: the Messiah himself would come in person to Palestine bringing peace and salvation to the whole world.

Joshua, the high priest, and Zorobabel, of David's royal line, led the first caravan back; with the help of Aggaeus and Zacharias they rebuilt the temple in 515 B. C. The next and most important figure in post-exile Judaism was Esdras, a scribe who led the second caravan of about 8,000 back to Jerusalem in 458 B. C. Through his influence the teachers (called the scribes and Pharisees in the New Testament) became the dominant force in Israel. The third important returnee was Nehemias, who came back and rebuilt the walls of Jerusalem in 445 B. C. With Esdras and the prophet Malachias, he carried out sweeping moral reforms among the Jews in Palestine.

Most of the wisdom literature dates from this period. These manuals of sanctified common sense were meant primarily for the instruction of youth. They also helped to prepare Israel for the Incarnation by their teaching on divine Wisdom as a subsistent Being.

In the fourth century B. C. Greece replaced Persia as ruler of Palestine. In the second century the Jews, under the leadership of Judas Machabeus and his brothers, staged a spectacular revolt against the Hellenizing attempts of Antiochus the Illustrious. In 63 B. C. Pompey captured Jerusalem; Rome was still ruling when Christ was born.

THE SONG OF SONGS

Bride: A kiss from those lips! Wine cannot ravish the senses like that embrace, nor the fragrance of rare perfumes match it for delight. Your very name spoken soothes the heart like flow of oil. Draw me after you where you will. To his own bower the king has brought me. Close my love is to my heart as the cluster of myrrh that lodges in my bosom all the night through.

Lover: See how fair is the maid I love! Soft eyes you have, soft as dove's.

Bride: And see how fair is the man I love, how stately! Count me no more than wild rose on the lowland plain, wild lily on the mountain slopes.

Lover: A lily, matched with these other maidens, a lily among the brambles, she whom I love!

Bride: An apple-tree in the wild woodland, shade cool to rest under, fruit sweet to the taste, such is he my heart longs for, matched with his fellows. Into his banqueting-hall the king has brought me, shown me the blazon of his love. His left hand pillows my head; his right hand, even now, ready to embrace me.

Bride: The voice I love! See where he comes, how he speeds over the mountains, how he spurns the hills. Gazelle nor fawn was ever so fleet of foot as my heart's love. And now he is standing on the other side of this very wall; now he is looking in through each window in turn, peering through every chink. I can hear my true love calling me.

Lover: Rise up, rise up quickly, dear heart, so gentle, so beautiful, rise up and come with me. Winter is over now, the rain

A DIALOGUE OF DIVINE LOVE

THE BRIDE RETURNS TO HER ROYAL LOVER. *The Song of Songs (Douay: Canticle of Canticles) has the same theme as that of the prophet Osee (p. 61) and Psalm 44 (p. 67), though it was probably written several hundred years later, towards the end of the Babylonian captivity.*

It is in the form of a dialogue between a lover (Dodi in Hebrew, a name used for God in Isaias 5, 1) and his bride (Rayati). She stands for Israel in the Old Testament, and for the Church, the new Israel of God. The poem is written in oriental imagery that is highly symbolical and full of deeper meanings than are apparent on the surface. The metaphors are all taken from Hebrew life in the holy land of Palestine. It must be remembered that the dialogue is in great part lovers' exaggerated talk.

The first scene is set in the royal palace. This is the temple at Jerusalem, the home of the Lord, the King of Israel. The Bride has returned from Babylonian exile with renewed love for her royal Bridegroom. In the New Testament fulfilment this is to be understood as the mutual expression of love between Christ and the Church.

SPRINGTIME OF LOVE. *The winter of captivity in Babylon has passed; the Lord himself, the divine lover of Israel his bride, has come to lead her back home to the land of promise. He is presented as standing outside the prison door of his bride as she languishes in exile under the roof of the Babylonian conqueror; he invites her to come with him to a new life, a springtime of happiness. This time Israel is to be united for ever to her Lord, because she will become the Church*

has passed by. At home, the flowers have begun to blossom; we can hear the turtle-dove cooing already, there at home. There is green fruit on the fig-trees; the vines in flower are all fragrance. Rouse you, and come, so beautiful, so well beloved, still hiding yourself as a dove hides in cleft rock or crannied wall. Show me but your face, let me but hear your voice, that voice sweet as your face is sweet.

Bride: I lie asleep; but oh, my heart is wakeful! A knock on the door, and then my true love's voice.
Lover: Let me in, my true love, so gentle, my bride, so pure! See how bedewed is this head of mine, how the night rains have drenched my hair!
Bride: I rose up to let him in; but my hands dripped ever with myrrh; still with the choicest myrrh my fingers were slippery, as I caught the latch. When I opened, my true love was gone; he had passed me by. How my heart sank within me when he turned his back! And now I searched for him in vain; there was no answer when I called out to him. As they went the city rounds, the watchmen fell in with me, that guard the walls; beat me, and left me wounded, and took away my cloak. Then, when I had scarce left them, I found him, so tenderly loved; and now that he is mine I will never leave him, never let him go.
Lover: How fair you are, my true love; how fair; eyes soft as dove's. Fair in every part, my true love, no fault in all your fashioning! What a wound you have made, my bride, my true love, what a wound you have made in this heart of mine! My bride, my true love, a close garden; hedged all about, a spring shut in and sealed! What wealth of grace is here! A stream bordered with garden; water so fresh never came tumbling

united to Christ, her eternal lover; the restoration from exile
is to be the final stage of the Old Testament preparation for
the coming of the Messiah.

As members of the Mystical Body of Christ we are the
object of our Lord's personal love. To each soul he addresses
the same invitation to leave the winter of our old selves and
enjoy the everlasting springtime of his love; a happiness that
will never end.

A REPENTANT BRIDE SEEKS HER HUSBAND. All through the
captivity God was knocking at the door of Israel's heart; he
is always the lover trying to regain entrance to the heart of
her whom he took as his bride when he made a covenant
with her at Sinai. The exile was meant by God to punish
Israel for her infidelity in worshipping false gods, which the
prophets called adultery. The unfaithful bride showed signs
of repentance by responding to the Lord's grace; but a long
period of testing was needed before she could be so purified
as to win the company of her lover once more. Israel had to
learn by sad experience in a foreign land what a terrible thing
it is to abandon the Lord her God. It is only when she has
undergone the sorrow of separation, and sought him out with
a repentant heart, that he will receive her back to his loving
embrace.

'A heart that is humbled and contrite you, O God, will
never disdain' (Ps. 50, 19). The Lord receives his repentant
bride just as the Father welcomes his prodigal son (Lk. 15).
This new relationship of love is spoken of in terms of the
Garden of Eden, that idyllic picture of holiness before mankind sinned against God.

Two of the expressions used by the lover are quoted frequently in the liturgy of our Lady. More than any other

down from Lebanon. North wind, awake; wind of the south, awake and come; blow through this garden of mine, and set its fragance all astir.

Bride: Where should he be, my true love, but among the his fruit.

Bride: Into his garden, then, let my true love come, and taste spices; where but in his garden, gathering the lilies? All mine, my true love, and I all his; ever he would choose the lilies for his pasture-ground.

Lover: Fair you are as Thersa, my heart's love; for beauty, Jerusalem itself is not your match; yet no embattled array so awes men's hearts. One there is beyond compare; for me, none so gentle, none so pure! Maid was none that saw her but called her blessed; queen was none, nor concubine, but spoke in her praise. Who is this, whose coming shows like the dawn of day? No moon so fair, no sun so majestic, no embattled array so awes men's hearts.

Bride: But when I betook me to the nut garden, to look at the blossoms in the valley, to see if vine had flowered there, and pomegranate had budded, all unawares, my heart had made me the blessed one of my kinswomen.

Lover: Ah, princely maid, how dainty are the steps of your sandalled feet! How graceful you are, dear maiden, how fair, how dainty!

Bride: My true love, I am all his; and who but I the longing of his heart? Come with me, my true love. Would that you were my brother; then I could meet you in the open street and kiss you, and earn no contemptuous looks.

Daughters of Jerusalem: Who is this that makes her way up the desert road, all gaily clad, leaning upon the arm of her true love?

human being she is the object of divine love. 'Fair in every part' (tota pulchra es) expresses Mary's Immaculate Conception; there is no sin at all in her. 'A close garden' (hortus conclusus), 'A spring shut in and sealed' (fons signatus) symbolize the virginity of our Lady; she belongs to God alone.

THE FINAL UNION OF TWO LOVERS. The consummation of the love of the repentant bride returned to her Lord and lover is marriage; this is symbolized by the bridegroom taking possession of his bride in the garden. Palestine was the place on earth chosen by God where this final act of his relationship with mankind would take place; that is why the garden element is so prominent; the land would flourish and blossom like the Garden of Eden. This final act was the Incarnation, the greatest proof of God's love for mankind. Christ is not only the lover of men; he is their brother as well.

The Daughters of Jerusalem represent the Gentiles. They are pictured as watching the wedding procession. Maybe they stand for the harem of king Solomon into which the bride has been taken from her shepherd lover; now at last she is free to leave the harem and return to her true love. Solomon then would represent the idolatry which made a captive of Israel during the Babylonian exile (3 Kg. 11); all the while she longed for her Shepherd Lover, the Lord. This view makes the Song of Songs a drama by introducing two male characters competing for the affection of the maiden. It was proposed by Pouget, and is followed by Knox in his notes to the text. In the first scene, the king is making love to the bride while she is longing for her absent shepherd husband; in the second scene she hears her husband calling her in a dream; in the third scene he visits the harem at night; in the final scene the two separated lovers are united at last.

Bride: Hold me close to your heart, close as locket or bracelet fits; not death itself is so strong as love, not the grave itself cruel as love unrequited; the torch that lights it is a blaze of fire. Yes, love is a fire no waters avail to quench, no floods to drown; for love, a man will give up all that he has in the world, and think nothing of his loss.

AGGAEUS 2, 2-10

On the twenty-first day of the seventh month, the Lord sent another message through the prophet Aggaeus. To Zorobabel, and Joshua, and all the people with them his word was: 'Tell me, those of you who saw this house in its former brightness, what make you of it now? It is no better in your eyes than a very nothing. Take heart, Zorobabel; Joshua, son of Josedec, take heart! And you, too, people of the land, the Lord of hosts bids you take heart and perform (is not he, the Lord of hosts, at your side?) the word which I covenanted with you when you escaped from Egypt; my own spirit shall be among you, do not be afraid.

'A little while now,' the Lord of hosts says, 'and I mean to set heaven and earth, sea and dry land rocking; **stirred all the nations shall be, so that the treasures of the whole world shall come in, and I will fill this temple with the brightness of my presence,'** says the Lord of hosts. 'Silver or gold, what matters it?' the Lord of hosts says. 'Both are mine! Bright this new temple shall be,' he tells you, 'as never the first was; here,' he tells you, 'his blessing shall rest.'

ZACHARIAS 2; 8

When next I looked up, I saw a man there that carried a measuring-line; so I asked him, whither he was bound? 'For

The phrase 'No moon so fair, no sun so majestic' (pulchra ut luna, electa ut sol) is used of our Lady's Assumption. This Marian usage is common in the liturgy; it is based on Mary's relation to the Church (p. 275). Bride of Christ has a deeper meaning when we remember that Mary is related to Christ in the deepest bonds of love.

THE LORD IN HIS TEMPLE

THE GLORY OF THE SECOND TEMPLE. It was almost twenty years since the Jews had returned from exile in Babylon. They had begun to rebuild the temple immediately on their arrival, but they had given up owing to opposition, and to serve their own selfish interests. So Aggaeus was sent with a message from the Lord to stir up the governor Zorobabel and the high priest Joshua to get on with the work.

As the building rose, the onlookers could not help contrasting it with the first temple built by Solomon. The post-exile Jews were poor, and their temple was drab and dingy compared with the magnificent edifice of Solomon. But the Lord tells them that this unpretentious building will far outshine the grandeur of the first temple. First, all nations will worship there (only Jews worshipped in Solomon's temple); the whole world will bring its treasures to the Lord (silver and gold are symbols of spiritual gifts dedicated to God). And most important, the Messiah himself will glorify it by his presence; Mary and Joseph present Jesus in the temple (Lk. 2, 22); later, our Lord will preach many times in the temple.

DIVINE PROTECTION OF THE CHURCH

AN ANGEL MEASURES JERUSALEM. Zacharias preached in Jerusalem to the returned exiles at the same time as Aggaeus.

Jerusalem,' said he, 'to measure the length and breadth of it.' And at that, my angel monitor would have gone out on his errand, but here was a second angel come out to meet him. 'Speed you,' said he, 'on your way, and tell that pupil of yours: "So full Jerusalem shall be, of men and cattle both, wall it shall have none to hedge it in; **I myself,"** the Lord says, **"will be a wall of fire around it, and in the midst of it the brightness of my presence."**

'Away, away, from the north country get you gone,' the Lord says; 'what if I have scattered you, far as the four winds? Away with you, Sion; would you still make your home with widowed Babylon? Sion, poor maid, break out into songs of rejoicing; **I am on my way, coming to dwell in the midst of you,'** the Lord says. 'There be nations a many that shall rally that day to the Lord's side; they, too, shall be people of mine, but with you shall be my dwelling.'

Juda the Lord shall claim for his own, his portion in a holy land; still Jerusalem shall be the city of his choice. Be silent, living things, in the Lord's presence; yonder in his holy dwelling all is astir.

A message from the Lord of hosts: 'Great ruth have I for Sion, and sore it grieves me. To Sion I will return,' so runs his promise, 'and make in Jerusalem my home; **"The loyal city,"** men shall call her, and that mountain where dwells the Lord of hosts, **"The holy mountain."'**

This too: 'Trust me, there shall yet be aged folk in the streets of Jerusalem, men and women both, that go staff in hand, they are so bowed with years; thronged they shall be, those streets, with boys and girls at play in the open.'

And this: 'Hard to believe? So now they find it, poor rem-

The first six chapters of his prophecy are a series of eight visions. In this, his third vision, he sees an angel measuring up Jerusalem—the preliminary stage of any building operation. His constant companion, the angel monitor, is informed by a third angel, who is the Lord's personal representative, that this new Jerusalem will have great glory and importance.

The most important part of a city in ancient times, and the first part to be built, was a high protecting wall; this ensured the safety of the city against attack from enemies. But in the new Jerusalem, the Church of Christ, there will be no need of material protection; the Lord himself will guard and defend his Church. The imagery used here ('a wall of fire . . . the brightness of my presence') is taken from the Shekinah, that bright, shining cloud which stood over the tabernacle during the forty years in the wilderness. It foreshadowed the real presence of Christ in his Church.

The time of exile and mourning is gone forever; instead there will be gladness and rejoicing in rebuilt Jerusalem. The Gentiles shall no longer be enemies, but true worshippers of the Lord in the Church of Christ.

THE LORD'S PITY FOR SION. In chapter seven, some exiles recently returned from Babylon put a question to the priests and prophets in Jerusalem: Should they still keep the fifth month of each year as a time of fasting in memory of the fall of Jerusalem? (This had been a Jewish custom all during the exile; Jerusalem had fallen in the fifth month of the year.)

The next three sections are part of the Lord's reply through the mouth of his prophet Zacharias. The answer to the exiles' question is No. The reason for the answer is that the restoration of the chosen people to the promised land is really an

nant of a people; but should I, the Lord of hosts, find it hard to perform?'

And this, too: 'See if I do not rescue my people from the east country and the west, bring them back to dwell here, in the midst of Jerusalem; **they my people, and I their God, in troth and loyalty either to other bound.'**

A message from the Lord of hosts: 'Take courage, then, you that still hold fast by the commands the prophets gave you, when the foundations of yonder house were a-laying, and the Lord of hosts had no temple yet. Before that time, labour went unrewarded, for men and beast; so hard pressed were you, none might come or go in safety; every man, in those days, I left at his neighbour's mercy. **But now,' says the Lord of hosts, 'this remnant of my people shall enjoy better fortune; a happier seed-time is theirs. Its fruit the vineyard shall yield, the land its harvest, heaven its rain, and all for this remnant to enjoy.** Breed of Juda, breed of Israel, by-words of misfortune once, when heathen folk fell to cursing their enemies; happy deliverance, they shall be names of blessing now!'

This promise I give you from the Lord of hosts: 'What alien throngs, from what far cities, shall make pilgrimage yet! And ever, as fresh towns they reach, says pilgrim, "Come with us, and welcome; court we the divine favour, to the Lord of hosts repair we"; says townsman, "Go with you I will." **No nation so populous, no kingdom so strong, but shall betake itself to Jerusalem, to find the Lord of hosts and court his divine favour.'**

This too: 'A time is coming, when there is never a man of

overture to Messianic times. It should be a time of rejoicing,
not of mourning.

There are three motives for gladness: the Lord has made
Jerusalem his home once again; the long life of old people and
the great numbers of young people is a sign of divine favour;
they are the chosen race.

THE REMNANT SHALL ENJOY BETTER FORTUNE. Like Aggaeus, Zacharias was prophesying about twenty years after the
return from exile. He recounts (compare Aggaeus 1) the early
struggles against enemies and the hardship caused by drought
and famine. Stirred by the divine message from Aggaeus and
Zacharias, the people overcame these two obstacles and rebuilt the temple of Jerusalem.

This was the turning-point of the Restoration. From now
on better times are coming for the returned remnant; it is the
inauguration of Messianic times. This is presented under the
familiar imagery of material prosperity; seed-time, fruit from
vineyard, harvest from crops, and rain from heaven are proverbial signs of divine favour in the Old Testament prophecies; they are symbols to a primitive people of spiritual
blessings.

ALL NATIONS SHALL WORSHIP THE LORD. This is the supreme
reward for all the effort needed by the Jews to rebuild the
temple at Jerusalem, and a high motive for rejoicing at their
present lot instead of mourning the days of exile in Babylon.
Jerusalem will once again be the centre of worship; nations
from the whole world will come there to join in offering true
worship to God.

The universality of salvation, the Gentiles finding their way
into the Catholic Church, is the most frequent note of Mes-

Jewish blood but shall have ten Gentiles at his heels, and no two of the same speech; clinging all at once to the skirts of him, and crying, "Your way is ours! The tale has reached us, how God is there to protect you." '

ZACHARIAS 3, 1-10; 6, 9-15

Another vision the Lord showed me; here was an angel of his, and before this angel stood the high priest Joshua, with the Accuser at his right hand bringing accusation against him. But to the Accuser the divine answer came, 'The Lord rebuke you, Satan; the Lord, that makes choice of Jerusalem, rebuke you! What, is not this a brand saved from the embers?'

Then, for he saw Joshua standing there in his presence very vilely clad, the angel gave it out to his attendants they should take away these vile rags from him: 'Guilt of yours,' said he, 'I have set by; you shall have new garments to wear instead.' A clean mitre they should give him besides. And so, when the new mitre was on his head and the new garments were about him, the angel of the Lord rose up and gave Joshua his commission from the Lord of hosts: 'My beckoning follow you, my commands keep you, people of mine you shall govern, house of mine shall have in your charge, and in their company, that here stand about you, shall come and go. This for the hearing of the high priest Joshua, and others of his co-assessors, names of good omen all.

'**Time is I should bring hither my servant, that is the Branch.** Stone is here I will set before yonder Joshua; a stone that bears seven eyes (what should they be, those seven, but eyes the Lord has, glancing this way and that to scan the earth?), device of my own carving,' says the Lord of hosts. '**All the guilt of this land I will banish in a single day.** That

sianic times in the Old Testament. In the time of St. Paul
they soon outnumbered Jews; the Jews lost their privileged
position when they rejected Jesus as the Messiah (Romans
9-11).

CHRIST THE BRANCH OF DAVID

A VISION OF JOSHUA CLOTHED IN NEW GARMENTS. This is
the fifth of Zacharias' eight visions. Himself a priest, Zacharias had special interest in the high priest Joshua and his
exalted position in restoring worship of God in the temple,
then in the course of reconstruction. The vile rags in which
Joshua is clothed signify the sinful and idolatrous state of the
priesthood before the exile. Joshua is like a log ('brand') saved
from the previous night's fire to start the morning fire; he is
the link with pre-exile Judaism, the source from which the
Lord will once again build up the priestly sacrifice. His new
status is symbolized by the clean mitre and new vestments;
once more the priesthood has won divine favour.

With one of those sudden leaps for which the prophets
are famous, Zacharias jumps the intervening years to him who
will remove the guilt of the world in a single day; his mind is
now on Christ and his sacrifice on Calvary, which was the
completion and fulfilment of all the Old Testament sacrifices.
He calls Christ the ZEMACH, a branch or shoot from the
stump of a tree; this stump represents the devastated state of
the house of David brought on by the sins of Israel and
punished by exile in Babylon. Isaias, Jeremias, and Ezechiel
all used the same metaphor when speaking of the Messiah,
who would restore the fortunes of the chosen people.

With another quick change of metaphor, Zacharias calls
Christ the foundation stone of the temple building, giving

shall be a day of good cheer,' the Lord of hosts says, 'friend making glad with friend under vine and under fig-tree.'

And a message from the Lord came to Zacharias: 'From yonder emissaries of the exiled Jews, Holdai, Tobias and Idaias, toll you must take; this very day bestir you, and make your way to the house of Josias, son of Sophonias, whither they have repaired, newly come from Babylon. Gold and silver you must take from them, and make a crown, to crown the high priest, Joshua son of Josedec.

'This message you shall give him from the Lord God of hosts: **"Here is one takes his name from the Branch; he will branch forth from that beneath him.** He it is shall rebuild the Lord's temple; builder of the Lord's temple, to what honours he shall come! **On princely throne he sits, throne of a priest beside him, and between these two, what harmony of counsel!"**

'For Helem, Tobias, Idaias, and the son of Sophonias, the crowns they gave shall win remembrance in the temple of the Lord. Men shall come from far away, to work at the temple's rebuilding; you shall not doubt, then, it was the Lord of hosts gave me my warrant. Will you but heed the voice of the Lord your God, this shall be your reward.'

ZACHARIAS 9, 1-10

Burden of the Lord's doom, where falls it now? On Hadrach's land; ay, and Damascus shall be its resting-place; the cities of Syria belong to the Lord, just as much as the tribes of Israel. Perilously near is Emath, and yonder cities of Tyre and Sidon, so famed for wisdom. This Tyre, how strong a fort-

unity and solidity to the structure. This image is better known in Isaias 28, 16, and from its application to our Lord by St. Peter (1 Pet. 2, 6) and St. Paul (Rom. 9, 33).

THE SYMBOLIC CROWNING OF JOSHUA. The Jews remaining in exile sent three delegates to Jerusalem with gifts for the construction of the temple. Zacharias, as the chief prophet of the Lord, is told to take a portion of the silver and gold to make a crown for the high priest Joshua. This is an unusual request; high priests were anointed with oil, not crowned. Some authorities think the crown was meant for Zorobabel.

But the prophet's mind is not really on Joshua or Zorobabel; he is thinking primarily of the ZEMACH, the branch that springs up from the trunk of David. The existing priest and king only serve as an occasion for a Messianic utterance. The temple in the thoughts of Zacharias is not the structure of wood and stone rising in Jerusalem, but the Church, the work of Christ in the future. This is clear from the fact that Gentiles shall take part in its building. The fact that king and priest are engaged in building the present temple reminds him that Christ will combine both offices in his own person, as King David foretold long before in Psalm 109.

PALM SUNDAY

THE PRINCE OF PEACE ENTERS JERUSALEM. Two of the countries bordering on Palestine were most prosperous in Persian times, when Zacharias wrote this prophecy. They were Syria to the north and Philistia to the west; they stand in this context for all the traditional enemies of the chosen

ress she has built, what silver and gold she has amassed, till they were common as clay, as mire in the streets! Ay, but the Lord means to dispossess her; cast into the sea, all that wealth of hers, and herself burnt to the ground! At sight of it, how Ascalon trembles, how Gaza mourns, and Accaron, for hopes belied; no chieftain in Gaza, no townsfolk left in Ascalon now; in Azotus dwells a bastard breed. So low will I bring the pride of yonder Philistines; snatch the blood-stained morsel from their mouths, the unhallowed food theirs no longer; servant of our God he shall be that is left surviving, a clansman in Juda; so shall Accaron be all one with the Jebusite. I have sentinels that shall march to and fro, guarding this home of mine, and none shall take toll of it henceforward; my eyes are watching now.

Glad news for you, widowed Sion; cry out for happiness, Jerusalem forlorn! See where your king comes to greet you, a trusty deliverer; see how lowly he rides, mounted on an ass, patient colt of patient dam! Chariots of yours, Ephraim, horses of yours, Jerusalem, shall be done away, bow of the warrior be unstrung; **peace this king shall impose on the world, reigning from sea to sea, from Euphrates to the world's end.**

ZACHARIAS 11—13

This message the Lord my God sent me: 'To this flock that is a-fattening for slaughter you must play the shepherd.' Poor sheep fattening for slaughter, take charge of your flock I must; and two staves I made me, for the better tending of it, one I called Favour, and the other Union. Before a month was up, of three shepherds I had rid them, yet had I no patience with them, and they of me grew no less weary. 'No more will I

people. Five cities are listed in Syria, and four in the land of
the Philistines; they will be conquered and incorporated into
the Church of Christ.

In contrast to the rich nations stands the still-ruined city
of Jerusalem (Zacharias wrote this prophecy about 480 B. C.,
forty years before Nehemias built the walls); but it will have
a glory of its own when the victorious Messianic king rides
through its gates in triumph. He will be a conqueror by peaceful means, not by force of arms. This is indicated by the animal on which he rides: military conquerors rode on horseback,
peaceful men on donkeys. The weapons Christ uses are spiritual: he will win the souls of men by preaching the gospel.
His victory will come through suffering and death, not by a
military campaign; by this means he will conquer the world.

This prophecy was fulfilled to the letter when our Lord
rode over the mount of Olives from Bethany into Jerusalem
on Palm Sunday. He was explicitly giving the Jews a sign
that he was the promised Messiah, and at the same time indicating his programme of peace. In his account of the incident,
St. Matthew (21, 1-7) has two donkeys; the foal only is mentioned by Zacharias; probably it would not lead without its
mother coming along too.

THE TRUE SHEPHERD PUT TO DEATH

ZACHARIAS ACTS THE PART OF A SHEPHERD. The prophets
used a variety of techniques in making known the divine
message to the people. One of the most effective was the one
employed here by Zacharias: it was a dramatic presentation of
God's message by acting a part, in this case that of the true
shepherd, the Messiah himself. Like Ezechiel, the most
famous of the play-actors, Zacharias takes the two staffs used

tend you,' said I; 'perish all of you that will perish, be lost all that will be lost; and for the residue, let them devour one another; I care not.' With that, I took the staff I called Favour, and cut it in two; in token that my covenant with all the world should be null. Then I took my other staff, Union, and cut it in two; token that all brotherhood was at an end between Juda and Israel.

'And now,' said I, 'pay me my wages, if pay you will; if not, say no more.' So they paid me for my wages thirty pieces of silver. 'Why,' the Lord said, 'here is princely sum they rate me at! Throw it to the craftsman yonder.' So there, in the Lord's temple, I threw the craftsman my thirty pieces of silver.

'Up, sword, and attack this shepherd of mine, neighbour of mine,' says the Lord of hosts. 'Smite shepherd, and his flock shall scatter; so upon the common folk my vengeance shall fall. Theirs on my name to call, their plea mine to grant: "My own people," so I greet them, and they answer, "The Lord is my own God."'

'Never a nation that marched on Jerusalem but I will hunt it down, when that day comes, and make an end of it. On David's clan, on all the citizens of Jerusalem, I will pour out a gracious spirit of prayer; towards him they shall look, him whom they have pierced through. Lament for him they must, and grieve bitterly; never was such lament for an only son, grief so bitter over first-born dead.

'When that day comes, great shall be the mourning in Jerusalem, great as Adadremmon's mourning at Mageddo; the whole land in mourning, all its families apart. Here the men of David's clan, yonder their women, here the men of Na-

by a shepherd, one for walking and counting sheep, the other a heavy cudgel used to beat off wild animals from the flock. These two sticks are inscribed with names which are explained when the prophet breaks the two sticks. When Favour is broken, the Lord has annulled his agreement to protect Israel from Gentile onslaught; they are now at liberty to attack the chosen people. As well as being exposed to persecution from without, the chosen people lose their national unity; this is signified by breaking the Union staff.

The reason for this abandonment by the Lord is that the Jews have rejected their true shepherd, the Messiah, played in this context by the prophet. Instead of appreciating the loving care of Christ, the Jews rate him no better than a slave. (Thirty pieces of silver was the price of a slave, Exodus 21, 32; the same price was paid for the betrayal of Jesus, Matthew 26, 15.) The Jews' hatred of Christ is the motive that makes them not only despise his ministrations but determine on his death; sorrowfully the Lord permits them to attack and kill his only Son, because he knows it will be the means of their salvation.

REPENTANCE OF THE JEWS AT THE CRUCIFIXION. Although the death of the Messiah was predicted by earlier prophets (the two classical passages are Psalm 21 and Isaias 53), this is probably the first time crucifixion is mentioned explicitly in Messianic prophecy. Crucifixion came to the Jews through the Persians; Zacharias prophesied during the Persian rule of Palestine. St. John (19, 37) says that this prophecy was fulfilled when the soldier pierced our Lord's side; but he is most likely thinking of the whole process of crucifixion, or piercing through.

At the moment of Jesus' death on the cross, a sudden

than's, yonder their women, here the men of Levi's, yonder
their women, here the men of Semei's, yonder their women;
apart they shall mourn, whatever families there be, and all
their women-folk apart. **When that day comes, clansmen of
David and citizens of Jerusalem shall have a fountain flowing
openly, of guilt to rid them, and of defilement.'**

ZACHARIAS 14

The Lord's appointed time is coming. Then the Lord will
go out to battle against those nations, as he did ever in the
decisive hour. There on the mount of Olives, that faces Jerusalem on the east, his feet shall be set; to east and west the
mount of Olives shall be cloven in two halves, with a great
chasm between, and the two halves shall move apart, one
northward, one southward. On, on he comes, the Lord my
God, with all his sacred retinue.

Heat there shall be none that day, nor frost, nor cold; one
continuous day there shall be (none but the Lord knows the
length of it), not day and night; when evening comes there
shall be light. Then a living stream will flow from Jerusalem,
half to the eastern, half to the western sea, winter and summer both; **and over all the earth the Lord shall be king, one
Lord, called everywhere by one name.**

Yet of all the nations that sent their armies against Jerusalem there shall be some remnant left; and these, year by
year, shall make pilgrimage, to worship their King, the Lord
God of hosts. Come and worship their King they must, the
Lord of hosts; else no rain shall fall on them, all the world
over.

change came over the crowd: 'And the whole crowd of those who stood there watching it, when they saw the issue, went home beating their breasts' (Lk. 23, 48). This repentance is what Zacharias predicted when he spoke of universal mourning at the death of an only, first-born son. The atoning death of Christ unloosed all the stored-up graces of divine love and pity; sin could now be washed away in the blood of the crucified Redeemer.

KING OVER ALL THE EARTH

THE LORD COMES TO JERUSALEM'S AID. The imagery here is taken from an earthquake on the mount of Olives, the usual encampment of enemy forces besieging Jerusalem. It is not meant to be taken literally; it is a symbol of how efficiently and unexpectedly the Lord intervenes on behalf of his Church. The Hebrews delighted in writing of dramatic comings of the Lord in time of trial; a storm (Ps. 17) or an earthquake was the usual way in which God manifested his power. It was a too literal interpretation of such phenomena that misled the Jews in the time of Christ; they failed to recognize him when he came quietly and unobtrusively among them (Lk. 17, 20).

Two common symbols used to express the blessings of Messianic times are used here by Zacharias; they are light and water. They both come from the creation account in Genesis: light where God dwells (1, 3), and water, the symbol of life in the Garden of Eden (2, 10-14). Probably the most famous use of light as a symbol of Messianic glory is Isaias 60; the best-known picture of the blessings Christ brings under the image of water is the stream that flows from the temple in Ezechiel 47, 8-12.

Spoils from the enemy's bridle-rein shall be consecrated on that day to the Lord's service, till there is never pot or pan in his temple but rivals the altar's bowls for costliness! Nay, never pot or pan in all Jerusalem but shall be consecrated to the Lord of hosts, for any who will come and take it and seethe victim in it; trafficking there shall be no more in the Lord's temple, when that day comes.

MALACHIAS 1, 6-11

'Son to father, servant to master gives his due. Your father I, where is the honour, your master I, where is the reverence you owe me?' Such complaint the Lord of hosts makes, and to whom? To you, priests, that care so little for his renown. 'Ask you what care is lacking, when the bread you offer at my altar is defiled, ask you what despite you have done me, when you write down the Lord's table a thing of little moment? What, no harm done, when victim you offer in sacrifice is blind? No harm done, when it is lame or diseased? Pray you,' says the Lord of hosts, 'make such a gift to the governor yonder, will he be content? Will he make favourites of you?

'Ay,' says the Lord of hosts, 'the guilt is yours. To the divine presence betake you, and sue for pardon; which of you finds favour with him? Never a man of you but must be paid to shut door, light altar fire; no friends of mine,' says the Lord of hosts, 'no gifts will I take from such as you. No corner of the world, from sun's rise to sun's setting, where the renown of me is not heard among the Gentiles, where sacrifice is not done, and pure offering made in my honour; so revered is my name,' says the Lord of hosts, 'there among the Gentiles.'

The Gentile forces on Olivet are at first hostile to the Church; but under the influence of divine grace they shall fall down in worship to the true God; this is the image of the universality of salvation recurring continually in the Messianic prophecies. The temple itself will be filled with treasures from the whole world; it shall be a holy place set apart for divine worship. That is why our Lord cleansed it of money-changers (Jn. 2, 16).

THE SACRIFICE OF THE MASS

A New Daily Sacrifice to replace the Old. 'If any beast has a blemish, or is lame or blind or misshapen or maimed in any way, it cannot be offered to the Lord your God' (Deut. 15, 21). This was the prescription of the Mosaic code which the Jews of Malachias' time were breaking; it was only rejected animals, of no value, that they used for the most important act of their lives, the worship of the one true God.

The divine gaze goes out into the future (although he speaks in the present tense, a common poetic device), when the perfect sacrifice shall be offered all over the world, a sacrifice that cannot be defiled by the unworthiness of the minister. Catholic tradition, confirmed by a definition of the Council of Trent, has always understood this as the sacrifice of the Mass, instituted by our Lord at the Last Supper.

The key word for this interpretation is 'pure offering,' which represents the Hebrew word MINCHAH, a technical word for unbloody sacrifice, such as bread and wine, not bloody animal sacrifices (ZEBACH). This was foreshadowed in Melchisedech's bread and wine (Gen. 14, 18), in the Manna (Ex. 16), and possibly in the girdle cake that strengthened the prophet Elias (3 Kg. 19, 6-8).

MALACHIAS 2, 17—3, 5; 4, 1-5

Oh, but the Lord is aweary of your doings! And little wonder, when you think so amiss of him; telling yourselves, 'Foul
is fair in the Lord's sight, and wrong-doing well likes him;
God that judges us is none.'

**'See where I am sending a messenger of mine, to make the
way ready for my coming! All at once the Lord will visit his
temple; that Lord, so longed for, welcome herald of a divine
covenant.** Ay,' says the Lord of hosts, 'he is coming; but who
can bear the thought of his advent? Who will stand with
head erect at his appearing? He will put men to a test fierce
as the crucible, searching as the lye that fullers use. From his
judgment-seat, he will refine that silver of his and cleanse it
from dross; like silver or gold, the sons of Levi must be re-
fined in the crucible, ere they can offer the Lord sacrifice duly
performed. Then once more the Lord will accept the offerings
of Juda and Jerusalem, as he did long since, in the forgotten
years. Come I to hold assize, not slow to arraign the sorcerer,
the adulterer, the forsworn, all of you that deny hired man
his wages, widow and orphan redress, the alien his right, fearing no vengeance from the Lord of hosts.

'Trust me, a day is coming that shall scorch like a furnace;
stubble they shall be before it,' says the Lord of hosts, 'all the
proud, all the wrong-doers, caught and set alight, and neither
root nor branch left them. **But to you that honour my name
there shall be a sunrise of restoration, swift-winged, bearing
redress;** light-hearted as frisking calves at stall you shall go
out to meet it; ay, and trample on your godless enemy, ashes,
now, to be spurned under foot, on that day when the Lord of
hosts declares himself at last.

THE LORD VISITS HIS TEMPLE

THE LORD WILL PURIFY HIS PEOPLE. Malachias prophesied
during the time of the Esdras-Nehemias reform, about the
middle of the fifth century B. C. (2 Esd. 8-13). He makes it
quite clear that both priests and people were living lives dis-
pleasing to God. The Lord himself, in the Person of his Incarnate Son Jesus Christ, would come into this sinful world
to purge it of all evil and make its people holy and pleasing
to him.

As in Aggaeus 2, 8, the temple is to be the first and most
important place visited by our Lord. When the infant Jesus
was brought to the temple for the Presentation (Lk. 2, 22-
38), and again when he came at the beginning of his public
ministry to cleanse the temple at Passover time (Jn. 2, 13-22),
he was fulfilling the prophecies of both Aggaeus and Malachias: 'All at once the Lord will visit his temple' (Mal. 3, 1).
These official entries of the Messiah heralded his work for
the redemption of the chosen people, a new 'divine covenant'
(Mal. 3, 1) that would be 'a sunrise of restoration' (Mal.
4, 2). Zachary, the father of John the Baptist, used the same
imagery when he spoke his Benedictus before Jesus present in
Mary's womb at the Visitation: 'Such is the merciful kindness
of our God, which has bidden him come to us, like a dawn-
ing from on high, to give light to those who live in darkness,
in the shadow of death, and to guide our feet into the way of
peace' (Lk. 1, 78).

Malachias is the only prophet to make mention of the work
of John the Baptist in preparing the way for our Lord. He
calls him 'a messenger of mine' (3, 1), and also refers to him
as 'Elias' (4, 5). The messenger text is quoted in Matthew

'And before ever that day comes, great day and terrible, I will send Elias to be your prophet; he it is shall reconcile heart of father to son, heart of son to father; else the whole of earth should be forfeit to my vengeance.'

JOEL 2, 12—3, 21

'Time now,' the Lord says, 'to turn the whole bent of your hearts back to me, with fasting and with mourners' tears. It is your hearts, not the garments you wear, that must be torn asunder.' **Come back to the Lord your God; he is ever gracious and merciful, ever patient and rich in pardon; threatens he calamity, even now he is ready to forgive.** People of a land well loved, he spares us yet. His answer comes: 'Here is corn and wine and oil to your hearts' content; no more will I let the nations mock you. Fear no more, land of Israel; in the Lord's wondrous doings triumph and rejoice! Fear no more, beasts that roam the countryside; grass grows on the upland meadows! There is fruit on the trees again; vine nor fig-tree ever bore so lustily. **Rejoice, men of Sion, and triumph in the Lord your God; proof he gives you of your restoration to favour, making the winter and the spring rains fall, as in time past.** Now the threshing-floor shall be piled with wheat, and the presses overflow with wine and oil. Drip now with sweet wine the mountain-slopes, bathed in milk the upland pastures; never a stream in all Juda but flows full and strong. What fountain is this that comes out from the Lord's temple, and waters the dry valley of Setim?

'Profitless years, when the locust ravaged you, Gnaw-all and Ruin-all and Spoiler, that great army of mine I let loose among you, they shall be made good. Eat you shall to your

11, 10, and the Elias reference is quoted as fulfilled in John
the Baptist (Mt. 17, 10-13). He was not Elias in person; he
came 'in the spirit and power of an Elias' (Lk. 1, 17). Some
authorities hold that John only partially fulfilled Malachias'
prophecy, and that Elias will return in person at the end of
time.

THE COMING OF THE HOLY SPIRIT

A PROMISE OF MATERIAL PROSPERITY.   The prophecy of Joel
is timeless and cosmic; it could fit into almost any period of
Israel's history. But, seeing that he mentions the exile as already past (Joel 3, 2), and refers to the Greeks (Joel 3, 6), it
seems more natural to place his prophecy in the period of the
post-exile prophets. There is no king mentioned, no divided
kingdom; the priests alone are mentioned as the dominant
power in the land, as they were in post-exile Palestine.

The prophecy begins with a terrifying description of a locust
plague; these oriental grasshoppers strip the whole land bare
of all vegetation: 'O great, O terrible day of the Lord; who
shall find strength to bear it?' (2, 11). Any like calamity, such
as the Flood (Gen. 6-7), was thought of by the Hebrews as
coming directly from the hands of God. It was a punishment
on sinners, in some way foreshadowing that final Day of the
Lord, the Second Coming that will conclude all God's dealings with mankind.

If Israel repents of her sins and turns back to the Lord, he
will be quick to forgive and restore his people to the divine
favour. With no clear knowledge of reward in a future life
after death, the Jews looked to temporal blessings rather than
eternal life. God accommodated his message through the
prophets to this materialistic outlook; it is the usual symbolic
way of describing the spiritual graces of the Messianic era.

hearts' content, praising the name of the Lord your God for his wondrous protection; never again shall Israel go away disappointed. **I will make myself known among you, I, the Lord your God, who alone am God;** Israel cheated of their hopes never again!

'And afterwards? Afterwards **I will pour out my spirit upon all mankind, and your sons and daughters will be prophets. Your old men shall dream dreams, and your young men see visions; everywhere servants of mine, handmaids of mine, inspired to prophesy!** I will show wonders in heaven, and on earth blood, and fire, and whirling smoke. The sun will be turned into darkness and the moon into blood before the day of the Lord comes, the great, the terrible day. And never a soul shall call on the Lord's name but shall find deliverance; here on mount Sion, here in Jerusalem there shall be refuge; for a remnant, a remnant of the Lord's own summoning, there shall be deliverance at last.

'Perilous those times shall be, when the hour has come for reversing my sentence against Juda and Jerusalem. Into the valley of Josaphat I will herd the heathen folk, one and all, and there hold assize over them for the wrong they did to my people, to Israel, my own domain.'
Cry it to the nations, they should do sacrifice and muster their tried warriors for battle; rally they, march they, all that bear arms. Ploughshare beat into sword, spade into spear; weakling is none but must summon up his manhood now! To arms, to the rendezvous, nations all about; doom of the Lord awaits you, warriors all! Up, up, to Josaphat's valley betake you; here, upon all neighbouring peoples, I will hold assize. The sickle, there! Harvest is ripe already. Down to the

Man, beast, and vegetation shall recover from the locust plague, when the Lord sees fit to cease his punishment; rain will fall, all the dry gullies will run again with water, even a fountain will spring up in the temple (Ezech. 47, 8-12); such will be the plenteous supply of grace in Messianic times.

THE DESCENT OF THE HOLY SPIRIT. When St. Peter began his sermon on Pentecost Sunday to the crowd assembled in the temple, he used this passage from Joel to prove that the Christians were not drunk; this ecstatic gift of tongues was the external manifestation of the presence of the Holy Spirit within them (Acts 2, 16-21).

The second part of this prophecy, quoted in part by St. Peter on Pentecost Sunday, seems to treat of the Second Coming of Christ, not of details associated with his First Coming to redeem mankind. It must be remembered that Joel, and the Old Testament prophets generally, did not distinguish the two Comings of Christ; the time lag was not revealed to them by God.

JUDGMENT IN THE VALLEY OF JOSAPHAT. Jews, Christians, and Moslems have all identified the valley of Josaphat with the Kedron valley between Jerusalem and the mount of Olives. Its slopes are covered with tombs of the dead, who have selected this place so that they will be present where and when the Lord comes in judgment on the Last Day. The identification is based on the various, repeated references to the Lord's dwelling-place in Jerusalem; it is natural to suppose that, since he lives in the temple at Jerusalem, he will come to judge at some place nearby. Josaphat is not mentioned elsewhere, and is probably not meant as a place name at all; in Hebrew it means 'The Lord judges.'

Uppermost in this presentation of the Day of the Lord is

vineyard with you! Are not the vats full, the presses overflow-
ing? Has it not come to a head, the measure of their wickedness?

Thronging, thronging they come, in yonder valley to try
their destiny, appointed trysting-place of a divine audit; dark
grow sun and moon, light of the stars is none. Loud as roaring of lion speaks the Lord in thunder from his citadel at
Jerusalem, till heaven and earth quake at the sound. To his
own people, the sons of Israel, refuge he is and stronghold:
'Doubt you shall have none thenceforward that I, the Lord
your God, have my dwelling-place at Jerusalem; a holy city
Jerusalem shall be, never again shall alien foe breach the wall
of her. **For Juda, for Jerusalem, there shall be peace undisturbed, long as time shall last; for these, guilt of blood that
went still unpardoned shall be pardoned now.**' Here, in Sion,
the Lord will have his dwelling-place.

ABDIAS 1, 15—18, 21

Be sure of this, a time is soon coming when the Lord will
summon all the nations to their account; then, as you did, it
shall be done to you, in your own coin you shall be paid. 'The
cup of vengeance you, my people, have drunk, there on that
mountain which is my sanctuary, all the heathen shall drink
henceforward; drink, ay, drink deep, and fall into forgetful-
ness, as if they had never been. **But here, on mount Sion, all
shall be deliverance, all shall be holiness,** and their spoilers
the men of Jacob shall despoil. A fire Jacob shall be, a living
flame the sons of Joseph, and Esau's race stubble before their
onset; the spark once kindled, all shall be consumed, and of
Esau's race no memory left.' The Lord decrees it. No lack
of champions Sion shall have, to do justice on the mountains

the divine judgment on the Gentiles, the heathen folk who
have persecuted, exiled, and fought against the chosen people.
The day will come when the Lord will punish them with an
eternal sentence of doom. This is the familiar outlook of the
Jewish prophets in all their prophecies against the pagan
nations.

The imagery of judgment as a harvest was also used by our
Lord in his Parable of the Weeds: 'Leave them to grow side
by side till harvest, and when harvest-time comes I will give
word to the reapers, "Gather up the weeds first, and tie them
in bundles to be burned, and store the wheat in my barn"'
(Mt. 13, 30). These words of Christ clearly distinguish the
lot of the good and the wicked. The same distinction is made
in Joel; he has the citizens of Jerusalem dwelling in 'peace
undisturbed,' in the friendship of God with all their sins
pardoned.

THE DAY OF THE LORD

DIVINE JUDGMENT ON IDUMEA. Jacob, otherwise known as
Israel, had a twin brother: 'The first to come was of red com-
plexion, and hairy all over as if he had worn a coat of skin;
this one was called Esau' (Gen. 25, 25). Esau means 'hairy'
and Edom means 'red'; the land where his descendants lived
was called Idumea. These two brothers were rivals right from
birth, and enmity continued between their descendants, the
Israelites and the Edomites, throughout the Old Testament.
Idumea is situated to the south of Palestine, and so there were
many opportunities to harass and persecute; when Jerusalem
fell to the Babylonians in 587 B. C., Edom came in to loot
and plunder; during the restoration after exile, they opposed
the reconstruction of the city. Edom represents the enemies

of Edom; **and of that empire the Lord himself shall be sovereign ruler.**

DANIEL 2, 1-3, 26-45

In the second year of his reign, Nabuchodonosor had a dream; and his mind, between sleep and waking, was all distraught. Diviner and sage, soothsayer and astrologer must be summoned without more ado, to pronounce on the royal dream; and when they were admitted to his presence, he said to them, 'I have had a dream, but my mind is so distraught, I cannot tell what it was.'

And Daniel spoke out in the royal presence, 'Never wizard or sage, never diviner or prophet, that can give the king's grace an answer! But there is a God in heaven, king Nabuchodonosor, that makes hidden things plain; he it is that has sent you warning of what must befall long hence. Let me tell you what your dream was, what visions disturbed your sleep. As you were lying there abed, my lord king, your thoughts still turned on future times; and he that makes hidden things plain revealed to you what the pattern of those times should be. If the secret was disclosed to me also, it is not that I have wisdom beyond the wont of living men; I was but the instrument by which the meaning of it was to be made known, and a king's thoughts unravelled.

'A vision you had of a great image; what splendour, how terrible an aspect it was that confronted you! Of fine gold the head, breast and arms of silver, belly and thighs of bronze; of iron the legs, and of the feet, too, part was iron, part was but earthenware. And as you were watching it, from the mountainside fell a stone no hands had quarried, dashed against the feet of yonder image, part iron, part clay, and shattered them. With that, down came iron and clay, down came bronze and

of the chosen people, the Church of the New Testament;
God will condemn them on judgment day.

THE EMPIRE OF CHRIST

Nabuchodonosor's Dream of the Great Statue. Daniel
was a young man in his teens when he was carried off as a
captive from Jerusalem to Babylon; this happened in 605
B. C., eighteen years before the fall of Jerusalem. Being of
'princely stock, in body well formed, handsome of mien, so
well versed and grounded, so keen of wit,' he was chosen by
king Nabuchodonosor to live in the royal palace, and be
taught 'the lore and language of the Chaldeans.' He was an
apt pupil, 'and of visions and dreams especially Daniel was
master' (Dan. 1).

All the ancients placed great importance on dreams; at the
royal court there were teams of learned men whose main
function was the interpretation of dreams. Their skill was
put to an unusual test one day early in Daniel's apprenticeship
at the Babylonian court. The king had a dream which he
could not remember on awaking; unreasonably, he demanded
that his wise men tell him the forgotten dream, and its meaning as well, under penalty of death. When they protested
that such a task was beyond mortal powers, and an impossibil-
ity, the king only grew angrier. Daniel's first knowledge of
these happenings was the information that he was to be put
to death with the others.

Immediately he fell to prayer with his three Jewish companions, Ananias, Misael, and Azarias. 'Then, in a vision by
night, the secret was revealed to Daniel' (2, 19). It was the
Lord himself who made this secret known to his prophet in
Babylon (as he did to Joseph, Genesis 41); and Daniel was
taken into the royal presence to recount and explain the king's

silver and gold; chaff of the threshing-floor was never so scattered on the summer breeze. They were gone, none knew
whither; **and stone that had shattered image grew into a high
mountain, filling the whole earth.**

'So much for the dream, and now we that know the secret
of it will tell the king's grace what it means. You have kings
for your vassals; royalty, power, dominion and great renown
the God of heaven has bestowed on you; every haunt of man
and wild beast and flying bird he has given over to you, all
alike he has made subject to you; the head of gold, who else
but you? Another and a lesser empire must follow yours, one
of silver, then another of bronze, still wide as the world; then
a fourth, of iron, breaking down and crushing all before it, as
iron has power all-conquering, all-subduing. But feet and toes
of the image were part iron, part clay; this fourth empire will
be divided within itself. Foundation of iron there shall yet
be, from which it springs; sure enough, in the feet you saw,
earthenware was mixed with true steel. Yet was true steel
mixed with base earthenware, token that this empire shall be
in part firmly established, in part brittle. Iron and clay
mingled; race of the conquerors shall be adulterated with common human stock; as well mix clay with iron!

'**And while those empires yet flourish, another empire the
God of heaven will bring into being, never to be destroyed,
never to be superseded; conqueror of all these others, itself
unconquerable.** This is that stone you saw none ever quarried,
that fell from the mountain-side, bringing clay and iron and
bronze and silver and gold to nothing; this was a revelation
the king's grace had from the most high God himself of

dream. The dream was about an immense statue. The sight of such a colossal image would not be wholly unfamiliar in the environs of Babylon, for the same king had set up one ninety feet high, probably on the occasion of the fall of Jerusalem in 587 B. C. (Dan. 3, 1). The statue of the dream was unusual in that it was made of four different materials.

DANIEL EXPLAINS THE MEANING OF THE DREAM. Most modern commentators see the hand of an inspired reviser in the interpretation of the four elements of the statue. Probably all that Daniel himself explained was the destruction of all (four stands for completeness) human kingdoms and their replacement by the kingdom of Christ (the stone from the mountain). The Machabean reviser took the basic story of Daniel and amplified it to fit the historical conditions of the times in which he lived. It is the fourth kingdom that is described in detail; this seems to be the divided kingdom (iron and clay) of Alexander the Great's generals, which ruled Palestine in the time of the Machabees. Its most important ruler, Antiochus the Illustrious, is the villain of the Book of Daniel. The profanation of the temple by Antiochus is regarded as the final act in the Old Testament Messianic drama.

According to this view, the reviser of Daniel is merely narrating historical events; he uses a literary device of telling history as though foreseen by the prophet Daniel. Commentators are not agreed on the identity of the four kingdoms. The identification most prevalent among modern Catholic scholars is: Babylon (gold), Persia (silver), Alexander the Great (bronze), Syrian-Egyptian coalition (iron-clay). This fourth kingdom was a mixture of hardness and violence (iron) and instability and weakness (clay); despite intermarriage, the two states never were united. The empire

what must come about; true was your dream, and this, past doubt, the meaning of it.'

DANIEL 7, 1-27

In the first year of the Babylonian king Baltassar, Daniel had a dream; sleep he might, but still his thoughts were busy. The substance of this dream he put on record, giving no more than the sum of it, in these words following: 'Night came, and brought with it a vision for my seeing. All the winds of heaven, I thought, did battle over the wide sea, and out of it came four great beasts, each of them different from the last. A lioness the first seemed, that yet had eagle's wings; but as I watched, these wings were plucked, and with that it rose up from the ground, standing on its feet like a man, and a man's heart was given to it. Then rose up another by its side, this one like a bear; three rows of teeth it had in its mouth, and a summons came to it, great part of mankind it should devour. What saw I next? A leopard it seemed, yet had a bird's wings, four of them, on its back, and four heads; this beast it was that now attained dominion. But still I dreamed on, and a fourth beast saw at last, fiercer, and stronger, and more power-ful yet. It had great teeth of iron, ready to crush and to devour, and ever what these spared it would trample down with its feet; match it those others might not; and out of its head grew ten horns. Even as I watched them, a new horn grew up in the midst of the others, and three of them must be plucked away to make room for it; eyes it had, this new horn, like a man's eyes, and a mouth that talked very boastfully.

'While I still watched, there were judgment thrones a-setting; and one took his seat there crowned with age.

of Christ will be permanent; it will last forever and embrace all nations of the world.

THE SON OF MAN

DANIEL'S VISION OF THE FOUR BEASTS. Nabuchodonosor was succeeded by Nabonidus, whose son Baltassar (Belshazzar) succeeded him; there is an interval of fifty-four years between the dream of Daniel and the dream recorded in the previous section; it is now 548 B. C. Instead of the statue of Nabuchodonosor, Daniel sees in a vision four ferocious wild animals; the two dreams are similar in that both are built on the number four, a symbol of all worldly powers, the four winds of heaven, the four points of the compass.

The vision is introduced by a storm at sea. It is not any particular sea, but stands for the empires of the entire world, with special emphasis on their power (the winds) to attack and harm the kingdom of God. From the midst of this turbulent scene four beasts rise up and play their part on the stage of human affairs. This is the same setting as that for St. John's vision of the beast from the sea in Apoc. 13.

The four beasts stand for the same four empires already outlined in the statue dream of Nabuchodonosor. The lioness represents Babylon (winged lions are a common feature of its architecture), the golden head of the statue. The bear is Persia, the silver body of the statue. The leopard is Alexander the Great's kingdom, the bronze of the statue. The fourth beast is a monster unlike any created animal; it stands for the Syrian (Seleucid) sector of Alexander's empire, the iron and clay of the statue.

THE LORD AND HIS MESSIAH. This is a judgment scene, in which God is presented in all the majesty of his heavenly

White as snow his garments were, his hair could match un-sullied wool for whiteness; his throne all of flame, the wheels under it glancing fire; and ever from his presence a stream of fire came rushing onward. A thousand thousand they were that waited on his bidding, and for every one of these, a thousand others were standing there before him. Assize should be held now, and the records lay open. And still I watched, to see what would become of the boasts yonder horn had made; and all at once I was aware the beast itself had been slain, and even the carcase of it had vanished, handed over to the flames; nor might those other beasts enjoy power any longer, though life they should enjoy for a while, until their turn came. **Then I saw in my dream, how one came riding on the clouds of heaven, that was yet a son of man; came to where the Judge sat, crowned with age, and was ushered into his presence. With that, power was given him, and glory, and sovereignty; obey him all must, men of every race and tribe and tongue; such a reign as his lasts for ever, such power as his the ages cannot diminish.**

'By this,' Daniel wrote, 'my heart was ill at ease; a dread sight it was, and as I dreamed, my thoughts bewildered me. So I drew closer to one that stood by, and asked to know the truth of all that had gone forward; he it was that read the riddle for me, and thus he unravelled it: "It is but earthly kingdoms they betoken, these four great beasts you have seen; **the servants of the most high God shall have dominion yet; theirs it shall be for ever and for evermore.**"

'But I was minded to know the truth more fully; what was the fourth beast, so different from all the rest, so dreadful; why must it have teeth and claws of iron, to crush and to

court; whiteness, fire, and flame are the biblical symbols of
the divine presence (Ezech. 1). It is particularly the fourth
beast, and its 'new horn' (Antiochus the Illustrious), that receive sentence from on high; the other three beasts also are
deprived of their power.

God the Father will not execute judgment personally; this
he delegates to his representative, the Messiah whose origin
is not of earth (like the beasts); he comes from the very
throne of the Almighty in heaven. His power is universal and
eternal; his kingdom, the Church, is to rule supreme over all
earthly kingdoms.

'Son of Man' is a Hebrew way of saying 'a human being'—
though he is of heaven, the Messiah is yet man. It is the title
ordinarily used by our Lord when he is speaking of himself
(eighty times in the gospels); as the Incarnate Son of God he
is the Son of man par excellence. Jesus claims to be this mys-
terious 'Son of Man' of Daniel when he is on trial for his life
before Caiphas; the Jewish leaders understood it as an explicit
claim to divinity.

MEANING OF THE FOURTH BEAST AND HORN. As in Zacharias 1-6, it is an angel ('one that stood by') who interprets
the dream for Daniel; possibly the angel was Gabriel, who is
named as the interpreter of the next scene (Dan. 9, 21). He
has a message of hope for the chosen people of God; they
shall possess the kingdom won for them by their Messiah;
what belongs to Christ belongs to his Church.

Daniel's further enquiry as to the significance of the fourth
beast and the horn that grew out of its head is probably
a Machabean addition to the original vision (as in the previous dream of the statue). It is a write-up of contemporary

devour, to trample on what was left? What of the ten horns on its head, and that other, before which three of them fell, the horn that had eyes, and a mouth to boast with, and grew greater than the rest? This horn it was I saw doing battle against the servants of the most High, and getting the better of them, until the Judge appeared, crowned with age, to give them redress, and their turn came to have dominion.

'And his answer was, this fourth beast was the fourth of those earthly kingdoms, and the greatest of them all, to crush and devour and trample down a whole world. Ten kings be the ten horns of that kingdom, and after these another shall rise, more powerful yet, and three of them shall bite the dust. Boastfully he shall challenge the most High, and do his servants despite; calendar and ordinance he shall think to set aside; for a space of time, and for twice as long, and for half as long, he must needs have his way. Then assize shall be held on him, and all his power be taken away, crushed down and forgotten for ever. Then what royalty, what empire, what earth-embracing dominion shall be theirs, the people set apart for the most High! Sovereignty everlasting; no monarch but must bow to its yoke.'

DANIEL 9, 1-6, 16-27

Then Darius the Mede, son of Assuerus, was raised to the throne of Chaldea; and in the year when his reign began who but I, Daniel, should discover, by the reading of old records, how to compute the seventy years of Jerusalem's widowhood? Such doom the Lord had foretold to the prophet Jeremias. And with that, I turned to the Lord my God; pray to him I

history by an inspired author living at the time of the persecution of Antiochus IV, the Illustrious; for dramatic effect it is presented as a vision of the future as seen by the famous seer of the Babylonian exile, the prophet Daniel.

The fourth beast is really the Seleucid kingdom of Syria that ruled Palestine after the death of Alexander the Great. The Jews of the Machabean age (second century B. C.) were subjected to a fierce persecution when they refused to abandon the Jewish faith and adopt paganism; the king chiefly responsible for this harsh treatment was Antiochus IV ('the horn'). He it was who sparked the revolt of the Machabees, men who fought and won the battle for their ancestral faith and religious liberty.

What angered the Jews most of all was the setting up of an idol in the temple of Jerusalem; this sacrilege of the boastful horn (Antiochus) was a direct insult to the Lord himself. The idol stood for three and a half years, which is the meaning of 'for a space of time, and for twice as long, and for half as long' (Dan. 7, 25; 8, 14; 12, 11-12; Apoc. 13, 5). Maybe the number 3½ is merely a symbol; it is half of seven, the perfect number. It could mean the repeated persecutions that will never succeed, never arrive at that total conquest which belongs to God.

SEVENTY WEEKS OF YEARS

Daniel's Prayer for Desolate Jerusalem. Ten years have passed since Daniel's vision of the four beasts; it is now 538 B.C. This was an important year in the life of the Babylonian exiles; it marked the fall of Babylon and the return of the Jews to Jerusalem. The prayer of Daniel, recorded in this paragraph, was made one afternoon in Babylon, soon after

would, and sue for mercy, fasting ever, sackcloth and ashes my only wear.

Prayed I then to the Lord my God, and made confession of my sins, in these words following: 'Mercy, mercy, Lord God, the great, the terrible; to those who love you, so gracious, with those who keep your commandments, troth keeping still! Sinned we have, and wronged you, rebelled we have, and forsaken you, turned our backs on decree and award of yours, nor heeded your servants, the prophets, that spoke to us in your name, to king and prince and the common folk that gendered us. But will you let your indignant anger fall on Jerusalem, on that holy mountain of yours? Too long, for our sins and the sins of our fathers before us, all our neighbours have held Jerusalem, and us your people, in contempt. God of our race, give audience at last to the prayer, the plea your servant brings before you; for your own honour, restore the sanctuary, that now lies forlorn, to the smile of your favour. My God, give ear and listen to us; open your eyes, and see how desolate is this city of ours, that claims to be your own. No merit of ours, nothing but your great love emboldens us to lay our prayers at your feet. Your hearing, Lord, and your pardon; your heed, Lord, and your aid! For your own honour, my God, deny yourself no longer the city, the people that is called your own!'

Thus prayed I, thus did I confess my own sins, and the sins of my fellow Israelites, pouring out supplication, there in the presence of my God, for that holy mountain which is his dwelling-place. And I was still at my prayer, when the human figure of Gabriel, as I had seen it at the beginning of my vision, flew swiftly to my side; it was the hour of the evening sacrifice when he reached me. And with these words he en-

that city had fallen to the Persian conqueror Cyrus but before
the decree had been signed permitting the Jews to return
home.

Daniel was one of the few who had lived through the entire exile in Babylon; he went into captivity with the first
group in 605 B.C. (Dan. 1, 1). He was excited at the fall of
the Babylonian empire in 538 B.C. Surely the Lord was beginning now to show mercy on his chosen people, to fulfil his
promise to bring them back again to their own land! In
searching through the Jewish records, Daniel came across a
passage in the prophet Jeremias: 'For seventy years this whole
land shall be a desert and a portent, and the king of Babylon
shall have all these peoples for his slaves' (Jer. 25, 11). It was
now sixty-seven years since the exile had begun; that was the
basis for Daniel's petition to the Lord for the restoration of
Israel; the promised return must be near at hand.

There is a problem of chronology in the first sentence of
this paragraph: Darius is said to be on the throne of Chaldea.
Actually he did not begin to reign until sixteen years later;
Cyrus was the first king of the new Medo-Persian empire to
rule in Babylon. It seems that some ignorant copyist put the
name of Cyrus in by mistake; maybe the person he was thinking of was Gobyras, the general of Cyrus, who actually captured Babylon.

GABRIEL DISCLOSES A SECRET.   Probably only the first of these
two paragraphs belongs to the time of Daniel; the second
paragraph (verses 25-27) seems to be a Machabean addition
with the usual emphasis on Antiochus the Illustrious, as in
the dream of the statue and the vision of the four beasts
(Dan. 2 and 7).

In common with the prophets of the exile, Daniel thought

lightened me: 'Daniel, my errand is to instruct you and give
you discernment. Even as your prayer began, a secret was disclosed, and I am here to make it known to you, so well heaven
loves you. Mark well, then, the message, and read the revelation aright: **It is ordained that this people of yours, that holy
city of yours, should wait seventy weeks before guilt is done
away, sin ended, wrong righted; before God's everlasting
favour is restored, and the visions and the prophecies come
true, and that which is all holiness receives its anointing.**

'Be assured of this, and mark it well: A period of seven
weeks must go by, between the promise to rebuild Jerusalem
and the coming of an anointed prince. Street and wall will be
built again, though in a time of distress; and then sixty-two
weeks must pass before an anointed priest is done to death,
one who was truly innocent. Then the army of an invading
leader will destroy both city and sanctuary, so that its taking
away will mean utter destruction; only a ruin is to be left
when that war is ended. High covenant he shall make, before
another week is done, and with folks a many; but when that
week has run half its course, offering and burnt-sacrifice shall
be none; in the temple all shall be defilement and desolation,
and until all is over, all is fulfilled, that desolation shall continue.'

PSALMS 84; 125; 149

What blessings, Lord, you have granted to this land of
yours, restoring Jacob's fortunes, pardoning your people's
guilt, burying away the record of their sins, all your anger

that the restoration of Jerusalem would be the beginning of Messianic times. The message of the angel Gabriel is meant to clarify this belief: final forgiveness of sin (the redemption of Christ) and the founding of the Church ('all holiness' is a Hebrew way of speaking of the temple) are not close at hand. A long period must yet pass before Messianic times come; this is the meaning of 'seventy weeks,' or seventy times seven (Mt. 18, 22). It seems contrary to Jewish symbolism to interpret it as 490 years till redemption; no New Testament writer does so.

The inspired reviser, who wrote the second paragraph, is not prophesying future events; he is merely writing history into the framework of the symbolical seventy times seven. His viewpoint is that of the final half week, the three and a half years of desecration of the temple and the abolition of Jewish sacrifices (1 Mach. 1, 57—4, 54). The 'invading leader' is Antiochus the Illustrious, the villain of Machabean times, who figures so prominently in the Machabean additions to Daniel.

This second paragraph has a Messianic colouring. The 'anointed prince' is Cyrus, a type of Christ (Is. 45, 1) because he liberated the Jews. 'An anointed priest' is Onias, who was slain in 171 B.C. (2 Mach. 4, 34); he resembled Jesus in his innocence. Our Lord alluded to Daniel's 'abomination of desolation' (Mt. 24, 15) when predicting the desecration of the temple.

DELIVERANCE FROM BONDAGE

A PRAYER FOR COMPLETE RESTORATION. This is Psalm 84, the first of nine psalms with a Messianic colouring which belong to the post-exile period. When the exiles returned to

calmed, your fierce displeasure forgotten! And now, God of our deliverance, do you restore us; no longer let us see your frown. Would you always be indignant with us? Must your resentment smoulder on, age after age? Will you never relent, O God, and give fresh life, to rejoice the spirits of your people? Show us your mercy, Lord, grant us your deliverance!

Let me listen, now, to the voice of the Lord God; it is a message of peace he sends to his people; to his loyal servants, that come back, now, with all their heart to him. **For us, his worshippers, deliverance is close at hand; in this land of ours, the divine glory is to find a home. See, where mercy and faithfulness meet in one; how justice and peace are united in one embrace! Faithfulness grows up out of the earth, and from heaven, redress looks down.** The Lord, now, will grant us his blessing, to make our land yield its harvest; justice will go before him, deliverance follow where his feet tread.

When the Lord gave back to Sion her banished sons, we walked like men in a dream; in every mouth was laughter, joy was on every tongue. Among the heathen themselves it was said, 'What favour the Lord has shown them!' Favour indeed the Lord has shown us, and our hearts are rejoiced.

Deliver us, Lord, from our bondage; our withered hopes, Lord, like some desert water-course renew! The men who are sowing in tears will reap, one day, with joy. Mournful enough they go, but with seed to scatter; trust me, they will come back rejoicing, as they carry their sheaves with them.

Sing the Lord a new song; here, where the faithful gather, let his praise be heard. In him, the maker of Israel, let Israel

Jerusalem in 538 B.C. they were expecting the commencement of Messianic times; instead they met with opposition from the inhabitants of the promised land; the countryside was barren and drought-stricken. In such distress as this they appealed to the Lord to send the long-promised Messiah.

The Incarnation was the fulfilment of their prayer; it was not made known to them that there would be a gap of centuries before this was realized. The divine glory was to find a home on earth when 'the Word was made flesh' (Jn. 1, 14). God's mercy and man's faithfulness, the divine justice from heaven 'and peace on earth to men that are God's friends' (Lk. 2, 14), would meet in perfect union on Christmas Day; from now on the Kingdom of God would be established for the salvation of men. This psalm is used frequently in the liturgy for Advent; it expresses the longing of the world for the coming of the Messiah to inaugurate a new relationship with God.

GOD CAN CHANGE SORROW INTO JOY. When the exile ended and the Israelites came back to their homeland, it seemed such a marvel of divine deliverance that they could hardly credit it; they thought they must be dreaming. Even the heathen peoples stood gaping in wonder at such a manifest intervention of the Lord.

The second paragraph deals with the sad conditions of the first resettlement in Palestine. The chosen people pray for a betterment of their lot; this fulfilment came only in Messianic times. There are two vivid images: that of a dry water-course running with plentiful streams and that of the harvest which comes after sowing.

PRAISE GOD BY WORD AND DEED. It would seem that this psalm (149) was written at the period when Nehemias re-

triumph; for him, the ruler of Sion, let Sion's children keep
holiday; let there be dancing in honour of his name, music
of tambour and of harp, to praise him. **Still the Lord shows
favour to his people, still he relieves the oppressed, and grants
them victory.** In triumph let your faithful servants rejoice, rejoice and take their rest.

Ever on their lips they bear the high praise of God, ever in
their hands they carry two-edged swords, ready to take vengeance upon the heathen, to curb the nations, to chain kings,
and bind princes in fetters of iron. Long since their doom is
written; boast it is of his true servants that doom to execute.
Alleluia.

PSALMS 95; 96; 97; 98

Sing the Lord a new song; in the Lord's honour, let the
whole earth make melody! Sing to the Lord, and bless his
name; never cease to bear record of his power to save. Publish
his glory among the heathen; his wonderful acts for all the
world to hear.

How great is the Lord, how worthy of honour! What other
god is to be feared as he? They are but fancied gods the
heathen call divine; the Lord, not they, made the heavens.
Honour and beauty are his escort; worship and magnificence
the attendants of his shrine.

Tribes of the heathen, make your offering to the Lord, an
offering to the Lord of glory and homage, an offering of glory
to the Lord's name; bring sacrifice, come into his courts, worship the Lord in holy array. Before the Lord's presence let
the whole earth bow in reverence; tell the heathen, 'The Lord

turned from Babylon in 445 B.C. to rebuild the walls of
Jerusalem. The enemies mentioned in the second paragraph
are the hostile forces of Sanballat and Tobias (2 Esd. 4) who
opposed Nehemias. They stand for all hostile forces that rise
up against God and 'the king he has anointed' (Ps. 2, 2). Such
enemies will always remain, so the children of God must be
prepared to do battle; victory will come only with the advent
of Christ.

When the enterprise of Nehemias was completed in fifty-
two days of feverish work (2 Esd. 6, 15), the whole nation in
Jerusalem celebrated it with the customary jubilation of song;
it was a happy holiday with much enthusiastic singing, dancing, and loud music.

THE LORD REIGNS AS KING

KING OF THE UNIVERSE. These four psalms were composed
probably for the inauguration of the second temple, built by
Zorobabel and the high priest Joshua twenty-two years after
the return from exile; they are the conclusion to the first
phase of resettlement in Jerusalem. After much opposition
and many problems, the house of the Lord had risen once
more in the holy city; this was an occasion for all Israel to
celebrate and proclaim to the whole world that the Lord's
power must be recognized universally; he it was who brought
them back from exile, as no heathen god could do; he is
worthy of all praise.

This advent of the Lord in power to his temple was regarded by the Jews as the beginning of a new era in human
affairs; it was the inauguration of the Messianic kingdom.
And so the Church has always interpreted these psalms in

is king now, he has put the world in order, never to be thrown
into confusion more; he gives the nations a just award.'

Rejoice, heaven, and let earth be glad; let the sea, and all
the sea contains, give thunderous applause. The fields, and
all the burden they bear, full of expectancy; no tree in the
forest but will rejoice to greet its Lord's coming. **He comes to
rule the earth; brings the world justice, to every race of men
its promised award.**

**The Lord reigns as king; let earth be glad of it, let the isles,
the many isles, rejoice!** See where he sits, clouds and darkness
about him, justice and right the pillars of his throne; see
where he comes, fire sweeping on before him, burning up his
enemies all around. In the flash of his lightning, how shines
the world revealed, how earth trembles at the sight! **The hills
melt like wax at the presence of the Lord; his presence, whom
all the earth obeys. The very heavens proclaim his faithfulness; no nation but has sight of his glory.** Shame upon the
men that worship carved images, and make their boast of
false gods! him only all the powers of heaven, prostrate, adore.

Glad news for Sion, rejoicing for Juda's townships, when
your judgments, Lord, are made known; are you not sovereign
Lord of earth, beyond measure exalted above all gods? They
are the Lord's friends, who were never friends to wrong; souls
that are true to him he guards ever, rescues them from the
power of evil-doers. **Dawn of hope for the innocent, dawn of
gladness for honest hearts!** Rejoice and triumph, just souls, in
the Lord, of his holy name publish everywhere the renown.

Sing the Lord a new song, a song of wonder at his doings;
how his own right hand, his own holy arm, brought him vic-

her liturgy; in practically every feast of our Lord, phrases are taken from them and applied to Christ the king; from his Nativity in Bethlehem until his death on Calvary he was working at his task of establishing the kingdom of God on earth. The writers of the psalms did not know that the Lord and the Messiah were to be one and the same Being; but the Holy Spirit, author of Sacred Scripture, did. The divinity of our Lord is the clue to understanding these psalms.

A POWERFUL KING. The mightiest and most awe-inspiring intervention of the Lord in the whole history of Israel was his appearing on mount Sinai, during the Exodus from Egypt under Moses. All the terrifying elements of a thunderstorm (darkness, thunder, and lightning) accompanied that great Theophany (showing of God), when his majesty and power were manifested to the chosen people (Ex. 19, 16-18). This is the imagery on which the psalmist here bases his picture of a new enthronement of the Lord over all his enemies and the heathen gods.

Historically it refers to the reign of the Lord on the return of the Jews to Palestine after the Babylonian exile. But that was only a dim foreshadowing of the Day of the Lord when the Second Person of the Trinity would make known his saving power by becoming Incarnate; he would then deliver his friends, bringing a new dawn of hope and gladness to those waiting for his coming. This deliverance came when Jesus was enthroned on the cross; that was the defeat of all his enemies. It is used most fittingly by the Church on feasts of his majesty, such as the Epiphany, Transfiguration, and Ascension.

A VICTORIOUS KING. The return from Babylon was proof that the Lord had the power to save his people; it was time

tory. The Lord has given proof of his saving power, has vindicated his just dealings, for all the nations to see; has remembered his gracious promise, and kept faith with the house of Israel; no corner of the world but has witnessed how our God can save.

In God's honour let all the earth keep holiday; let all be mirth and rejoicing and festal melody! Praise the Lord with the harp, with harp and psaltery's music; with trumpets of metal, and the music of the braying horn! Keep holiday in the presence of the Lord, our King; the sea astir, and all that the sea holds, the world astir, and all that dwell on it; the rivers echoing their applause, the hills, too, rejoicing to see the Lord come. **He comes to judge the earth; brings the world justice, to every race of men its due award.**

The Lord is king, the nations are adread; he is throned above the Cherubim, and earth trembles before him. **Great is the Lord who dwells in Sion, sovereign ruler of all peoples!** Let them all praise that great name of yours, a name terrible and holy. He reigns in might, that right loves, to all assuring redress, giving the sons of Jacob doom and award. Praise, then, the Lord our God, and bow down before his footstool; that, too, is holy.

Remember Moses and Aaron, and all those priests of his, Samuel and those others who called on his name, how the Lord listened when they called upon him. His voice came to them from the pillar of cloud; so it was they heard the decrees, the command he gave them. And you, O Lord our God, listened to them, and they found you a God of pardon; yet every fault of theirs you were quick to punish. **Praise the Lord our God, and do worship on the holy mountain where he dwells; the Lord our God is holy.**

to compose a new song of rejoicing at victory, to replace the old song of the first great deliverance from Egypt under Moses. It was a tumultuous welcome for the coming of the King in victory to Jerusalem. In all oriental displays music played a big part; the joyful Jews would make such a noise that all the world would hear it. Even inanimate nature, the noise of waves, of running torrents, of wind roaring in the trees on the hillside, would join in melody to the Lord.

When our Lord did come triumphantly into Jerusalem on Palm Sunday, seated on the back of a donkey, such a welcome was given him by the Jewish pilgrims assembled on mount Olivet (Mt. 21, 9). When he was asked to restrain his disciples, he answered: 'If they should keep silence, the stones will cry out instead' (Lk. 19, 40).

A HOLY KING. The atmosphere of this psalm is entirely different from that of the preceding; no longer the joyous welcome to a victorious king, but respect, fear, and worship of the Lord most holy. The psalmist's mind is on the temple just rebuilt in Jerusalem; this was the dwelling-place of God among his people. The Jews pictured the Lord seated over the Cherubim in the Holy of Holies; the ark of the covenant there was the footstool under his feet. He is a holy king to be feared; he dispenses justice to Israel and all the nations of the world.

When the angel Gabriel appeared to Mary at Nazareth, he announced the holiness of her son: 'Thus this HOLY offspring of yours shall be known for the Son of God' (Lk. 1, 35). St. Paul says: 'That is why God has raised him to such a height, given him that name which is greater than any other name' (Phil. 2, 9). This refers to the holy name of Jesus, a name to be loved, not feared.

PSALMS 116; 117

Praise the Lord, all you Gentiles, let all the nations of the world do him honour. Abundant has his mercy been towards us; the Lord remains faithful to his word for ever.

Give thanks to the Lord; the Lord is gracious, his mercy endures for ever. Echo the cry, sons of Israel; the Lord is gracious, his mercy endures for ever. His mercy endures for ever, echo the cry, sons of Aaron; his mercy endures for ever; echo the cry, all you who are the Lord's worshippers.

I called on the Lord when trouble beset me, and the Lord listened, and brought me relief. With the Lord at my side, I have no fear of the worst man can do; with the Lord at my side to aid me, I shall yet see my enemies baffled. Better trust the Lord than rely on the help of man; better trust the Lord than rely on the word of princes. Let all heathendom ring me round, see, in the power of the Lord I crush them! They cut me off from every way of escape, but see, in the power of the Lord I crush them! They swarm about me like bees, their fury blazes up like fire among thorns, but see, in the power of the Lord, I crush them! I reeled under the blow, and had well-nigh fallen, but still the Lord was there to aid me. Who but the Lord is my protector, my stronghold; who but the Lord has brought me deliverance?

The homes of the just echo, now, with glad cries of victory; the power of the Lord has triumphed. The power of the Lord has brought me to great honour, the power of the Lord has triumphed. I am reprieved from death, to live on and proclaim what the Lord has done for me. The Lord has chastened me indeed, but he would not doom me to die.

Open me the gates where right dwells; let me go in and

CHRIST THE CORNER-STONE

GENTILES AND JEWS PRAISE THE LORD. The first paragraph is Psalm 116, the shortest in the psalter, a mere four lines. It is familiar to us as the psalm sung at Benediction. St. Paul says it was fulfilled when the Gentiles entered the Church (Rom. 15, 11); both Jews and Gentiles can now sing the one song of praise to the Lord, being united in Christ, the corner-stone that binds the two walls of the building together.

The remaining five paragraphs all belong to Psalm 117. It was probably composed for the feast of Tabernacles in 445 B.C. to celebrate the completion of the building of the walls of Jerusalem by Nehemias (2 Esd. 8, 13-18). The psalm develops through a vivid description of victory over fierce enemies, followed by a procession of thanksgiving to the temple. It is the mention of 'a screen of boughs' that is the main evidence for identification with the feast of Tabernacles, when branches of trees were used to make huts in memory of the wandering life in the wilderness during the Exodus.

The psalmist writes in the first person; but this is merely a literary device to make the narrative more vivid. It is almost certainly the nation of Israel that is being described. The difficult times during the building of the city walls of Jerusalem fit in quite well with the situation pictured in the psalm; the neighbouring peoples, under the leadership of Sanballat and Tobias, made open war on the wall-builders, who worked with one hand and held a sword with the other (2 Esd. 4, 17).

Continuing the imagery from building a wall, the psalmist likens the Jewish nation to 'the chief stone at the corner.' This was the binding-stone at the angle of the walls that gave solidity to the structure: Israel, despised and rejected by the

thank the Lord! Here is the gate that leads to the Lord's presence; here shall just souls find entry. Thanks be to you, Lord, for giving me audience, thanks be to you, my deliverer. **The very stone which the builders rejected has become the chief stone at the corner; this is the Lord's doing, and it is marvellous in our eyes.** This day is a holiday of the Lord's own choosing; greet this day with rejoicing, greet this day with triumph!

Deliverance, Lord, deliverance; Lord grant us days of prosperity! **Blessed is he who comes in the name of the Lord!** A blessing from the Lord's house upon your company! The Lord is God; his light shines out to welcome us; marshal the procession aright, with a screen of boughs that reaches to the very horns of the altar. You are my God, mine to thank you, you are my God, mine to extol you. Give thanks to the Lord; the Lord is gracious, his mercy endures for ever.

PSALM 129

Out of the depths I cry to you, O Lord; Master, listen to my voice; let but your ears be attentive to the voice that calls on you for pardon.

If you, Lord, will keep record of our iniquities, Master, who has strength to bear it? Ah, but with you there is forgiveness; be your name ever revered.

I wait for the Lord, for his word of promise my soul waits; patient my soul waits, as ever watchman that looked for the day.

Patient as watchman at dawn, for the Lord Israel waits, the Lord with whom there is mercy, with whom is abundant power to ransom. **He it is that will ransom Israel from all their iniquities.**

pagan nations opposing the building, will become the key-stone in God's plan for the unity of all the nations of the world. This will take place only in Messianic times. The Holy Spirit is thinking of the place of the Church in the divine plan; and what is said of the Mystical Body can be said in a more perfect manner of the Head, Christ our Lord. That is why Jesus quotes this text of himself, in the parable of the Unfaithful Vine-dressers (Mt. 21, 42), and St. Peter also quotes it as fulfilled in our Saviour, Jesus Christ (1 Pet. 2, 7).

The contrast is between the Passion and the Resurrection of our Lord; the Jewish nation rejected him and put him to death, but he triumphed on Easter Sunday. This was a day of rejoicing in the heavenly court, 'a holiday of the Lord's own choosing.' The Death and Resurrection of Jesus was the true deliverance of Israel and all the Gentiles. For this reason the Church gives thanks to Almighty God, because 'his mercy endures for ever.'

FORGIVENESS OF SINS

A Prayer for Pardon.   From the fall of Adam to the Baby-lonian exile, the history of man is full of his sinfulness. God's chosen people were continually rebuked by the prophets for their abandonment of God. This psalm expresses the Hebrew consciousness that they were all sinners in need of God's pardon. Forgiveness would come to them only through the re-demption of Christ.

Israel is pictured as a watchman on the city walls, with eyes searching the eastern sky for the first sign of dawn. It is the same image Simeon used when describing his wait for the Messiah to come to his temple (Lk. 1, 29-31). This psalm is called the De Profundis, and is used by the Church as a prayer for the souls in purgatory.

PROVERBS 8, SIRACH 24, WISDOM 7

And, all the while, the wisdom that grants discernment is crying aloud, is never silent; there she stands, on some high vantage-point by the public way, where the roads meet, or at the city's approach, close beside the gates, making proclamation. To every man, high and low, her voice calls: 'The Lord made me his when first he went about his work, at the birth of time, before his creation began. Long, long ago, before earth was fashioned, I held my course. Already I lay in the womb, when the depths were not yet in being, when no springs of water had yet broken; when I was born, the mountains had not yet sunk on their firm foundations, and there were no hills; not yet had he made the earth, or the rivers, or the solid framework of the world.

'I was there when he built the heavens, when he fenced in the waters with a vault inviolable, when he fixed the sky overhead, and levelled the fountain-springs of the deep. I was there when he enclosed the sea within its confines, forbidding the waters to transgress their assigned limits, when he poised the foundations of the world. I was at his side, a masterworkman, my delight increasing with each day, as I made play before him all the while; made play in this world of dust, with the sons of Adam for my playfellows.

'Listen to me, then, you that are my sons, that follow, to your happiness, in the paths I show you; listen to the teaching that will make you wise, instead of turning away from it. Blessed are they who listen to me, keep vigil, day by day, at my threshold, watching till I open my doors. The man who

CHRIST THE WISDOM OF GOD

Wisdom, the Master-workman at Creation. It was not
revealed to the people of Old Testament times that there
were three persons in God. When the angel Gabriel appeared
to the virgin Mary at Nazareth, he brought the first message
to human ears that God is Father, Son, and Holy Spirit. The
final preparation for this revelation of the Blessed Trinity is
found in the doctrine of Wisdom personified, chiefly in these
three passages from the wisdom literature of post-exilic Judaism.

The first selection is from Proverbs 8, 22-36. Wisdom is
presented as a prophet proclaiming her (wisdom is a feminine
noun) teaching publicly. Genesis 1 and Psalm 103 relate the
creation of the world from the point of view of man; Proverbs
8 tells the same story from God's viewpoint. God manifested
his wisdom in the creation of an orderly universe. Wisdom is
presented as the intelligence of God personified, assisting him
in planning and carrying out the works of creation, the
'master workman' executing the divine decrees. And that is
how St. John sums up the work of the Second Person of the
Trinity: 'It was through him that all things came into being,
and without him came nothing that has come to be' (Jn.
1, 3).

By presenting wisdom as present with God before creation
began, Proverbs implies its divine origin. Sirach is even more
explicit: 'All wisdom has one source; it dwelt with the Lord
God before ever time began' (Ecclus. 1, 1). This is how St.
John opens his Gospel: 'At the beginning of time the Word
already was' (Jn. 1, 1).

Man is the crown of God's creation; so wisdom is mainly

wins me, wins life, drinks deep of the Lord's favour; who fails, fails at his own bitter cost; to be my enemy is to be in love with death.'

Hear now how wisdom speaks in her own regard, of the boast she utters among the nation that is hers. In the court of the most High, in the presence of all his host, she makes her boast aloud: '**I am that word that was uttered by the mouth of the most High;** it was I that covered, as with a mist, the earth. In high heaven was my dwelling-place, my throne a pillar of cloud; none but I might span the sky's vault, pierce the depth of the abyss, walk on the sea's waves; no part of earth but gave a resting-place to my feet.

'People was none, nor any race of men, but I had dominion there. Yet with all these I sought rest in vain; it is among the Lord's people that I mean to dwell. **He who fashioned me, he, my own Creator, has found me a dwelling-place; and his command to me was that I should find my home in Jacob, throw in my lot with Israel, take root among his chosen race. From the beginning of time, before the worlds, he had made me, unfailing to all eternity; in his own holy dwelling-place I had waited on his presence; and now, no less faithfully, I made Sion my stronghold, the holy city my resting-place, Jerusalem my throne.** My roots spread out among the people that enjoys his favour, my God has granted me a share in his own domain.

'I grew to my full stature as cedar grows on Lebanon, as cypress on mount Hermon; or a palm tree in Engaddi, or a rose bush in Jericho; grew like some fair olive in the valley, some plane-tree in a well-watered street. Cinnamon and odorous balm have no scent like mine; the choicest myrrh has no such fragrance. Perfumed is all my dwelling-place with

concerned with human relations. In the final paragraph, Proverbs shows that obedience to wisdom's teaching will bring man life eternal with God.

WISDOM INCARNATE IN THE MOSAIC LAW. One of the most famous professors of the rabbinical school at Jerusalem was Jesus ben Sirach. Shortly after 200 B.C. he wrote down under divine inspiration the notes of his lectures delivered to the young men of Israel over the years of a long life. Because of its use by the Church, particularly in the instruction of converts, this work became known as Ecclesiasticus, the Church Book. The chapter here treated is 24, which was written in praise of wisdom.

Sirach begins with wisdom in heaven with God, and assisting him in the work of creation, as in Proverbs 8. Wisdom has universal dominion over all creation; it is pictured as roaming the world, looking for a place to reside permanently among men. God himself selects the people among whom his wisdom is to make its dwelling-place; the chosen nation in Israel. This coming of wisdom from heaven to earth took place at mount Sinai, in the thirteenth century B.C. during the course of the Exodus of the Jews under Moses from the bondage of Egypt.

Sirach himself, in the final paragraph of chapter 24, tells in what form the wisdom of God came down on earth in the Old Testament: it was the law of Moses, that 'life-giving book that is the covenant of the most High.' Basically the Law was the ten commandments, the codification of the rules by which Israel was to live: 'You will live on in my love, if you keep my commandments, just as it is by keeping my Father's commandments that I live on in his love' (Jn. 15, 10).

Acting on a divine command, the Israelites built a tent

galbanum, and onycha, and stacte, like the odour of incense in the holy place. Mastic-tree spread not its branches so wide, as I the hopes I proffer of glory and of grace. No vine ever yielded fruit so fragrant; the enjoyment of honour and riches is the fruit I bear.

'Hither turn your steps, all you that have learned to long for me; take your fill of the increase I yield. Never was honey so sweet as the influence I inspire, never honey-comb as the gift I bring. Eat of this fruit, and you will yet hunger for more; drink of this wine, and your thirst for it is still unquenched. **He who listens to me will never be disappointed; he who lives by me will do no wrong.**'

What things are these I write of? What but the life-giving book that is the covenant of the most High? What but the law Moses enjoined, as an inheritance to the community of Jacob? What but this can make wisdom flow, deep as the stream Phison sends down, or Tigris, in the spring; make the tide of prudence run, strong as Euphrates' own, or Jordan's tide in the month of harvest; make obedience rise to its full height, like Nile or Gehon when men gather the vintage? The first man never finished comprehending wisdom, nor will the last succeed in fathoming her; so deep are her thoughts, sea-deep, so dark her counsels, dark as the great abyss.

What wisdom is, whence came its birth, I will now make known to you. All the mysteries and all the surprises of nature were made known to me; wisdom herself taught me, that is the designer of them all.

Mind-enlightening is the influence that dwells in her; set high apart; one in its source, yet manifold in its operation;

(the tabernacle of the wilderness) to house the tablets of the law, placed inside the ark of the covenant. This was the dwelling-place of wisdom in the midst of the chosen people of God. In the course of time, the Israelites settled in the promised land of Palestine and built a permanent home for the Ark in Jerusalem; this was called the temple. It was Solomon who constructed it, three hundred years after the law was first given at Sinai. From then on Sion (Jerusalem) was wisdom's home.

Wisdom brings supernatural life to man. This is presented by Sirach under the imagery of the Garden of Eden with its trees, perfumes, and abundant rivers of water. All this fertility is a symbol of the life-giving grace that wisdom supplies to those who seek her. 'Come to me, all you that labour and are burdened; I will give you rest' is our Lord's invitation (Mt. 11, 28).

The prophet Baruch alludes to wisdom incarnate in the Mosaic law in a passage that surely foreshadows the Incarnation of the Second Person of the Trinity: 'Not till then would he reveal himself on earth, and hold converse with mortal men' (Bar. 3, 38). And Sirach's message in chapter 24 is understood in the same way; it surely prefigures the coming of Jesus Christ, the Wisdom of the Father, to take up his dwelling on earth: 'And the Word was made flesh, and came to dwell among us' (Jn. 1, 14).

WISDOM IS SIMPLE AND LIKE GOD. This is 7, 22—8, 1 of the Book of Wisdom, the most precise statement of wisdom's relation to God to be found in Scripture.

The author lived about 100 B.C. at Alexandria in Egypt. It was one of the great university cities of Greek thought and culture; many of the Jews living there came under the

subtle, yet easily understood. An influence quick in move-
ment, inviolable, persuasive, gentle, right-thinking, keen-
edged, irresistible, beneficent, kindly, gracious, steadfast, proof
against all error and all solicitude. Nothing is beyond its
power, nothing hidden from its view, and such capacity has
it that it can pervade the minds of all living men; so pure and
subtle an essence is thought. Nothing so agile that it can
match wisdom for agility; nothing can penetrate this way and
that, etherial as she.

**Steam that ascends from the fervour of divine activity, pure
effluence of his glory who is God all-powerful, she feels no
passing taint; she, the glow that radiates from eternal light,
she, the untarnished mirror of God's majesty, she, the faithful
image of his goodness.**

Alone, with none to aid her, she is all-powerful; herself ever
unchanged, she makes all things new; age after age she finds
her way into holy men's hearts, turning them into friends and
spokesmen of God. Her familiars it is, and none other, that
God loves.

Brightness is hers beyond the brightness of the sun, and all
the starry host; match her with light itself, and she outvies it;
light must still alternate with darkness, but where is the conspiracy can pull down wisdom from her throne? Bold is her
sweep from world's end to world's end, and everywhere her
gracious ordering manifests itself.

WISDOM 2, 1, 10-20; 4, 20-25, 5

Reason the wicked offer, yet reason all amiss: 'Helpless innocence,' they say, 'shall lie at our mercy; might shall be our
right, weakness count for proof of worthlessness. Where is he,

influence of Greek ideas. Our author begins by listing twenty-one qualities of wisdom; they emphasize the immaterial, spiritual nature of wisdom. Wisdom is in the category of spiritual beings; freed from dependence on matter, wisdom is more efficient and powerful in operation. It is a gift of God: 'Your purpose none may know, unless you grant your gift of wisdom, sending out from high heaven your own holy spirit' (Wis. 9, 17).

Five illustrations deal with the likeness of wisdom to God. 'Steam' is the vapour caused by heat, by the fire of divine love; 'effluence' is an image from water, the clear, undefiled stream that flows out from divine omnipotence; 'glow' is an effect of light, a radiation from eternity; 'mirror' is the perfect reflection of divine majesty; 'image' is from a picture or a statue, the likeness of the divine goodness in created things.

St. Paul begins the Epistle to the Hebrews by proving the divinity of our Lord; the two expressions he uses are taken from this passage of the Book of Wisdom: 'A Son, who is the radiance of his Father's splendour, and the full expression of his being' (Heb. 1, 3). Even in the full light of New Testament revelation, Paul still uses the terminology of the Book of Wisdom: 'He is the true likeness of the God we cannot see' (Col. 1, 15).

CHRIST'S PASSION AND DEATH

THE WICKED ATTACK THE JUST MAN.   Good and evil are opposed to each other as light to darkness. That is how St. John presents the coming of our Lord into the world: 'When the

the just man? We must plot to be rid of him; he will not lend himself to our purposes. Ever he must be thwarting our plans; transgress we the law, he is all reproof, depart we from the traditions of our race, he denounces us. **What, would he claim knowledge of divine secrets, give himself out as the son of God?** The touchstone, he, of our inmost thoughts; we cannot bear the very sight of him, his life so different from other men's, the path he takes, so far removed from theirs! No better than false coin he counts us, holds aloof from our doings as though they would defile him; envies the just their future happiness, boasts of a divine parentage.

'Put we his claims, then, to the proof; let experience show what his lot shall be, what end awaits him. **If to be just is to be God's son indeed, then God will take up his cause, will save him from the power of his enemies.** Outrage and torment, let these be the tests we use; let us see that gentleness of his in its true colours, find out what his patience is worth. **Sentenced let him be to a shameful death; by his own way of it, he shall find deliverance.'**

Alas, the long tally of their sins! Trembling they shall come forward, and the record of their misdeeds shall rise up to confront them. How boldly, then, will the just man appear, to meet his old persecutors, that thwarted all his striving! And they, in what craven fear they will cower at the sight of him, amazed at the sudden reversal of his fortunes! Inward remorse will wring a groan from those hearts: **'Why, this is the man we made into a laughing-stock and a by-word! We, poor fools, mistook the life he lived for madness, his death for ignominy; and now he is reckoned as God's own son, now it is among the holy ones that his lot is cast.'**

light came into the world, men preferred darkness to light; preferred it, because their doings were evil. Anyone who acts shamefully hates the light, will not come into the light, for fear that his doings will be found out' (Jn. 3, 19-20). This principle is valid for any just man; his conduct is a standing reproach to all men of evil lives; they are so filled with hatred towards him that they will go to any length, even fiercest persecution and death, to destroy him.

The situation visualized by the author of the Book of Wisdom is the fate of any just man who lives according to the law of God. Religious pogroms were not uncommon in Alexandria, where he wrote about 100 B.C. Degenerate pagans and faithless Jews joined forces in opposing those true Israelites intent on observing the divine law in their pagan surroundings. A consideration of these facts, with the help of divine revelation, led the author to the belief that God would reward the just by eternal life and punish the wicked with damnation for ever (Wis. 2, 23; 5, 16-17). It is only in the second century B.C. that reward and punishment in the next life are presented in clear, explicit terms in the Old Testament.

In describing this conflict, the Book of Wisdom uses terminology that seems to be far in advance of the times in which it was written. The fate of the just man is described in words reminiscent of Psalm 21 and Isaias 53. The Holy Spirit, the primary author of Sacred Scripture, probably intended to portray Christ's death under the figure of the just man, seeing that our Lord was the just man par excellence. The taunts of the Jews against Christ on the cross seem to be taken from this passage: 'He trusted in God; let God, if he favours him, succour him now; he told us, "I am the Son of God"' (Mt. 27, 43).

2 MACHABEES 7, 1, 7-19

Seven brothers there were, that lay under arrest, and their mother with them; these too were tortured at the king's command, to see if whip and thong would not make them eat swine's flesh, for all their scruples.

When the hair was torn from the head of the second brother and the skin with it, they asked, 'Would he eat, or must his whole body pay for it, limb by limb?' And he answered, eat he would not; whereupon he, in his turn, suffered like the first. 'Ay, miscreant,' he said with his last breath, 'of this present life it lies in your power to rob us; **but he, who is ruler of the whole world, he, for whose laws we perish, will raise us up again, and to life everlasting.'**

And now they had their will with the third, who was no sooner bidden than he put forth tongue and hands very courageously: 'Heaven's gift these be,' he said, 'and for God's law **I make light account of them, well assured he will give them back to me.'** Well might they marvel, king and courtiers both, at one so young that recked so little of his sufferings. Such was the manner of his passing; the fourth, too, when with like tortures they assailed him, died with these words on his lips: **'Man's sentence of death, what matters it, so there be hope in God, that shall raise up the dead? For you, resurrection to new life shall be none.'**

And when the fifth was put to the question, he looked Antiochus in the face, thus warning him: 'Mortal, at your own whim free to govern your fellow men, think not God has abandoned this race of ours! Wait but a little, and good proof you shall have of his sovereign power, such torments you and yours awaits.' So they came to the sixth, and this was his

RESURRECTION OF THE BODY

THE MARTYRDOM OF THE SEVEN BROTHERS.   It is surprising
how often St. Paul in his Epistles speaks of the resurrection
of the body. For him it is the final completion of Christ's
redemption; not till our bodies are glorified on the last day
will the full effects of Calvary be realized. St. Paul makes it
clear, in the classic passage on resurrection (1 Cor. 15), that
we shall rise only because Christ has won this right for us:
'Christ has risen from the dead, the first-fruits of all those who
have fallen asleep; a man has brought us death, and a man
should bring us resurrection from the dead' (1 Cor. 15, 20-
21).

The doctrine of our Lord's own personal resurrection appears in the Old Testament as early as king David, in Psalm
15, 10. But the revelation that those redeemed by him will
also share in his bodily resurrection is not made until the
time of the Machabean revolution in the middle of the second century B.C. At the same time the Jews first began to
look to life after death as the final place where all wrongs
would be righted: 'Many shall wake, that now lie sleeping in
the dust of earth, some to enjoy life everlasting, some to be
confronted for ever with their disgrace' (Dan. 12, 2).

Antiochus IV, the Illustrious, reigned in Antioch of
Syria from 175 to 164 B.C. During his ten years' reign he
tried to impose Greek culture and religion on the Jewish
nation to the south. He had a simple test to find out whether
his subjects were following his orders: he demanded that they
publicly eat pork, which was expressly forbidden by the
Mosaic law (Lev. 11, 7). Among those so tested were seven
brothers and their mother; they all refused to abandon their

dying utterance: 'Never flatter yourself with vain hope; speed we amiss, it was our own doing, that sinned against our God. Strange be his dealings with us, yet think not you to defy God unpunished.'

2 MACHABEES 12, 38-46

And now, recalling his men from the pursuit, he made his way to the city of Odollam; the week had gone round, and here, duly cleansed from defilement, they kept the sabbath. Next day, with Judas at their head, they went back to recover the bodies of the slain, for burial among their own folk in their fathers' graves; and what found they? Each of the fallen was wearing, under his shirt, some token carried away from the false gods of Jamnia. Here was defiance of the Jewish law, and none doubted it was the cause of their undoing; none but praised the Lord for his just retribution, that had brought hidden things to light; and so they fell to prayer, pleading that the sin might go unremembered. Judas himself, their gallant commander, gave public warning to his men, of fault they should evermore keep clear, with the fate of these transgressors under their eyes.

Then he would have contribution made; a sum of two thousand silver pieces he levied, and sent it to Jerusalem, to have sacrifice made there for the guilt of their dead companions. Was not this well done and piously? **Here was a man kept the resurrection ever in mind; he had done fondly and foolishly indeed, to pray for the dead, if these might rise no more, that once were fallen!** And these had made a godly end; could he doubt, a rich recompense awaited them? **A holy and wholesome thought it is to pray for the dead, for their guilt's undoing.**

ancestral law and died martyrs for the faith. The words of
the second, third, and fourth brothers express explicit belief
in the resurrection of the body. The remainder of the chapter
is a touching story of the fate of the youngest brother and the
mother.

PRAYERS FOR THE DEAD

THE FALLEN OF JUDAS' ARMY. The amulets found on the
soldiers killed in battle had been worn in express violation of
the Lord's command: 'All their images you shall commit to
the flames, with no eye for the gold and silver they are made
of; keep nothing for yourself, or it will lead you into sin'
(Deut. 7, 25). But, seeing they were fighting for God in the
Machabean war of liberation, it is clear that they had not
thrown off their allegiance to the Lord. Their superstitious
wearing of the amulets is what we could now call a venial
sin; it did not condemn the wearers to hell but to a state we
now call purgatory. This text is the classic proof in the Old
Testament of the Jewish belief in the existence of such a
place.

The Jews did not clearly distinguish the First and the Second Coming of Christ. The resurrection of the body was pre-
sumed as an essential condition of existence for the members
of the kingdom established by the Messiah. When the good
thief made the request of Jesus on the cross, 'Remember me
when you come back in the glory of your kingdom,' he was
thinking of life on earth in a resurrected body. The basis for
this way of thought was philosophical: the Jewish mind could
not comprehend the existence of a spiritual soul apart from
the body. The inert, shadowy existence in Sheol (the abode
of the dead) could not really be called life; to live completely
a man must have his body united to his soul.

CONTENTS: Chapter 6

GEN. 3	Adam, the Representative Man	263
GEN. 6–7	Noah's Ark: Baptism and the Church	263
GEN. 14, 18-20	Melchisedech: A Priest Forever	263
GEN. 22	Isaac: The Wood of the Cross	264
GEN. 27	Jacob: The Sins of Others	265
GEN. 41	Joseph: Saviour of the World	265
EX. 13–14	Moses: from Bondage to Freedom	265
EX. 12	The Paschal Lamb: Redemptive Blood	265
EX. 14	The Red Sea: Sacrament of Baptism	266
GEN. 17	Circumcision: Sacrament of Baptism	266
EX. 16	Manna: The Blessed Eucharist	266
EX. 17, 6	Water from Rock: Sanctifying Grace	266
LEV. 16	The Scapegoat: Vicarious Expiation	267
NUM. 19	The Red Heifer: the Blood of Christ	267
NUM. 21, 4-9	Bronze Serpent: the Crucifixion	267
OS. 11, 1	Exodus: Christ's Return from Egypt	267
PS. 94	Palestine: Eternal Rest in Christ	267
JOSH. 3	Joshua: Entry into the Promised Land	268
JG. 7	Gedeon: Victory with a Small Army	268
JG. 13–16	Samson: Victory by his Death	268
2 KG. 16–17	David: betrayed by a Close Friend	268
3 KG. 3	Solomon: Glory and Wisdom	268
3 KG. 17–4 KG. 2	Elias: Persecution and Mental Anguish	269
JON. 2, 1	Jonah: Three Days and Three Nights	269
JER. 11, 19	Jeremias: The Suffering Messiah	269
JOB 16, 7-9	Job: Intense Mental Anguish	271

Is. 45, 1   Cyrus: Return from Exile   272
Ag. 2, 24   Zorobabel: King with Divine Authority   272
Zach. 6, 9-14   Joshua: High Priest and King   272
Dan. 9, 26   Onias: Death of Innocent Priest   265

6. Types of Christ

THIS chapter deals with a unique phenomenon; it is found as a distinct pattern only in the Bible, not in any other literature. Many incidents (thirty are listed here) in the Old Testament have a double meaning; the obvious meaning of the words in their original setting is called the literal sense; yet sometimes the actions or persons there described have a further meaning to be realized later in Christ; this second meaning is what is known as the typical sense.

There are two reasons why this does occur in the Bible. The Old Testament was a preparation for the New; in the preparatory stage God wished to give glimpses of what was to come. It is as though Calvary, the central fact of God's plan for mankind, cast a shadow back over the whole Old Testament. A second unique fact about every book in the Bible is that each has two authors: God, the primary Author, and the actual man who wrote it under inspiration. The human author and his Old Testament readers need not fully comprehend all that God intended to be understood in these types; that would come only with the fulness of New Testament revelation.

How can we be certain that God meant these Old Testament incidents to be types of Christ? The only answer to this is revelation: God himself must tell us. For more than half of the thirty types we have a passage in the New Testament telling us that they are types of Christ. For the rest we rely on the authority of the Church to interpret Scripture; we are aware of the Church's teaching in this matter chiefly through the writings of the early Fathers and through the liturgy (missal and breviary). At times it is not easy to tell whether the passage in question is merely a parallel to something in our Lord's life or whether God intended it to be an actual type.

These types are found throughout the Old Testament, but most abundantly during the Exodus (twelve types). They are listed in biblical order in the Index. At the end of this chapter there is a summary of our Lady's place in the Old Testament with a list of types (ten) of her.

ADAM is the first type of Christ. Both were representative men; each in his own way represents the whole race. Adam brought death to the human race (Gen. 3), Christ healed the breach between the human race and God: 'Mankind begins with the Adam who became, as Scripture tells us, a living soul; it is fulfilled in the Adam who has become a life-giving spirit' (1 Cor. 15, 45). The classic contrast between Adam and Christ is Romans 5, 12-21; there St. Paul explicitly states that 'Adam was the type of him who was to come' (Rom. 5, 14).

NOAH'S ARK was the means used by God to save a family from destruction (Gen. 6-7). St. Peter says: 'That ark in which a few souls, eight in all, found refuge as they passed through the waves, was a type of the baptism which saves us now' (1 Pet. 3, 20). Christian baptism signifies passing through the waters of death; it is the plank by which men are carried to salvation (Wis. 14, 7). Many of the Fathers also see in Noah's Ark a type of the Church, by which men are saved from the waters of destruction.

As Abraham was returning from a victorious battle to his home in Hebron, he passed through Jerusalem; nearby he was met by the king of that city, MELCHISEDECH: 'And he, priest as he was of the most high God, brought out bread and wine with him, and gave him this benediction, "On Abram be the blessing of the most high God, maker of heaven and earth, and blessed be that most high God, whose protection has brought your enemies into your power." To him, Abram gave tithes of all he had won' (Gen. 14, 18-20). David is the first to link up Melchisedech with the person of Christ: 'You are a priest forever in the line of Melchisedech' (Ps. 109, 4). St. Paul, in the Epistle to the Hebrews, demonstrates how Melchisedech is a type of Christ: Jewish priests received their priesthood by descent; their power to offer sacrifice came from their genealogy. Melchisedech stands alone, like Jesus; his priesthood is directly from God (Heb. 7). Patristic writers liken Melchisedech to Christ in that both offered bread and wine, not sheep and oxen, as the material of their sacrifice to God.

ISAAC was mocked by his half-brother Ishmael (Gen. 21, 9). St. Paul sees in this a foretelling of the persecution that is to afflict the Church, 'the son whose birth is a spiritual birth' (Gal. 4, 29). Probably he means this only as an illustration, not as a true type intended by God. But the Fathers see in another incident of Isaac's life a foreshadowing of Christ carrying his cross to Calvary. This is Genesis 22, where Isaac carried the wood of sacrifice up the hill of Jerusalem (p. 15).

Readers of the breviary are familiar with St. Augustine's attempt to explain Jacob's deception of his father Isaac by pretending to be his brother Esau (Gen. 27). According to Augustine (Second Sunday of Lent) JACOB, also called Israel, was a type of Christ: the goatskin in which he dressed himself represents sin, not his own but the sins of others (it was our sins Christ bore, Isaias 53, 4). There is no certain proof that God intended Jacob to be a type of Christ; it seems more

likely that it is only an ingenious explanation thought up by
St. Augustine.

There is a close parallel between the life of JOSEPH, the
favourite son of Jacob, and that of Jesus. Joseph was sold by
his brothers out of hatred (Gen. 37), yet he eventually was
to become the saviour of his people. In Egypt he was imprisoned on a false accusation, but rose to great eminence
and became known as 'Saviour of the World' (Gen. 41). But
again there is no certain evidence that God wished to foreshadow the life of the Messiah in these incidents of the life
of the patriarch Joseph.

MOSES gave up his life at Pharaoh's court to share the sufferings of his own people, the Hebrews. St. Paul sees in this
a foreshadowing of Christ giving up the glories of heaven
to redeem mankind (Heb. 11, 26). There is an obvious parallel between Moses and Christ in that both led their people
from bondage to the freedom of the promised land (Heb. 3-
4). Both inaugurated covenants with the chosen people of
God (Mt. 26, 28; Heb. 9, 12–22), though the New Covenant
far surpassed the Old: 'Through Moses the law was given to
us; through Jesus Christ grace came to us, and truth' (Jn. 1,
17).

Many incidents from the Exodus under Moses had a typical
sense in the mind of the Holy Spirit. When the prophet Osee
later referred to the Exodus in the words, 'I called my son
out of Egypt' (Os. 11, 1), St. Matthew sees, in the call of
the chosen people from exile, the return of Jesus from Egypt
after his flight there from Herod (Mt. 2, 15).

The PASCHAL LAMB (Ex. 12) is the best known type of
Christ in the Old Testament (p. 19). St. John the Baptist is
probably referring to it when he points out Jesus to his disciples with the words, 'Look, this is the Lamb of God' (Jn. 1,

29). St. John the Evangelist concludes his account of the crucifixion, in which not a bone of Jesus' body was broken, with a reference to it: 'Not a single bone of his shall be broken' (Jn. 19, 36).

St. Paul sees in the PILLAR OF CLOUD (Shekinah), and the passage of the RED SEA (Ex. 14), a type of baptism: 'Our fathers were hidden, all of them, under the cloud, and found a path, all of them, through the sea; all alike, in the cloud and in the sea, were baptized into Moses' fellowship' (1 Cor. 10, 1-2). Moved and guided by God (the Shekinah), men must cross from the bondage of sin to the kingdom of Christ through the waters of baptism (Ex. 14). The rite of initiation into the chosen people, CIRCUMCISION (Gen. 17), was also a type of baptism. (It is the opinion of St. Thomas Aquinas that although it was not a sacrament, it was the occasion when God remitted original sin because of the future merits of Christ.) St. Paul mainly brings out the contrast, rather than the parallel with Christian baptism (Rom. 2, 29; Col. 2, 11).

When the Israelites were hungry, the Lord gave them bread from heaven. This food which fell in their camp for forty years was called MANNA, which means 'What is it?' (Ex. 16). According to St. Paul (1 Cor. 10, 3) and St. John (6, 31ff.), it was a type of the food of the New Covenant, the Blessed Eucharist. Likewise the WATER from the rock (Ex. 17, 6; Num. 20, 10-11) was a type of the graces to come through Christ (1 Cor. 10, 4). Jesus himself seems to allude to it: 'If any man is thirsty, let him come to me, and drink' (Jn. 7, 37).

All the blood shed in animal sacrifices in the Old Testament pointed to the perfect Victim who would one day atone for all sin by shedding his blood on Calvary. The paschal lamb was the most important annual sacrifice; next in importance was the Day of Atonement, when the SCAPEGOAT was sacrificed for the sins of the people (Lev. 16): 'God laid on his shoulders our guilt, the guilt of us all' (Is. 53, 6). Just as the scapegoat was put to death outside the camp of Israel, so Jesus died outside the city walls (Heb. 13, 11-12). The RED HEIFER (Num. 19) also was immolated, like Jesus, outside the camp (Heb. 13, 11). The lustral water made from her ashes was used by the Hebrews to cleanse those who had incurred legal defilement; this was a foreshadowing of the blood of Christ, which cleanses sin from the souls of men (Heb. 9, 13-14).

When the Israelites were complaining against God, towards the end of the forty years in the desert, he sent serpents upon them, and many died of the serpents' bites. When they had confessed their sin, the Lord told Moses to make a BRONZE SERPENT and set it up on a pole; and as many as looked towards it were healed (Num. 21, 4-9). Our Lord quoted this incident to Nicodemus: 'And this Son of Man must be lifted up, as the serpent was lifted up by Moses in the wilderness; so that those who believe in him may not perish, but have eternal life' (Jn. 3, 14-15). As the nonvenomous image of the serpent, looked upon with faith, healed the poisoned wounds, Christ, incarnate in the likeness of sinful man, heals the wounds of sin (2 Cor. 5, 21).

The text of Osee 11, 1 is quoted by Matthew 2, 15 as fulfilled in Christ: 'I called my son out of Egypt.' Christ's return from Egypt to Palestine is understood by Matthew as a spiritual exodus; in Christ all humanity was journeying from the Egypt of sin to the promised land of peace with God. In Psalm 94, St. Paul (Heb. 3-4) gave a Christian meaning to the exodus from Egypt; it had more of a lesson for the

Christians of his day than for the Jews for whom the psalm was written. He bases his argument on two words in the psalm, 'Today' and 'Rest.' It is an eternal Today of Rest in Christ.

JOSHUA is the Hebrew form of Jesus. He crossed the Jordan (a symbol of baptism, like crossing the Red Sea) and led his people into the promised land (Josh. 3). So too, Jesus brings us through Baptism into his Church.

GEDEON won a spectacular victory over the Madianite host with a puny force of three hundred men (Jg. 7); our Lord sent twelve apostles to conquer the world. SAMSON (Jg. 13-16) was a combination of great strength and weakness. He was betrayed by his kinsmen and handed over to the Philistines, just as Jesus was sold by Judas and handed over to his enemies. Samson offered his life when he pulled down the house on the Philistines; so Jesus offered himself as a victim for all mankind.

The title most in use for the Messiah when our Lord was born was 'Son of David' (Ezechiel 37, 24 simply calls him 'David'). We would expect this greatest person in the Old Testament to foreshadow his most famous Son (p. 35). DAVID was born in Bethlehem; so too was our Lord. David slew the Philistine Goliath (1 Kg. 17); Jesus slew the giant Sin with the wood of the cross and his five wounds (David carried a staff and five stones). During the rebellion of his son Absalom, David was betrayed by Achitophel, his trusted counsellor (2 Kg. 16-17). Psalms 40 and 54 (p. 47) were written about this incident. Our Lord himself quoted a verse from Psalm 40 as being fulfilled in the treason of Judas Iscariot: 'The man who shared my bread has lifted his heel to trip me up' (Jn. 13, 18).

The name SOLOMON means 'peace.' Isaias predicted the

coming of the Messiah as 'The Prince of peace' (Is. 9, 6). Solomon had the most glorious reign of all the kings of Israel; our Lord's kingdom would far outshine it with all the treasures of divine grace. Solomon was noted for his wisdom, a gift of God (3 Kg. 3); Jesus is the Wisdom of God personified, 'in whom the whole treasury of wisdom and knowledge is stored up' (Col. 2, 3). Solomon raised up a temple of cedar and stone; our Lord raised the temple of his body by his resurrection (Jn. 2, 19-22). The Queen of Sheba brought costly presents to Solomon (3 Kg. 10); the Wise Men from the East brought their gold, frankincense, and myrrh to the Christ-child (Mt. 2).

ELIAS was one of the most colourful characters in the Old Testament (3 Kg. 17—4 Kg. 2). In one sense he foreshadowed John the Baptist (Mal. 4, 5; Mt. 17, 10). He also appeared at the Transfiguration in company with Moses. He seems to have been a type of the Messiah in that he was persecuted and felt great mental anguish, even to the point of death, like Jesus in the garden of Gethsemani. He too was comforted by an angel and was taken up bodily from this earth. Two other incidents of his life bear a close resemblance to our Lord's: he raised a widow's son to life and miraculously multiplied food.

Whether JONAH was a real, historical person or merely a fictional character from the book that bears his name, he is presented by our Lord himself as a type of his own resurrection after three days in the tomb: 'Jonah was three days and three nights in the belly of the sea-beast, and the Son of Man will be three days and three nights in the heart of the earth' (Mt. 12, 40).

The importance of the prophets is mainly in the message they speak to the people from the Lord; but with JEREMIAS

it is his own personal living of the life of the suffering Messiah. He bears the closest likeness to Jesus of all the persons
in the Old Testament. He preached to the Jewish leaders in
Jerusalem, shortly before it fell to the Babylonians in 587
B.C. His message, like our Lord's, went unheeded, and like
our Lord he aroused so much animosity that his enemies
plotted to take his life: 'Hitherto, I had been unsuspecting as
a cade lamb that is led off to the slaughter-house; I knew
nothing of the plots they were hatching against me, as they
whispered, "Let us give him a taste of the gallows-tree; let
us rid the world of him, so that his very name will be forgotten!"' (Jer. 11, 19). Often the words he uses could have
been spoken by Jesus himself: 'They thought to compass my
death by their clamour; to all my warnings would pay heed
no longer' (Jer. 18, 18). Those words remind us of the attempt to throw our Lord over the precipice at Nazareth (Lk.
4, 39), as well as the scene of Jesus' Trial and Death. When
the scribes and Pharisees tried to trap our Lord with the question of tribute to Caesar, he might have replied in the words
of Jeremias: 'Cunning the snare they laid, deep the pit they
dug to entrap me' (Jer. 18, 22). Actually our Lord does quote
Jeremias (7, 11) when he cleanses the temple: 'My house
shall be known for a house of prayer, and you have made it
into a den of thieves' (Mt. 21, 13). Jeremias wept over the
fallen city of Jerusalem in his Lamentations; he reminds us
of Jesus weeping over the same city (Lk. 19, 41): 'Keen
anguish for the overthrow of an unhappy race, that dims eye
with tears, that stirs my being to its depths, as my heart goes
out in boundless compassion!' (Lam. 2, 11). The words of
Lamentations are put on Jesus' lips in the liturgy of Holy
Week. The Temple soon to be destroyed was not made of
wood and stone, it was Jesus' own body (Jn. 2, 19-21). That

is why the Church puts these words on the lips of Christ: 'Look well, you that pass by, and say if there was ever grief like this grief of mine' (Lam. 1, 12).

Back in the time of Abraham there lived a man famous for his patience under affliction; his name was JOB. His story was written up into a powerful drama by a Hebrew poet (some argue from Ecclesiasticus 49, 11 that Ezechiel was the author), probably after the Babylonian exile. The literary figure of Job presented in the dialogue of the book that bears his name is a type of Christ: 'Poor man nor helpless orphan cried to me in vain; how they blessed me, souls reprieved from instant peril; with what comfort the widow's heart rejoiced! Dutiful observance was still the vesture I wore, my robe and crown integrity; in me, the blind found sight, the lame strength, the poor a father' (Job 29, 12-15). Those words could have been spoken by our Lord of his public ministry; they show his charity and his concern with doing his Father's will at all times. But it is mainly his intense mental anguish that makes Job a type of Jesus in the garden of Gethsemani: 'But here is grief words cannot assuage, nor silence banish; grief that bows me down till my whole frame is lifeless; these furrowed cheeks are the witness of it' (Job 16, 7-9). Like Jesus, Job was an innocent man; unlike our Lord, he did not know the cause of his sufferings. But he expresses his reactions to physical and mental suffering more deeply than any other character in the Old Testament. The whole of Job's words can be read with profit, particularly the final two chapters (30-31) of the dialogue.

The sad state to which the Jewish people were reduced because of their sinful lives is vividly pictured in Isaias 1, 5-6: 'Everywhere bowed heads, and faint hearts; no health anywhere, from sole to crown, nothing but wounds, and bruises,

and swollen sores, that none binds up, or medicines, or anoints
with oil.' Since Jesus bore all the sins of mankind in his body
during his Passion, these words take on a deeper significance
when applied to him, particularly after his Scourging at the
Pillar by the Roman soldiers.

The return from exile in Babylon was looked upon by the
Hebrew prophets as a second Exodus (Is. 44, 26—46, 14).
As in the first Exodus under Moses, we find here also some
types of Christ among those who led the exiles back to the
promised land. There is not the same wealth of type, actually
only three. The first is CYRUS, the Persian king who signed
the decree permitting the Jews to return to their homeland
(1 Esd. 1, 1-4). Isaias calls him a king anointed by the Lord
(Is. 45, 1); he is the Lord's shepherd, appointed to carry out
the divine purpose (Is. 44, 28). He also seems to be 'an
anointed prince' of Daniel 9, 25 (p. 223). He is a type of
Christ because on him rested the task of rescuing the chosen
people from bondage and exile from the Lord. His high prin-
ciples made him a suitable instrument to carry out the divine
command.

The two Jewish leaders who led the exiles back to Jerusalem
in 538 B.C. are types of Christ; he would lead all peoples
home to the friendship of God by his death on the cross.
ZOROBABEL was the grandson of the last king to reign in
Jerusalem; with the high priest JOSHUA, he marched at the
head of the returning exiles. Zorobabel is called the Lord's
'signet ring' (Ag. 2, 24); this meant he was acting with the
authority given him by God (documents were signed by
stamping with a ring, Genesis 41, 42). The prophet Zacharias
(6, 9-14) was told to make a crown for Joshua (p. 203). This
unusual procedure (priests were anointed, not crowned)
seems to point to Christ, the priest and king of the New
Covenant.

The last person to prefigure our Lord lived in the time of the Machabean revolt in the second century B.C. He was the high priest ONIAS, who was murdered as he left the temple in Jerusalem (2 Mach. 4, 34). He is alluded to in Daniel 9, 26: 'An anointed priest is done to death, one who is truly innocent' (p. 233). He is a type of Christ both in his death and his innocence.

CONTENTS: Chapter 7

Genesis 3, 15—Isaias 7, 14—Micheas 5, 3—Jeremias 31, 22—
   Psalm 44—The Song of Songs—Proverbs 8, 22-36—
   Sirach 24   275
Types of Mary: Eve—Burning Bush—Moses' Sister—Ark
   of the Covenant—Jahel—Gedeon's Fleece—Lamentations—
   Porta Clausa—Esther—Judith—Valiant Woman   276

7. Our Lady in the Old Testament

WHEN God decreed the redemption of the human race through the Incarnation of his only Son, at the same time he chose Mary to be his Mother, and co-redemptress. The first Messianic Promise (Gen. 3, 15) indicates the part to be played by our Lady (p. 13). In the Latin Vulgate the reading 'she is to crush your head' has replaced the original 'he' (Christ). This is not inspired Scripture, but a witness of tradition to the co-redemptress role to be played by Mary in the redemption of the human race. In two other passages, Isaias 7, 14 (p. 75) and Micheas 5, 3 (p. 105), the mother alone of the Messiah is mentioned. A further mention is made in the Vulgate text of Jeremias 31, 22 (p. 131): 'Weak woman is to be the protectress of man's strength.' This is not an inspired text, but like Genesis 3, 15 it is a traditional interpretation of the part of our Lady in the Incarnate life of her Son.

In Psalm 44 (p. 67) and The Songs of Songs (p. 189) the Bride stands for the Church, the Mystical Body of Christ. Since Mary is the Mother of the Mystical Christ, as well as of the physical Christ, it seems that the Holy Spirit intended some allusions to her when speaking of the Bride. Mary is not only bound to Jesus in the closest bonds of personal love (Sponsa Verbi); she is the exemplar and archetype of the Church; she personalizes the abstract collectivity of the Church. The main proof for this is the continuous use in the liturgy of the Church of passages from these writings for the various feasts of Mary.

The doctrine of divine Wisdom contained in the books of Proverbs and Sirach (p. 247) literally refers to the Second Per-

son of the Trinity. The liturgy also aptly applies these texts
to Mary, the Seat of Wisdom. She is the Mother of God;
and, with due proportion, what is said of her Son can be said
of her. She is associated with her Son in the creative govern-
ment of the world (Proverbs). She is also associated with the
Redeeming Wisdom in the work of salvation and sanctifica-
tion (Sirach). She, in the power of her Son, brings the whole
universe to the feet of God.

Spiritual writers and the liturgy of the Church have seen
Mary foreshadowed in several Old Testament persons. None
of these are expressly cited in the New Testament, so that we
have not absolute certitude that God intended them to be
types of Mary. Just as Christ is the Second Adam (p. 263), so
Mary is the SECOND EVE. Eve brought death to mankind,
Mary brought life; Eve's disobedience to God's command was
righted by Mary's acceptance of divine Motherhood (Lk. 1,
38); Mary's humility is contrasted with Eve's pride.

God appeared to Moses in the desert of Sinai in a BURNING
BUSH: 'And here the Lord revealed himself through a flame
that rose up from the midst of a bush; it seemed that the
bush was alight, yet did not burn' (Ex. 3, 2). This was a
symbol of the perpetual virginity of Mary; she gave birth to
the redeemer without losing her virginity.

MARY, the sister of Moses and Aaron, sang a song of
gratitude to God for delivery from Egypt after crossing the
Red Sea (Ex. 15, 20-21); Mary, the mother of Jesus, sang her
Magnificat at the beginning of mankind's spiritual liberation.

A third type from the Exodus period is the ARK OF THE
COVENANT, a title applied to our Lady in the Litany. The
ark was the container of God's way of life for his people, the
Mosaic law; it was the holiest object of the Old Testament.
Over it stood the cherubim, symbols of the divine presence

(Ex. 25, 10-22); the luminous cloud overshadowed it. Mary carried the divine child in her womb after the Incarnation, when the power of the most High overshadowed her (Lk. 1, 35).

JAHEL, wife of Haber, is presented as a type of Mary when she slew Sisera (Jg. 4, 17—5, 31). Mary triumphed over the power of the enemy by giving birth to the redeemer; for this she was 'blessed above all women' (Jg. 5, 22).

In GEDEON'S FLEECE (Jg. 6, 33-40) both the birth of Christ from Mary and her sinlessness are typified. When the fleece alone was filled with dew, the ground staying dry, it signified the Son of God assuming a human nature from Mary the Virgin. When the fleece alone remained dry it signified Mary's Immaculate Conception; she alone was preserved free from original sin.

The LAMENTATIONS OF JEREMIAS are put on the lips of both Jesus and his Mother for their sorrowful feasts. Since Mary shared in the redemption as co-redemptress, she too experienced the mental anguish expressed in Lamentations: 'Look well, you that pass by, and say if there was ever grief like this grief of mine' (Lam. 1, 12).

A text from Ezechiel's vision of the ideal temple has been understood of our Lady: 'Shut this gate must ever be, nor open its doors to give man entrance again, since the Lord, the God of Israel, entered by it' (Ezech. 44, 2; p. 153). This PORTA CLAUSA is Mary, through whom the Creator came into his world; for this reason Mary remained a virgin ever after; it was not fitting that any other person should be born to her after the Incarnation.

In the fifth century B.C. ESTHER became queen of Persia because of her beauty; through her queenship she was able to save her people, the Jews, from destruction. Mary is the queen of heaven, with a beauty both of body and soul; through her co-operation the whole world was saved from sin. A century later, JUDITH rose up as the saviour of the city of Bethulia (house of God); she went out and killed the besieging general Holofernes. She was greeted by her townspeople: 'You are the boast of Jerusalem, the joy of Israel, the pride of our people' (Jud. 15, 10). In this she foreshadowed the part played by Mary in our redemption, and is so honoured in the liturgy. THE VALIANT WOMAN of Proverbs 31, 10-21 may be regarded as a type of Mary, the ideal woman. Her worth, her industry in looking after her household, her virtuous life in the home at Nazareth, made her the most perfect woman of the human race.

Index of Messianic Texts

The Letter T is placed before all typical texts
An Asterisk * is placed before the key texts

* GEN. 3, 15	Redemption from Sin	11
T GEN. 2—3	Adam, the Representative Man	263
T GEN. 2—3	Eve, a Type of Mary by Contrast	276
T GEN. 6—7	Noah's Ark: Baptism and the Church	263
T GEN. 14,18–20	Melchisedech: Priesthood of Christ	263
T GEN. 17	Circumcision: Sacrament of Baptism	266
GEN. 22, 18	Son of Abraham	17
T GEN. 22	Isaac: The Wood of the Cross	264
T GEN. 27	Jacob: The Sins of Others	264
T GEN. 41	Joseph: Saviour of the World	265
GEN. 49, 10–12	Lion of the Tribe of Juda	17
T EX. 3	The Burning Bush: Mary's Virginity	276
*T EX. 12	The Paschal Lamb: Redemptive Blood	19, 266
T EX. 13—14	Moses: from Bondage to Freedom	265
T EX. 14	The Red Sea: Sacrament of Baptism	266
T EX. 15, 20–21	Mary, Sister of Moses: Our Lady	276
T EX. 16	Manna: The Blessed Eucharist	266
T EX. 17, 6	Water from the Rock: Sanctifying Grace	266
T EX. 25, 10–22	Ark of the Covenant: Mary's Motherhood	276
T LEV. 16	The Scapegoat: Vicarious Expiation	267
T NUM. 19	The Red Heifer: the Blood of Christ	267
T NUM. 21, 4–9	The Bronze Serpent: the Crucifixion	267
NUM. 24, 17	A Star out of Jacob	23
* DEUT. 18, 18	The Prophet of the Lord	23
T JOS. 3	Joshua: Entry into the Promised Land	268
T JG. 4—5	Jahel: Blessed above all Women	277
T JG. 6, 33–40	Gedeon's Fleece: the Immaculate Conception	277
T JG. 7	Gedeon: Victory with a Small Army	268
T JG. 13—16	Samson: Victory by his Death	268
* 2 KG. 7, 13, 16	Son of David	29
T 2 KG. 16—17	David: betrayed by Achitophel	268
T 3 KG. 3	Solomon: Glory and Wisdom	268
T 3 KG. 17—19	Elias: Persecution and Mental Anguish	269
TOB. 13, 11–23	The Glory of the Church	183
T JUD. 15,10	Judith: Mary, Co-redemptress	278
T ESTH. 2	Esther: Mary, Queeen of Heaven	277
T JOB 16, 7–9	Job: Suffering of Body and Mind	271
* PS. 2	A Universal and Divine King	31
PS. 8, 6–7	Universal Dominion of Second Adam	35
* PS. 15, 10–11	Belief in Resurrection of the Body	37
PS. 19, 5,7	Divine Protection for the King	35
PS. 20, 5	A King who will reign Forever	35
* PS. 21	Passion, Death, and Resurrection	39

* PS. 30	Filial Confidence during the Passion	43
* PS. 39, 7–9	Obedience to the Divine Will	45
T PS. 40, 10	Achitophel: Betrayal of Judas Iscariot	47, 268
* PS. 44	Royal Bridegroom and Bride	67
PS. 46	God is a Universal King	109
T PS. 54, 13–15	Achitophel: Betrayal of Judas Iscariot	47, 268
PS. 66	All Nations honour God	110
PS. 67, 30	Obedience and Worship of Nations	111
PS. 68	Prayer for Help during the Passion	49
* PS. 71	A Just and Peaceful King	107
PS. 84	A Prayer for Complete Restoration	233
PS. 86	The Church our Universal Mother	113
* PS. 88, 28–30	Eternal Reign of the Davidic King	155
PS. 89, 14–16	Restoration of Divine Friendship	157
T PS. 94	Palestine: Eternal Rest in Christ	267
PS. 95	King of the Universe	237
PS. 96	A Powerful King	239
PS. 97	A Victorious King	239
PS. 98	A Holy King	241
PS. 108, 4, 25	An Innocent Soul Misjudged	53
* PS. 109	King, Priest, Divine Sonship	33
PS. 116	Gentiles Praise the Lord	243
PS. 117, 22–23	The Corner-stone of the Building	243
PS. 125	God can change Sorrow into Joy	235
PS. 129, 8	Forgiveness of Sins	245
PS. 131, 17–18	A Davidic King in God's Presence	155
PS. 149	Praise God by Word and Deed	235
* PROV. 8, 22–36	Wisdom, the Master-workman at Creation	247, 276
T PROV. 31, 10–21	Mary, the Ideal Valiant Woman	278
SONG OF SONGS	A Dialogue of Divine Love	189, 275
* WIS. 2, 10–20	Passion and Death of the Son of God	253
* WIS. 7, 21—8, 1	Wisdom, Simple and like God	251
* SIRACH 24	Wisdom incarnate in the Mosaic Law	249
IS. 2, 2–3	The Church Visible and Universal	69
T IS. 1, 5–6	The Passion of Christ	271
IS. 4, 5	Divine Protection of Purified Sion	71
* IS. 7, 14	Mary, Virgin Mother of God	73
* IS. 9, 6	The Prince of Peace	75
IS. 10, 21–22	A Remnant will return	79
* IS. 11, 1–2	The Seven Gifts of the Holy Ghost	79
IS. 11, 6–9	Idyllic Peace of the Garden of Eden	81
IS. 12, 1–6	The Exiles' Hymn of Praise	83
IS. 13, 10, 13	The Day of the Lord	85
IS. 16, 5	The Chosen People return to God	87
IS. 19, 20–21	The Gentile World converted	87
IS. 24, 23	The City of God	89
IS. 25, 6	The Messianic Banquet	91
IS. 27, 3	The Vineyard of the Lord	93
IS. 28, 16	Christ the Corner-stone	95
IS. 30, 19, 26	True Citizens of Sion	95

	IS. 30, 33	Divine Judgment by Fire	85
	IS. 31, 5	The Security of Divine Protection	97
	IS. 33, 17	The King in his Royal Beauty	99
	IS. 35, 2, 4, 10	God himself the Saviour	101
	IS. 40, 1–11	Deliverance and Salvation	159
*	IS. 42, 1–9	A Gentle and Humble Saviour	165
	IS. 45, 8	Deliverance and Salvation	165
T	IS. 45, 1	Cyrus: Return from Exile	272
	IS. 45, 23	Worship of God, not Idols	163
*	IS. 49, 1–9	Obedience of Christ	167
*	IS. 50, 4–11	Christ's Constancy under Suffering	171
*	IS. 52, 13—53, 12	Handed over to Death for our Sins	171
	IS. 54, 5	The Church, the Bride of Christ	175
	IS. 55, 1–3	A New and Eternal Covenant	177
	IS. 56, 7	The Conversion of the Gentiles	179
	IS. 60	The Glory of the Church	179
*	IS. 61, 1–2	Divine Vocation of the Messiah	167
*	IS. 63, 1–6	A Champion bringing Deliverance	179
	JER. 3, 16	The Old Covenant abrogated	121
T	JER. 11, 19	The Passion of Our Lord	270
	JER. 23, 5–6	A Faithful Scion of David's Stock	46
	JER. 31, 15	Sorrow of Exile Turned to Joy	129
	JER. 31, 22	Love of Christ and the Church	131
*	JER. 31, 31–34	The New and Eternal Covenant	131
	JER. 33, 8, 11	God's Mercy to his Guilty People	125
	JER. 33, 15	A Faithful King in Jerusalem	127
	JER. 33, 22	The King, the Priests, the Nation	127
T	LAM. 1, 12	Suffering Messiah and Sorrowful Mother	270, 277
	BAR. 3, 38	Wisdom incarnate in the Mosaic Law	249
	BAR. 5, 3	The Splendour of the Church	133
	EZECH. 17, 22–23	A King of David's House	135
*	EZECH. 34, 16, 23	One Flock and One Shepherd	139
	EZECH. 36, 25–26	The New Christian Spirit	145
*	EZECH. 37, 24–25	The Good Davidic Shepherd	141
	EZECH. 38—39	Antichrist, the Champion of Wickedness	147
	EZECH. 43, 2	The Glory of the Church	151
T	EZECH. 44, 2	The Perpetual Virginity of Mary	153, 277
	EZECH. 47, 8–12	The Stream of Grace from the Temple	153
	DAN. 2, 35, 44	The Eternal Empire of Christ	221
*	DAN. 7, 13–14	The Son of Man's Universal Reign	225
	DAN. 9, 24	Seventy Weeks of Years till Redemption	229
T	DAN. 9, 26	Onias: Death of Innocent Messiah	273
	DAN. 12, 2	Resurrection of the Body	257
	OS. 2, 14–24	God's Everlasting Betrothal to Church	61
T	OS. 11, 1	Exodus: Christ's Return from Egypt	267
	OS. 14, 2–9	The Triumph of Divine Love	65
	JOEL 2—3	The Day of the Lord	215
	JOEL 2, 28	The Coming of the Holy Spirit	215
	AMOS 5, 18	The Day of the Lord	57
	AMOS 9, 11–15	Blessings of Messianic Times	59

ABD. 1, 15–18	The Day of the Lord	219
T JON. 2, 1	Resurrection after Three Days	269
MIC. 4, 2–4	Church Visible and Universal	103
* MIC. 5, 2	The Messiah born at Bethlehem	105
MIC. 7, 14	The Flock of the Lord	103
SOPH.1, 7–17	The Day of the Lord	117
SOPH. 3, 8–20	The Church One and Holy	119
AG. 2, 7–10	The Lord in his Temple	195
T AG. 2, 22–24	Zorobabel: King with Divine Authority	272
ZACH. 2, 5,10	Divine Protection of the Church	195
ZACH. 3, 8	The Branch of David	201
ZACH. 6, 12	The Branch of David	203
T ZACH. 6, 9–14	Joshua: Messianic Priest and King	269, 272
ZACH. 8	Divine Protection of the Church	197
* ZACH. 9, 9	The Prince of Peace enters Jerusalem	203
ZACH. 11, 12–13	The True Shepherd put to Death	207
* ZACH. 12, 10	Repentance of the Jews at the Crucifixion	207
ZACH. 14, 9	King over all the Earth	209
* MAL. 1, 11	The Sacrifice of the Mass	211
MAL. 3, 1	The Lord visits his Temple	213
MAL. 4, 2	A Sunrise of Restoration	213
MAL. 4, 5	Elias in the Person of John the Baptist	213
2 MACH. 7, 7	Resurrection of the Body	257
2 MACH. 12, 44	Prayers for the Dead	259